Understanding Internet Protocols
Through Hands-On Programming

J. Mark Pullen

Wiley Computer Publishing

John Wiley & Sons, Inc.
NEW YORK · CHICHESTER · WEINHEIM · BRISBANE · SINGAPORE · TORONTO

Publisher: Robert Ipsen
Editor: Carol Long
Managing Editor: Micheline Frederick
Associate New Media Editor: Louis Umerlik
Text Design & Composition: Benchmark Productions, Inc.

Designations used by companies to distinguish their products are often claimed as trademarks. In all instances where John Wiley & Sons, Inc., is aware of a claim, the product names appear in initial capital or ALL CAPITAL LETTERS. Readers, however, should contact the appropriate companies for more complete information regarding trademarks and registration.

This book is printed on acid-free paper. ∞

This publication is designed to provide accurate and authoritative information in regard to the subject matter covered. It is sold with the understanding that the publisher is not engaged in professional services. If professional advice or other expert assistance is required, the services of a competent professional person should be sought.

Library of Congress Cataloging-in-Publication Data:

ISBN 0471-35626-3

Printed in the United States of America.

10 9 8 7 6 5 4 3 2 1

This book is dedicated to the late Robert Swartwout of West Virginia University, who many years ago taught me so well the value of simulation software in education, and to my students, who have contributed to the Network Workbench both a strong functionality and an important reason for its existence.

CONTENTS

ACKNOWLEDGMENTS

I wish to thank my colleagues Peter Denning, Yih Huang, Daniel Menasce, and Robert Simon for their helpful comments on my software and drafts; my editor Carol Long for her coaching and useful ideas; and my wife Cheryl for her great patience during the many late-night and weekend sessions that resulted in the Network Workbench and this book.

This book was written to explain how the most important Internet protocols work. The text assumes that you, the reader, are an information technology professional, either still in college or already employed. The method of teaching is a series of hands-on projects in which you will program the central algorithms of the protocols. Each chapter describes an important protocol by presenting its technology context and explaining its principal algorithm(s). In this process you will learn something about a number of technologies associated with the Internet, but that is not why this book was written. In fact, there are several other books that cover a range of networking technologies in more depth and breadth. So, you might ask, what is different about this book?

The thing that is unique about this book is that each chapter contains a project in which the reader must program the central algorithm of a protocol. You won't be simply reading about the protocols, you will be *doing* something. In the process of doing, you will gain deeper understanding of the algorithm that makes the protocol work. To work through the projects, you must know the basics of probability and statistics and have the ability to program in C. To confirm that the protocol has been programmed correctly, you will execute it in a simulation system called the Network Workbench (NW). This custom software provides a complete, Internet-like protocol stack with working versions of protocols, and it gives you with the ability to observe the network's operation in detail. The CD-ROM in the back of the book contains the NW software in forms compatible with several major computing platforms and compilers.

You can use this book by itself to gain a basic understanding of the Internet protocols, or you can use it the way my students do: In conjunction with a textbook intended to provide in-depth coverage of data communications and networking principles and protocols. For those interested in the second approach, Appendix D provides suggested pairings of the chapters and projects in this book with several major textbooks.

A very significant part of learning about networking is the vocabulary (or, to be more honest, the jargon). Every chapter in this book introduces many new terms, which are printed in italics. Each of these terms is defined again in the Glossary at the end of the book.

The projects in this book have been used for several years by my intro-
ductory computer networking classes at George Mason University. My
students have confirmed what many information technology profes-
sionals know: A good way to really understand a process is to program it yourself. My intention in writing this book has been to enable
readers to gain this higher level of understanding. Experience has
shown that this understanding can make a big difference if you are
involved in making the Internet work, or in programming or main-
taining Internet applications.

The book is organized to make learning easy. The first chapter provides an introduction to the protocol stack concept and an overview of
NW. Chapter 2 expands on this overview by presenting the "big picture" of network topology. After that, the chapters (and the hands-on
projects they contain) start at the bottom of the Internet protocol stack
and work to the top in small steps. In this way, the chapters progress
through all of the protocols most important to the Internet, as follows:

CHAPTERS	TOPICS
3, 4, 5	Data link characteristics and data link control software
6, 7	Local area networks
8, 9	Wide area networking and Internet routing
10	Transport protocols
11	Multicasting and multimedia networking
12	Application layer servers and clients

At this point, you will know the basic aspects of the whole stack well
enough that the last two chapters can go back to big-picture issues:

CHAPTER	TOPIC
13	Network security and firewalls
14	Making your whole stack work together on the Internet

Following Chapter 14 are several appendices that are intended to help
you get more out of the book and out of NW:

APPENDIX	PURPOSE
A	Tells you how NW simplifies the real protocol
B	Provides directions for loading the software

C	Copy of the NW header file for reference
D	Suggestions for using this book with networking textbooks
E	References and other information resources
Glossary	Networking vocabulary

Creating a book or a sizable piece of software is a labor of love. That is certainly true of this book and the Network Workbench. My hope and wish for you is that you gain from them a level of understanding that will enable you to function well, as an information technology professional working with the Internet.

Mark Pullen

The Internet Protocol Stack and the Network Workbench

The Language of Networking

What is a network? Few people in our technological society can avoid hearing this term several times every week, but most of us would be hard pressed to define the word *network*. Definitions abound, often differing slightly from author to author. We use the following descriptions of network technologies in this book (see the Glossary for more definitions).

Communication. The process of passing information from a *sender* to a *receiver*. This process requires a *channel* or *medium* between the two and a way of representing information that is shared between the two. Figure 1.1 shows the basic communication process. In all real communications, there are occasional lapses in the quality of information received so that not all of the information sent by A reaches B. We refer to this garble added to the information as *noise*. The sort of communication that interests us in this book is *telecommunication*—that is, communication achieved by electronic means at a distance, usually under circumstances in which old-fashioned communication by human voice alone is impossible.

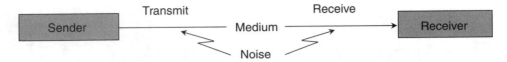

Figure 1.1   Basic communication process.

Data communication. In the case of computer communication, the information has a clear, definable value. In this book, we assume that A and B are computers, and that they can communicate in both directions at the same time (A to B **and** B to A). When this happens, the communication is called *full-duplex* communication. If communication can take place in only one direction at a time (A to B **or** B to A), that is *half-duplex* communication. Computers work with *binary digits (bits)*, so the rate at which the information is passed is measured in *bits per second*. In computer communication, the noise takes the form of *errors*, meaning that the received information does not match what was sent. As we will see later, the "data" being communicated between computers today may represent the traditional sort of data (numbers or text), or it may represent computer-encoded audio, video, or graphic images (known as *multimedia* communication). You will learn more about data communication in Chapters 3, 4, and 5 on Data Link Control (DLC).

Network. A collection of processing elements that have the ability to communicate with each other. The elements of the network are generally called *nodes*. Nodes represent fixed points to which

Units of Data Communication

Link data rates may be measured in:
- Kilobits per second (kbps): thousands of bits per second
- Megabits per second (Mbps): millions of bits per second
- Gigabits per second (Gbps): billions of bits per second

When using these values in C and C++ programs, we use *exponential notation*. For example, one megabit per second, which also can be expressed as 1.0×10^6 bps in scientific notation, is 1.0E6 bps in exponential notation.

Sometimes the data rate is given in *bytes* per second (Bps), where one byte = 8 bits, thus 1 kbps = 125 Bps.

communication *links* connect. Communication in the network can happen either directly, through a link between two communicating elements, or indirectly, in which case the two participants pass the information through one or more other, intermediary elements (which of course, requires a path of links and nodes between the two). Figure 1.2 is a diagram of a simple network, in which the nodes are shown as circles and the links as lines. We can see that some pairs of nodes are able to communicate directly (for example, nodes 1 and 4). Other pairs—for example, nodes 1 and 7—must pass information through other nodes. The ability to share resources for communication is one reason networks have become used so widely. Many networks, such as the one in Figure 1.2, also provide more than one path between any pair of nodes for improved reliability.

Local area network (LAN). A network that spans a small distance, typically a single building or a few buildings on a campus. Most LANs offer high data rates (from 2 megabits per second upward) but do not provide multiple (or *redundant*) paths between nodes. LANs are relatively inexpensive and generally are owned by the organizations that use them. Figure 1.3 shows a simple LAN in which several computers communicate with each other over a shared wire, known as a *bus*. It uses a simple mechanism called *broadcast*, whereby each transmission is received by all stations. You will learn more about LANs in Chapters 6 and 7.

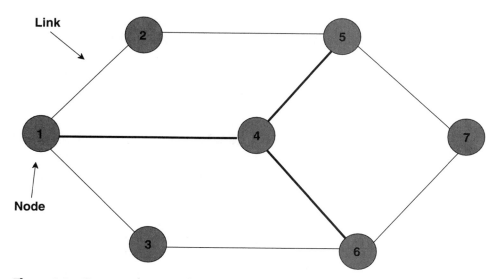

Figure 1.2   Seven-node network.

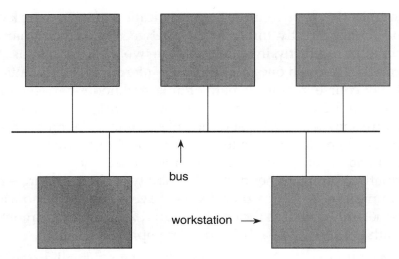

Figure 1.3   Bus LAN with five nodes.

Wide area network (WAN). A network that spans a larger geographic distance, ranging from a few separated buildings to worldwide locations. WANs normally are assembled from *leased links*, provided by a commercial telecommunication *carrier*: a company that is in business to move information electronically between distant points. The computers at which the links terminate are known as *routers* because they typically have the ability to route the information toward the destination over more than one link, using multiple paths to other router nodes. A typical WAN might be organized as in Figure 1.2. The routers might be operated by the carrier, by the using organization, or by a third organization, known as a *value-added network provider,* that provides more powerful network services using the carrier's communication circuits. Today the most common type of value-added provider is an *Internet Service Provider (ISP).*

The network illustrated in Figure 1.2 is known as a *switched network* because the routers pick specific paths among the links and nodes for information flows. That is, they switch the information into different parts of the network rather than broadcasting it to all parts of the network.

internet. This term means a network of networks. Figure 1.4 shows how several WANs can be interconnected so that any two computers connected to any of them can communicate. This process involves installing *gateways*—computers that interconnect the participating

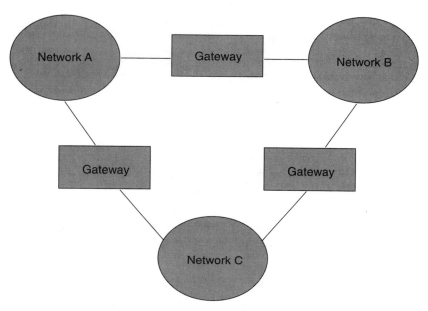

Figure 1.4   Network of networks.

networks. Internetting provides improved reliability: when the direct path between two networks is out, they may be able to communicate via a third network. Spelled with a lower-case *i*, an internet is any such network of networks. Spelled with an upper-case *I* (as in Internet), the word is the name for the worldwide network of networks that interconnect using the Internet Protocol (IP). You will learn more about IP in Chapters 8 and 9.

Intranet: Note that a LAN can participate in an internet. At one time, most WANs interconnected large computers called *hosts*. Today it is common for smaller computers (PCs and desktop workstations, still called hosts) to be connected to a LAN, with the LAN in turn connected to a WAN router. The WAN may support a private corporate network of LANs, known as an *intranet*, or it may be part of the Internet.

The Protocol Stack

The Internet consists of many millions of computers on tens of thousands of networks. It is arguably the most complex system ever assembled by mankind. How can such a complex system function reliably, particularly when it grows several times larger every year? The answer is that the Internet is assembled from components that have been built by many manufacturers to a common set of standards. The most fundamental of these standards, the ones we consider in this book, relate to a basic set of functions that has been defined collectively by the networking industry. At the core of these functions is a set of rules for exchanging information. These rules are known as *protocols*.

Networking technology is highly *modular*: Its systems are divided into "chunks" of well-defined functions. We organize our study of the Internet protocols around the model that has been defined by their developers, the *Internet Engineering Task Force (IETF)*. We present this in the form of a five-layer model, shown in Figure 1.5, which separates the various functions of network communication into *layers*. Each layer has a different purpose. Layering promotes software modularity and reuse because it facilitates creation of products that can be combined on a "mix and match" basis to provide a system solution to any networking problem. Because of the way they are layered on top of each other, the arrangement of protocols shown in Figure 1.5 is called a *stack*. One well-known stack with seven layers is called the *Open Systems Interconnect (OSI) Reference Model*. In this book, we use a simpler five-layer stack that is associated with the Internet. This stack is sometimes shown with only four layers, with the DLC and Physical layers combined into a single *host-to-network layer*. The five-layer stack is illustrated in Figure 1.5.

The functions of the five layers are:

Application Layer. Responsible for whatever the user wants the computer to do, such as interacting with a remote computer, transferring files, or displaying graphics obtained over the World Wide Web

Why Are They Called "Protocols"?

Diplomats learned a long time ago that, where different cultures come together, you need rules for accurate transfer of information. For example, in some cultures shaking your head up and down means "yes," but in other cultures it means "no." If you don't ensure accurate communication by developing rules for communicating your meaning, you will soon have a war on your hands! The rules diplomats develop for communicating are called protocols. Because we have a similar function in networks, we use the same name for our rules.

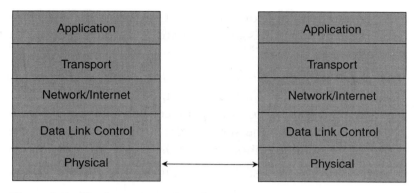

Figure 1.5   Five-layer protocol stack.

(which we refer to in this book simply as the Web). This interaction is achieved by sending *messages*.

Transport Layer. Responsible for packaging data for host-to-host delivery. For long streams of data, this requires dividing the information into *segments*. This layer also provides a means to identify how messages are to be used in the receiving host in that a set of messages is associated with a particular application. In many cases, this layer also keeps track of information flow between sender and receiver (which can be anywhere in the network) so that no information is lost or presented to the receiving application layer out of order.

Network Layer. Responsible for putting the segments into "electronic envelopes" called *packets* and providing the organization necessary to get the packets from sender to receiver. This process involves providing a consistent means of *addressing* (locating) the sender and receiver as well as a workable means of *routing* the packets through the communications links, routers, and gateways of the Internet. With good routing, the packets will flow efficiently and will be moved to another path quickly if problems arise.

Data Link Control (DLC) Layer. Responsible for controlling operation of a single data communication link to move information efficiently from end to end, even though the link may be experiencing transmission errors. An important function of this layer is Media Access Control (MAC), which allows multiple computers to share a single information channel, as shown in Figure 1.3. Other DLC functions include putting delimiters around the packet to make a *frame*, detecting (and possibly correcting) transmission errors, and controlling the rate at which the sender transmits so the receiver is not overwhelmed with data.

Physical Layer. Responsible for passing information between two physical locations. In its simplest form, the physical layer is a wire. In most cases, it is considerably more complex, being derived from a larger telecommunications system that supports a variety of uses (mostly commercial telephone service).

Data units. Notice in the list shown in Figure 1.6, each layer has its own name for the unit of data it transmits. The formal term for these is *protocol data units*.

The layers can be identified by number, starting from the bottom. In particular, it is common to refer to DLC as "layer two" and the network layer as "layer three."

From Figure 1.5 we can see that no less than four independent software modules (sometimes more) are required for a computer to communicate over the Internet. Of these, only the application layer normally is under the user's control. The transport, network, and DLC layers almost always are built into the computer's operating system. Although not separately visible to the user, each layer has a separate function and affects the performance seen by the user in a different way. These layers are designed and specified separately, but each conforms to the general notion of a "layer" shown in Figure 1.7. Each protocol has an *interface,* or "connection point," with the protocols immediately above and below it in the stack. The function it offers to the next higher protocol layer is called a *service.* Its communication with the protocol at the same level in the stack at the other end is called a *peer connection* and is possible only if the peers use the same protocol.

Layer	Common Data Unit
application	message
transport	segment
network	packet
data link control	frame
physical	bit

Figure 1.6   Protocol stack layers with common data units.

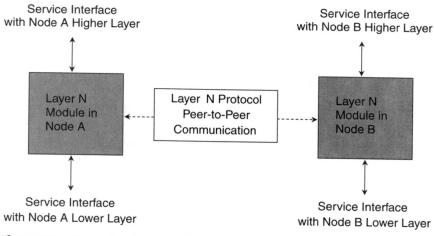

Figure 1.7   Generalized protocol layer.

Network Workbench Basics

Now we are ready to take a look at an actual protocol stack. The unique aspect of this book is the Network Workbench (NW for short). NW is *simulation* software. That means it uses a computer to model a real-world process or system in such a way that its important aspects are *abstracted*. In other words, a good simulation captures the important properties of whatever is being studied and models its behavior with regard to those properties to a good degree of accuracy. The question of what constitutes "good" is a critical one for the simulation developer. Too much accuracy slows down the simulation and may obscure the important properties being studied; too little accuracy can make the simulation misleading. Network simulators are available in a very wide range of levels of abstraction and accuracy. NW was designed to have accuracy sufficient for understanding the basic workings of protocols, without overwhelming its user with unnecessary details. NW does not have the power to depict network operations with timing accuracy less than a single bit, but it does represent the operation of each protocol in detail.

The concept behind NW is that the operation of each protocol is implemented in software that is nearly identical to that of a real network but without many of the features and details of normal network software.

The intention is that people who want to understand how the protocols work can program the protocol modules of NW. In arriving at a working program, they also arrive at a good understanding of the way the protocol works. The NW protocols have been abstracted with care to expose the fundamental works of the protocols used in the Internet.

To achieve good accuracy and efficient operation, NW uses a method known as Discrete Event Simulation (DES) which is useful for studying the behavior of systems over time. DES is useful with interconnected systems, such as networks, where the complexity of the system and its components makes it difficult to predict what it will do, given a particular set of inputs. The concept behind DES is to define the smallest increment of time that is required to represent the simulated process accurately. All actions in the simulation are then described in terms of this unit (in NW it is called a simulation time "tick"). It is important that this increment be small enough that using it as a basic unit does not mask fine details of the behavior of the system but still large enough that the count of ticks for the total time simulated can be represented easily within a long integer. The default tick in NW is 100 nanoseconds (10^{-7} seconds). Using this tick size, a time duration of 200 microseconds would have the following value:

```
200E-6/1E-7= 2000 ticks
```

Once the basic time increment has been selected, a discrete event simulation is programmed to keep track of all actions by system components. Typically, the result of an action by one component triggers an action by another component. For example, a message sent by the application layer in the protocol stack triggers action in the transport layer, which in turn triggers action in the network layer, etc. The length of time each event requires can be predicted with good accuracy. For example, if we are sending a 1000-bit packet on a 100 kbps link, we know it will take 10 milliseconds (.01 second) for the packets to be transmitted, so we set up the DES to produce an event indicating transmission is complete in 100,000 ticks = .01 second. At the heart of NW lies DES software that keeps track of all the events "waiting to happen." The code for this is in module des.cpp.

Built around the DES function, NW has a five-layer protocol stack like the one in Figure 1.5. Only one accommodation is needed to make the simulation work: Instead of directly invoking the next layer down,

---

About Typography

Computer file names, program algorithms, and C/C++ program code are identified in this book by a nonproportional typeface. For example, the NW header file is `code/nw.h`. Important concepts are identified by **boldface type**, and words with Glossary entries are identified by *italic font*.

---

each layer passes the function call to the next layer through the DES. In addition to providing for appropriate amounts of delay in the simulation, this process also provides a place for NW to print a trace as the simulation proceeds and collect statistics about the operation of all aspects of the network.

NW provides five basic services for network simulation. In the next few chapters, you will learn how to take advantage of these:

- DES, as discussed above
- All software required to make the five-layer stack work
- A set of input files representing networks and electronic mail (also called *email*) data, with functions to show the values being used at the beginning of the simulation
- A user-selected trace of actions happening in the simulated network as time proceeds
- A summary of network performance statistics at the end of the simulation

NW Files

Whether you download NW over the Internet or use the copy on the CD that accompanies this book, you will receive the same collection of files. If you download, you can select a version for your particular computer and compiler, whereas the CD contains several versions. In either case, you will find the files are organized into directories or folders, where xxx stands for a supported system—for example, sun for Sun Microsystems and bcb for Borland C++ Builder. For each version, the top-level nw directory contains the following directories plus some general descriptive files such as `nw-description.txt`, a general description of NW:

code: Contains C++ code for all available modules and stubs for student solutions

data: Contains the email files and network descriptions used by NW

xxx: Contains any special software for system xxx

The NW Header File nw.h

It is customary to organize large C and C++ programs into modules and to create a common *header file* that defines the data structures and C++ classes used across the collection of modules. The Workbench has been developed in this way, with all key definitions in file nw.h. A copy of the header file for NW version 4.0 is included in this book as Appendix C. The file is organized as follows:

- Narrative description of the Network Workbench (NW). Brags, boasts, disclaimers, warnings, and advice.

- Compilation constant definitions. Names associated with constants to be used when the compiler generates NW. For example, #define MAX_MSG_SIZE 101 defines the size of the largest message NW will support, which in turn is used in the data definitions that follow.

- Global NW type definitions. Data types that are used in the various NW classes. For example, message defines a structure with six header bytes (size, source_net, etc.) and a text field of size MAX_MSG_SIZE. Types are not actual program variables; rather, they describe generic data structures that are used by the classes that follow.

- NW class definitions. This is where C++ becomes important. A C++ *class* defines a collection of data elements associated with an instance of the class and the functions that manipulate those data elements. An important property of classes is *inheritance*, which means one class can pick up all the properties of another *base class* and add its own properties. The C++ functions in the Workbench create and use instances of these classes, which are called *objects*. To complete the projects in this book, you will not need to write any classes of your own. You can use the classes in nw.h to complete all of the projects. In effect, this means that you can do the projects if you know the C language, because the C++ part is all provided for you.

Finding Things in nw.h

The header file nw.h is sizable—over 60,000 characters. Finding the particular definition you are looking for can take a long time if you must read clear through the file. Fortunately, modern programming environments include an editor with search capability, making it easy to find what you are seeking. For example, you might want to find the definition of packet used in NW. To do this, you would load nw.h into the text editor program on your computer and invoke the "search" function. Because packet is used in the narrative and constant sections of the header file, you would need to search forward through about a dozen instances of packet, but after a few clicks you would come upon what you need: the data type packet with eight bytes of header and a segment payload.

 # Hands-On Activities

Every chapter in this book contains one "homework" problem, which may require use of the computer but does not entail a significant programming effort. Each chapter also contains one project, which in most cases will require a few hours to complete, depending on the skill of the reader. The problem and programming assignment for this chapter follow.

Problem: Identifying Stack Modules in NW

The "master index" to the Network Workbench is in file code/nw.h. (There is a copy in Appendix C of this book.) This is a C/C++ "header" file that defines all of the constants, data types, and C++ classes (functions and associated data structures). Your assignment is to become familiar with nw.h by reading it. In the process of reading, you are to produce a one-line description of each class and write out the names of the major software modules representing the five layers in the NW stack.

Project: Loading and Running NW

1. Run the appropriate NW setup program to create a working directory of files for the Network Workbench. If you intend to load NW onto your own computer, you will have to do that first. See Appendix B for instructions. There are two steps: *install* and *setup*. You can

find these processes and the directions for running them in
`nw*/xxx-install` and `nw*/xxx-setup`, where * is the current
version of NW, and xxx is the system you are using (for example,
nw40/Sun-setup). After running `install`, look in directory xxx
for program `setupn`, which will load the program and data files
appropriate to your computer and compiler. Here, n identifies the
size of the network to be used. To start, you should run `setup7`,
which will load a seven-node network.

2. After completing the setup, run the built-in NW solution to project
   DLC1. To do this, go to your `working` directory and edit program
   `dlc1.cpp`, which stands for "NW project DLC1, C++ code." The
   edit you should make is to insert two slashes (//) at the beginning
   of the line that contains:

```
#include "stuff.cpp"
```

This makes the line into a C/C++ comment, so it is ignored by the
compiler and is called "commenting out" the line. Now compile
and run `dlc1.cpp`. The output will pass by quickly on your
screen, but it will also be written into file `working/diskout.txt`.

3. Now load `diskout.txt`. in a text editor program to analyze it.
   You should be able to identify:

   - The various NW software modules loaded
   - The simulation parameters to be used
   - The nodes and links in the network
   - The operation of this simulation, in which the application sends
     only one message
   - The flow of data between layers, down the stack at the sending
     node from application to DLC layer, and back up the stack to the
     receive node
   - The statistics at the end of the simulation, which in the case of
     DLC1 show that only one frame was transmitted and one frame
     was received

CHAPTER 2

Wide Area Network Topology

Networks and Topologies

In this chapter, you will learn how computer software can capture and use network topologies. We begin our study of network components at the bottom of the stack, with the physical layer. This chapter sets the stage by describing how the physical links are assembled to form a WAN and how network software captures essential interconnection information regarding the WAN. In the next three chapters, we work our way through the most common link-layer technologies and the essential DLC protocol needed to make them usable in a network.

Figure 2.1 shows several common topologies. The *star*, *ring*, and *bus* topologies are used mainly in LANs. You will learn more about them in Chapters 6 and 7 on LAN protocols. The *mesh* topology, in its most general form, applies to a network in which every node is connected to every other node. This topology offers high reliability because every node has not only a direct way to reach all other nodes, but it also has many indirect paths that pass through other nodes. However, for a large network, the complexity of installing so many links would be impractical; there are $(N^2-N)/2$ links in a full mesh. So it is common in

Top of What?

A specific configuration of links and nodes is called a *topology*, after the branch of mathematics that studies such interconnections.

WANs to use a partial mesh, in which each node has links to a few others. This arrangement offers good reliability at a practical level of complexity and cost.

Figure 2.2 shows the diagram we called a network in the previous chapter and now recognize to be a WAN. However, in truth, this simple diagram does not show the network in very much detail. It really shows only how the nodes are interconnected. It is common to show the topology as a diagram, but it is possible to capture the same information represented by the diagram in a matrix. For example, if the network of Figure 2.1 has the usual sort of bidirectional links, its topology can be represented as shown in Figure 2.3.

Upon closer analysis, you'll see that this matrix holds a 1 in every position where the row and column nodes are directly connected by a

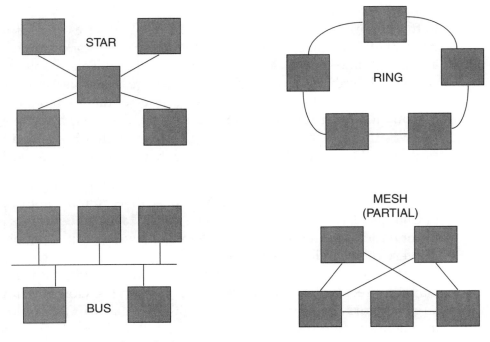

Figure 2.1   Network topologies.

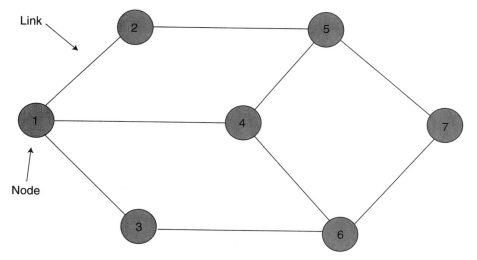

Link

Node

Figure 2.2 WAN topology.

link, a 0 in every case where they are not directly connected, and a dash (–) where the question of connection makes no sense because the node is always connected to itself.

TO NODE	1	2	3	4	5	6	7
FROM NODE							
1	-	1	1	1	0	0	0
2	1	-	0	0	1	0	0
3	1	0	-	0	0	1	0
4	1	0	0	-	1	1	0
5	0	1	0	1	-	0	1
6	0	0	1	1	0	-	1
7	0	0	0	0	1	1	-

Figure 2.3 Simple topology matrix.

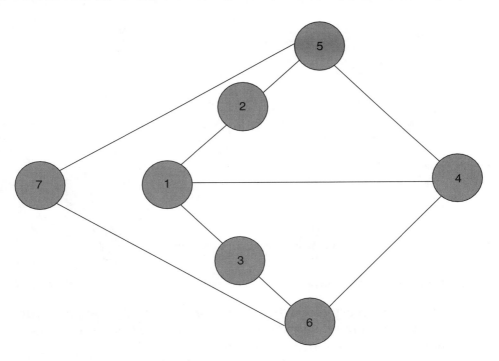

Figure 2.4   Another drawing with the same topology.

This topology matrix is *symmetric*. That is, if (row a, column b) holds a 1, then so does (row b, column a). Comparison tells us that there is no information in the diagram that is not captured in the matrix. However, there is more than one graphic depiction for this topology; for example, Figure 2.4 shows another one. On close inspection, every pair of nodes in Figure 2.3 is interconnected in exactly the same way as the same nodes in Figure 2.2. It therefore comes as no surprise that the two have the same topology matrix.

Practical Topology Matrices

Now we consider how to create practical topology matrices that NW can use to describe a network simply and accurately. The matrix we developed previously has some interesting mathematical properties, but it does not contain all the information we need to describe a network. For example, it says nothing about the bit-per-second capacities of the links, a very important parameter in a real network. We can add these link data rates to the matrix by putting a value in place of the 1 in our previous matrix, as shown in Figure 2.5.

Comparing this matrix with the earlier one reveals that we have replaced each 1 with a data link rate in kilobits per second. We also have used 0 on the matrix diagonal (those entries where row = column) in place of the dash (-) because we must have some numeric value, and 0 will do as well as any. In NW this is called the `links` matrix and is used to describe the basic topology of the WAN.

In the previous chapter, we looked at the idea of an *interface* between two layers in the stack. There are several different sorts of interfaces in a network. The word also applies to the point at which a link goes into a node. The next step toward a complete description of a network in NW is to identify each such interface by a number. If we assign numbers to each node's interfaces starting from zero and always go in order of lowest to highest neighboring node, we get the diagram shown in Figure 2.6, which also includes the link capacities contained in our most recent matrix.

TO NODE	1	2	3	4	5	6	7
FROM NODE							
1	0	64	64	128	0	0	0
2	64	0	0	0	64	0	0
3	64	0	0	0	0	64	0
4	128	0	0	0	128	128	0
5	0	64	0	128	0	0	64
6	0	0	64	128	0	0	64
7	0	0	0	0	64	64	0

Figure 2.5 The `links` matrix.

Principle of Simple Abstraction

The way the interface numbers are assigned here illustrates a principle that is used throughout NW: If any aspect of a network need not be considered in order to understand the important ideas in the Internet protocols, NW takes the simplest possible approach to representing that aspect. In real networks there is some messy bookkeeping associated with the interfaces of a node, but this level of detail does nothing to illustrate how the protocols work. Therefore, NW adopts a simple rule: Each interface is represented by a single digit, assigned in increasing order of neighbor nodes.

Now that we have the diagram it is easy to create another matrix, known in NW as exit_interfaces. Like links, the entries in exit_interfaces are organized by:

```
row = from node
column = to node
```

However, exit_interfaces contains the interface number in the same positions in which links contains the link data rates. Because later we will need to have an interface number 0 on some nodes, the entry -1 is used for positions in exit_interfaces where there is no interface. For example, at row 1, column 5 the value is -1 because there

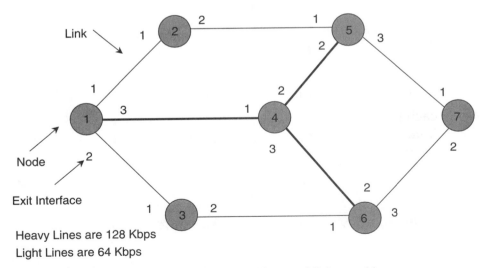

Figure 2.6 WAN topology with interface numbers and link capacities.

TO NODE:	1	2	3	4	5	6	7
FROM NODE							
1	-1	1	2	3	-1	-1	-1
2	1	-1	-1	-1	2	-1	-1
3	1	-1	-1	-1	-1	2	-1
4	1	-1	-1	-1	2	3	-1
5	-1	1	-1	2	-1	-1	3
6	-1	-1	1	2	-1	-1	3
7	-1	-1	-1	-1	1	2	-1

Figure 2.7   The `exit_interfaces` matrix.

is no direct link from node 1 to node 5 in our sample network. Continuing with the same example, the `exit_interfaces` matrix is shown in Figure 2.7.

Now that we have `exit_interfaces`, we have only one more matrix to create in order to complete the description of WAN topology as it is used in NW. Our third matrix is called simply `interfaces` and, unlike `links` and `exit_interfaces`, it is not square. Instead, it has one column for each interface in the network (all eighteen of them) and three rows. The number identifying a column is called a port identifier (`port` or `portnum` for short). Port numbers start at zero, and each is unique in the entire network. The rows stand for aspects of the interface that will be important when we use the topology data to compute results about the network. These are:

- `node`. The router node at which the interface connects
- interface number (abbreviated `ifacenum`). The value of `exit_interfaces` corresponding to the interface
- `other_end`. The `port_id` at the other end of the link

Figure 2.8 shows the corresponding `interfaces` matrix that completes the example.

PORT:	0	1	2	3	4	5	6	7	8	9	10	11	12	13	14	15	16	17
ROUTER:	1	1	1	2	2	3	3	4	4	4	5	5	5	6	6	6	7	7
IFACE:	1	2	3	1	2	1	2	1	2	3	1	2	3	1	2	3	1	2
OTHER END:	3	5	7	0	10	1	13	2	11	14	4	8	16	6	9	17	12	15

Figure 2.8 The `interfaces` Matrix.

 # Hands-On Activities

Algorithm for WAN1

Close inspection will show that the `interfaces` matrix was derived by first filling in each node/interface pair from `exit_interfaces` in order of increasing node, then putting in the "cross-reference" to the other end of each link. To see how `other_end` works, note that port 3 is interface 1 of node 2. Now look at the link that ends at this interface; its other end is interface 1 of node 1, which is port 0. Therefore, we find that for port 0, `other_end` is 3; and for port 3, `other_end` is 0. Thus `interfaces` makes it easy for us to find both ends of the link that connects to a particular port. The value of these matrices is evident; the question of how to find them is something like a puzzle. To solve this problem in a computer program, we need an *algorithm*, a set of steps that will solve the problem. We summarize the steps that must be programmed to create the two new matrices in the following algorithm:

```
Algorithm to produce exit interfaces and nports from links
do for each row in links,
{
  do for each column in the row of links, generating a row of
  exit_interfaces from this rule,
  {
    if an element of links is zero,
      the corresponding element of exit_interfaces is -1;
    do for non-zero elements in links,
    {
      set the corresponding element of exit_interfaces to an integer
      that starts at 1 for the first instance and increases by 1
      with each instance;
    }
  }
}
```

```
set the value of net_state_data[ ]->nports, in the position
corresponding to the row, to the number of interfaces on which
the node has connections;
}.
```

Algorithm to produce interface from exit interfaces
```
do for each row in exit_interfaces, starting with row 1, column 1,
{
  do for each column in the row,
    whenever you find an element greater than zero start a new
    position in interfaces,
    {
      set interfaces[position].net to the row number (this is the
      router);
      set interfaces[position].host to 1;
      set interfaces[position].ifacenum to the value of the
      element of exit_interfaces that is greater than zero
      (do not set the value of interfaces[position].other_end yet);
    }
  do for each column in interfaces to set the value of other_end,
  {
    get the net (router) number and the ifacenum;
    look in exit_interfaces row number for net to find the column
    that holds ifacenum;
    this [row][column] in exit_interfaces represents one end of a
    link;
    the other end of this link is the element with indexes
    reversed: [column][row];
    the value of net at the other end will be the [column] value and
    its ifacenum will be in position[column][row];
    now that you know the net and ifacenum for other_end, do for
    each column in interfaces,
    {
      test to find the position with these values,
        put the number of that position in the other_end for the
        position of interfaces you are filling in;
    }
  }
}.
```

Problem: Drawing a Topology Diagram

Obtain the NW solution to project WAN1 by commenting out the line #include topo.cpp in file wan1.cpp and running NW for this project. The output of NW includes the three matrices links, exit_interfaces, and interfaces. Use these matrices to draw a diagram of your network. *Answer (for seven node network): see figure 9.2.*

Algorithm Notation

The algorithms in this book are written in a semistructured language that is intended to tell you **how** your program should work, without telling you exactly what code to write. The language purposely falls short of formal algorithmic notation. Here is the notation I use:

- To label the purpose of something, a phrase ending in a colon (:)
- For an "aside" comment, parentheses ( )
- To describe a condition under which an action is to be taken, such as if, while, do for, a phrase ending in a comma (,)
- Phrases that are conditional (if, while etc.) or iterative (do, for etc.) are indented
- To group statements that fall under a particular control logic, matched pairs of braces as used in C/C++ { } with indentation of the lines contained
- At the end of an action phrase, a semicolon (;)
- At the end of the algorithm, a period (.)

Project: The WAN Topology Module

Look again at nw.h, which has all the data structures for the workbench. There is a copy in Appendix C of this book. In the section on the class network, you will find definitions for arrays links, exit_interfaces, and interfaces and scalar variables nnets (number of subnets, and therefore of routers) and nlinks (number of links).

Your assignment for project WAN1 is to write a C++ function network::create_topology that uses the values of nnets, nlinks, and the links matrix to complete the topology matrices, exit_interfaces, nports, and interfaces, as defined in nw.h, which will be used in various parts of the network simulation.

Notes

- This assignment deals with WAN interfaces. Nodes on the WAN are called *routers* and are identified as individual *subnets* (this concept will make more sense after we study more about internetting). The identifying number for a router node is found in interfaces[i] .netnum. The C++ variable interfaces[i].host will be used later to identify hosts on the subnet's LAN. For part1, your function should set the interfaces.host to 1 (the NW code for a router node).

C/C++ Refresher: Arrays

A *scalar* is a program variable with a single value—for example, x.

A *complex data type* consists of multiple values associated with the same name; for an example, look in nw.h for type tl_storage, which consists of two parts, tl_storage.sent_time and tl_storage.sent_seg. (If you dig deeper and look at the definitions of Sim_Timer and segment, you will find that each of these parts consists of other parts, further illustrating the concept of complex data.)

An *array* is a program variable holding multiple values; you indicate the particular value you want to use by an integer called a *subscript*, which can be a constant such as 2, a variable such as n, or a computed quantity such as n*m+1.

In C/C++, an array is indicated by brackets [ ] after a variable name. The variable must have been declared as an array by a statement such as float x[10];. Then you can put data in and get data out for any of the 10 positions of x, which run from x[0] to x[9].

An array may be of any data type, thus for the complex type iface, which consists of a net, a host, an ifacenum, and an other_end, we could define iface x[10], which would define ten successive sets of the four values, accessed by statements such as x[3].host = 5;.

C arrays can have multiple subscripts. NW uses two subscripts for links and exit_interfaces. To define a doubly subscripted array, use a statement such as float x[10][15];. Then you can use statements such as x[i][j] = 0; that access individual values of x.

Note: A statement such as z[i]->x = 5 represents a variation on the array theme. The algorithm for project WAN1 uses one array of this form. The characters "->" mean that z is an array of a special data type known as a *pointer*. We deal with pointers in more detail in Chapter 5. To complete WAN1, you only need to know that this represents a way of storing data in a different and more powerful form of array.

- Net number 0 and host number 0 are not used in the Workbench. Because of the way C arrays are defined, for any array that relates to net or host, position 0 must be present, but NW does not use it.

- net_state_data[netnum]->nports will always be one greater than the number of WAN host interfaces. This is because interface 0 is used for the LAN associated with this netnum. The LAN interface is always there, even if there are no other LAN hosts.

- There is a "stub" for the function in module topo.cpp in directory code. It is one of the files that are copied by setup to your

Programming Network Workbench Output

After you write your `topo.cpp` function, you will need to check it for errors (debug it). A tried and true way to resolve problems that come up in debugging is to print out the value of any variable that has a questionable status.

While C output functions such as `printf` and C++ output techniques such as `cout` generally work in NW, they may display results that are not synchronized with other NW output. To avoid this, use the NW `output` function, which puts a character string on your computer console and into file `diskout.txt`.

`output` is flexible in that you can use it with up to six parameters to print a sequence of strings, as in `output("string contains:",text, "\n");`. The string `"\n"` is a newline character. You should print this character at the end of your output; otherwise, the next NW output will come on the same line as your debug output.

The related function `outputn` puts an integer number in the same places. For example, you might want to print the value of position [2][4] in the `links` array. A statement that will achieve this is `outputn(links[2][4]).outputn` will print up to six parameters of type `int`, or any type that can be converted to `int` by the compiler. However, you will need to follow that with `output("\n");` for a newline.

Warning: NW has built-in number-to-character conversion functions such as `char* twodigs(int);` these are useful in formatting output, but they will **not** give proper results if invoked multiple times in the same call to `output`. Therefore, while `output("SN=",twodigs(SN), "\n");` will give good results, `output(twodigs(SN),twodigs(RN),"\n");` will give unsatisfactory results.

---

working directory. This and other stub functions do not provide any functionality, but they do have a working interface to the other Workbench code to get your project started.

- You should compile and run WAN1 using the same procedure as for Chapter 1. Assuming you have already run `setup`, you will not need to run it again. The WAN1 main program invokes the beginning part of the Workbench simulation. It reads the links matrix from file `wan.txt`, runs `topo.cpp`, and prints the internal values of the data structures `links`, `exit_interfaces`, and `interfaces`.

CHAPTER 3

Data Link Control—Framing

This chapter begins our study of the lower layers in the Internet stack. We will concentrate on the protocols of data link control (DLC), the second layer from the bottom. First, we need to understand the characteristics of the data link that needs to be controlled: the physical layer. Strictly speaking, the physical layer and DLC layer are not "Internet" protocols in that bodies other than the IETF set their standards. The Internet protocols are specifically designed to work over a wide variety of "host to network" lower layers. However, the lower layers have a profound impact on the performance of the higher layers, so it is essential to understand their operation.

The Physical Layer

The bottom layer in the protocol stack consists of the medium or channel that transmits the data bits between two physical locations. As shown in Figure 3.1, the binary values (0 or 1) of the data are represented by some physical quantity that the medium can convey, such as electrical charge, electromagnetic waves, or light pulses. Several media that are in common use are described next.

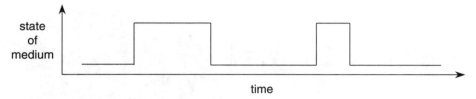

state
of
medium

time

Figure 3.1   Data as transmitted.

Twisted pair copper wire. Ordinary copper is good for data rates up to 100 Mbps, for short distances, and considerably longer distances at lower data rates (for example, 10 miles at 9.6 kbps). Data rates also depend on the quality of electrical insulation. Twisting the wires increases immunity to electromagnetic noise that causes data errors.

Dial-up telephone. By using a *modem* (modulator-demodulator), a channel intended for telephone voice communication can carry digital data. Such a communication link is called an *analog* channel, because the voice is carried over an electronic signal analogous to the acoustic pattern rather than being converted to a digital form. Analog dial-up can support data rates up to 28.8 kbps and, under special circumstances, up to 56 kbps. This capability extends to long-distance telephone connections, although longer distances often mean lower data rates and higher error rates due to lower-quality connections. Local access takes the form of a standard RJ-11 telephone jack from a pair of copper wires.

Digital telephone. In many locations it is now possible to order Integrated Services Digital Network (ISDN) telephone service. An *ISDN Basic Rate Interface (BRI)* makes two 56 or 64 kbps digital connections available to home or office over twisted copper pairs. This is a *switched* (dial-up) service in that a connection is set up when a call starts. The service can support voice through an ISDN telephone set, and data through an ISDN adapter.

Leased telephone lines. When communicating with another location outside of your own building or campus, you can lease a connection from a "telecommunications carrier," a company that is in the business of interconnecting physically separated sites. Normally, this will be the local telephone company, perhaps supplemented by a long-distance carrier if the other location is outside of the local telephone area. Data rates up to 1.5 Mbps are commonly available, and rates of 155 Mbps and higher are available in some locations. Local access is normally via two twisted pairs of copper wires. The latest form is "xDSL" (various forms of Digital Subscriber Line) to home or office.

Coaxial cable. This is a single wire, surrounded by high-quality insulation, then covered with braided copper shield. "Co-ax" supports data rates to 500 Mbps at distances as far as two miles, and much farther when amplifiers called regenerative repeaters are used to restore the signal every two miles (see Figure 3.2).

Microwave radio. At extremely high frequencies (in the gigaHertz range), radio can be transmitted only in a line-of-sight path, but uses a small parabolic dish antenna and experiences little interference. Digital microwave supports data rates up to hundreds of megabits per second, with moderate error rates. Typically, it is used where its high initial cost is offset by not having to pay a monthly lease. Figure 3.3 shows a microwave system in a typical arrangement, with the dish antennas mounted on top of buildings.

Satellite microwave. One way to avoid obstacles is to place the microwave antenna in space. The Earth is ringed with communications satellites at a distance of about 22,300 miles above the equator, where the "geostationary" orbit causes the satellite to always be over the same point on the Earth so that a fixed antenna can be used. These satellites house transmitter-receiver pairs called "transponders" that reflect a signal from one ground station to another. They have an end-to-end delay of about 1/4 second due to the time it takes the radio wave to propagate over 44,600 miles. Satellite channels tend to be noisy because of background signals from space. This and their relatively long delay (*latency*) make them less desirable in most cases than the next (and final) medium.

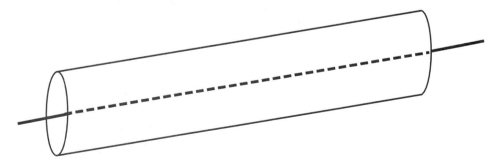

Figure 3.2 Coaxial cable.

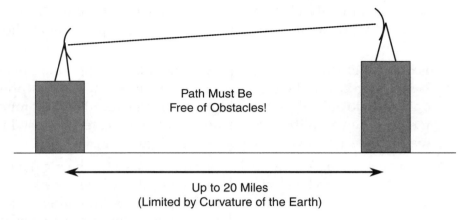

Figure 3.3 Microwave radio.

Optical fiber. This is ultra-clear glass, drawn out into very long, thin strands and wrapped in a protective cover. It will convey light from a low-power laser for long distances. It comes in various qualities, but even the lowest will carry data at rates of 100 Mbps for thousands of feet. Its best characteristic is an extremely low error rate arising from near-total immunity to electromagnetic noise. However, it is extremely difficult to splice, and therefore is used mostly in industrial installations. Long-distance carriers use fiber almost exclusively because of its high data rate, low error rate, and low maintenance. Transcontinental and transoceanic fiber cables are behind the availability of high data rates that support the global Internet. These are organized around the Synchronous Optical Network (SONET) standard, and in many cases use Asynchronous Transfer Mode (ATM) switching as a way of deriving high data rate paths over long distances. (While the carrier thinks of ATM and SONET as the underlying "network," from the standpoint of the Internet they are at the bottom of the protocol stack.)

Physical Layer Coding

What do the bits transmitted over the medium mean? In general, communication requires a *shared symbol set*. In other words, sender and receiver must agree on the value of the bit patterns, or information cannot be exchanged. Some data is exchanged using private codes agreed between sender and receiver, and some data is exchanged as binary numbers; for example:

Bandwidth versus Channel Capacity

If you spend much time talking to a person in the networking business, the term *bandwidth* is almost certain to be heard. Properly speaking, bandwidth is the range of analog frequencies that a telecommunications channel is capable of passing (as in "plain old telephone service," sometimes called *POTS*). However, a formula known as "Shannon's law" tells us that analog bandwidth can be related to digital channel capacity (data rate) by the formula:

```
max_channel_capacity = bandwidth * log2(1 + signal_power/noise_power)
```

The proportional relationship means that data rate is in fact related to bandwidth; hence, the common tendency to refer to the two as the same thing. The logarithm base two means channel capacity grows as the binary order of magnitude of the ratio of signal power to noise power at the receiver. For example, if the ratio goes from 15 to 31, Shannon's law tells us the maximum channel capacity grows by a ratio of 4:5 ($\log_2 16 : \log_2 32$).

$$1001001101_2 = 2^9 + 2^6 + 2^3 + 2^2 + 2^0 = 589_{10}$$

The largest amount of data is exchanged using the *American Standard Code for Information Interchange (ASCII)*. The ASCII code is commonly used for text data. The code patterns are seven bits long, so there can be $2^7 = 128$ different values. Figure 3.4 shows the ASCII code. You can see that all normal computer keyboard letters (upper and lower case), numeric digits, and special characters are represented. The remaining values represent special codes, some of which have been around since the days of the teletype. To look up a code value in this figure, look across the top for the first three bits and down the left side for the remaining four bits.

We will see in the next section that most computer communication is transmitted as eight-bit bytes (sometimes called *octets* in communication systems). How does seven-bit ASCII turn into eight bits for transmission? One simple way is to add a zero at the left; for example, the

Bet You Didn't Know This!

The ASCII code BEL rang the bell on teletype machines. Today it causes an audible sound on most computers.

letter A would become 01000010. Another way is to add a *parity* bit at the right end, chosen to allow a check for correctness of the other bits (more on this in Chapter 4 on DLC error detection).

What Is Data Link Control?

The frame is said to *propagate* through the channel, a process that takes place at the speed of light. Each of the physical media listed previously displays three characteristics that have a pronounced effect on its use for data communication:

Data rate (channel capacity). The maximum number of bits per second the channel will pass from sender to receiver.

Latency. The delay in seconds from the time a bit leaves the transmitter until it is available at the receiver (the speed of light is fast, but the transfer still takes time; if the channel is very long, this time becomes important in some cases).

$$B = 1000010$$

			b_7	0	0	0	0	1	1	1	1
			b_6	0	0	1	1	0	0	1	1
			b_5	0	1	0	1	0	1	0	1
b_4	b_3	b_2	b_1								
0	0	0	0	NUL	DLE	SP	0	@	P	`	p
0	0	0	1	SOH	DC1	!	1	A	Q	a	q
0	0	1	0	STX	DC2	"	2	B	R	b	r
0	0	1	1	ETX	DC3	#	3	C	S	c	s
0	1	0	0	EOT	DC4	$	4	D	T	d	t
0	1	0	1	ENQ	NAK	%	5	E	U	e	u
0	1	1	0	ACK	SYN	&	6	F	V	f	v
0	1	1	1	BEL	ETB	'	7	G	W	g	w
1	0	0	0	BS	CAN	(	8	H	X	h	x
1	0	0	1	HT	EM	)	9	I	Y	i	y
1	0	1	0	LF	SUB	*	:	J	Z	j	z
1	0	1	1	VT	ESC	+	;	K	[	k	{
1	1	0	0	FF	FS	,	<	L	\	l	|
1	1	0	1	CR	GS	-	=	M	]	m	}
1	1	1	0	SO	RS	.	>	N	^	n	~
1	1	1	1	SI	US	/	?	O	_	o	DEL

Figure 3.4 ASCII bit patterns with letter B highlighted.

Error rate. The fraction of all bits that are in error, normally expressed as a power of 10; for example, a microwave system might have an error rate of one in a million bits, written $1/10^6$ or 10^{-6}. Usually we assume these are random, single-bit errors, so we would say the *bit error rate* (BER) is 10^{-6}. However, in some cases errors occur in bursts, a fact that we will consider further in the next chapter.

No usable data communication system can ignore these three characteristics. Their effect is so great that a whole layer in the stack, DLC, is devoted to dealing with them. A fourth characteristic, the ability to share a data link, is the focus of the *media access control* (MAC) sublayer, which we address in Chapters 6 and 7 on LANs. For now, we will focus on DLC, and we will assume the link is *full duplex*, meaning it can send data between two stations in both directions at the same time.

The functions of DLC are:

- *Framing.* Creating markers such that a block or frame of data can be identified when it arrives at the receiver.
- *Error control.* Making arrangements to detect transmission errors and, in some cases, for retransmission.
- *Flow control.* Establishing rules by which the receiver can inform the sender when it is ready to accept data.
- *Link management.* Procedures for startup and shutdown of link protocols.

Framing

In this chapter, we will deal with the first function of DLC. Framing is needed because there is always something passing over a communications link. Whether the link is being used to pass information, or is just sitting there idle, the receiver is seeing data bits. We must arrange for our transmitted frame to be recognized when it comes across the link. There are two possible ways to do this. Using *asynchronous transmission*, every character is marked with "start" and "stop" bits, and the characters are sent one at a time. This is not very efficient, so higher-performance systems send blocks of data in *frames*, called *synchronous transmission*. Each frame begins and ends with a special pattern that is used to synchronize sender and receiver in the sense that the receiver knows the sender means for the frame to start or stop at that point.

A problem that must be dealt with in synchronous data transmission is that whatever pattern is used to mark the start and end of a frame must never appear in the data. The original solution to this problem, *byte-oriented* transmission, used a "SYN" (synchronous idle) pattern between frames, with a special bit pattern "STX" to start the frame, and another pattern "ETX" to end it. These characters were a holdover from the very first data communication system, teletype. Because binary data can take on any possible pattern, byte-oriented transmission had another special character "DLE" (data link escape). Whenever a STX, ETX, or DLE code showed up in the data, the sending DLC would insert a DLE before that character, and the receiving end would remove it.

Using DLE means that an extra eight bits must be transmitted any time one of the three special patterns occurs. A later approach to framing overcomes this inefficiency, using a technique known as *bit stuffing*. The frame is set off at each end with the eight-bit pattern 01111110, and the data is modified to ensure that six one bits never appear in sequence. This is achieved by the transmitting DLC, which inserts a zero after any sequence of five ones. (It must do this even if the next data bit is zero, in order to make the protocol work.) If the receiving DLC sees six one bits in a row, that must be the beginning or end of a frame. With this done, if the receiving DLC sees five one bits followed by a zero, it removes the stuffed zero because this pattern does not exist in the data. This is quite a simple arrangement, but it is essential to effective high-speed data communication.

In the next two chapters, we will consider error control and flow control. At this point, we are ready to consider a problem and project involving bit stuffing.

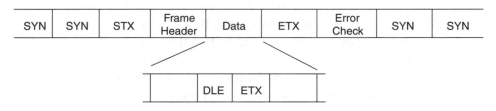

Figure 3.5 Byte-oriented stuffing.

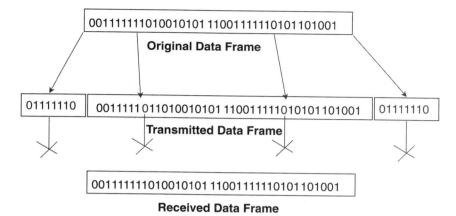

Figure 3.6 contents:

| 0011111110100101011001111110101101001 |
| **Original Data Frame** |

| 01111110 | 00111110110100101011001111101010110100 1 | 01111110 |
| | **Transmitted Data Frame** | |

| 0011111110100101011001111110101101001 |
| **Received Data Frame** |

Figure 3.6 Bit stuffing and unstuffing.

Hands-On Activities

Algorithm for Stuffing a Bit Frame

```
Copy the first eight bits to the output string without stuffing;
Scan the data bits from left to right for length minus sixteen,
{
  copy from input to output,
  {
    maintain an index, starting at 8, in the input bit array;
    another index, starting at 8, in the output array;
    and a counter, starting at zero;
    when copying a bit,
    {
      move the input bit to output;
      if it is a zero bit, set the counter to zero;
      if it is a one bit, add one to the counter;
      if the counter value is five,
      {
        insert a zero in the output;
        zero the counter;
        add one to the output index;
      }
      add one to input index;
      add one to output index;
    }
  }
}
Copy the last eight bits without stuffing.
```

```
Unstuffing: Left as an exercise for the student (it is very much
like stuffing)
```

Problem: Framing a Data Block

The following block of data needs to be framed for transmission using a bit-stuffing DLC. Show what bits need to be added to achieve this.

```
00111101 00000000 00000010 00000000 00000000 00000000 00000000 00110010
00000001 00000001 00000010 00000001 00001110 00000000 00000000 00101010
00000001 00000001 00000010 00000001 00000000 00000000 00000000 00000000
00000000 00000000 00011111 00000001 00000001 00000010 00000001 00000000
01000011 01101000 01101001 01100011 01101011 01100101 01101110 00100000
01001100 01101001 01110100 01110100 01101100 01100101 00100000 01110111
01100001 01110011 00100000 01110010 01101001 01100111 01101000 01110100
01111110 00000010 00010110
```

Answer: Run nNW solution to DLC1 to see stuffing for a similar frame.

Project: Bit Stuffing and Unstuffing Protocol

- Project DLC1. Starting with module stuff.cpp, develop a bit stuffing/unstuffing routine for framing, using the algorithm provided in this chapter. Stub code for bit stuffing/unstuffing is available in code module stuff.cpp, functions stuff() and unstuff().

- The length of the frame to be stuffed in stuff() is unstuffed_length. The frame contains initial and final flags; be careful not to stuff them, and to move them to the output frame. Note that while the stuff() stub provides a usable unstuffed_length, no such length is possible in unstuff(), because the input frame might have stuffing in the length field. Therefore, to find the end of the frame, look for the end flag (01111110).

- NW stores its data type bit in a C char (character). This may seem wasteful of storage, but it saves a lot of manipulation that would be needed to get the bits in and out of bytes. Computers today generally have more than enough storage to meet NW's needs. You can invert the NW bits using the C operator !; thus, the logical inverse of A is !A.

What Do All the Bits Mean?

A natural question regarding the data frame is, "where did all those bits come from?" The full answer to this question will have to wait a few chapters, but we can make a down payment on the answer now. If you completed the Chapter 1 project, this is not the first time you have seen these bit patterns. They come from running the Network Workbench (NW) solution to project DLC1. You may recall that the "email" message sent in that project is "Chicken Little was right~". This and the other enlightening email messages provided with NW are produced by the "fortune" program in the Unix operating system.

So, we know that somewhere embedded in the bits is this gem of wisdom about Chicken Little. Where could they be? Recalling from earlier in this chapter that the data is probably encoded in ASCII, let's look for the "C." The ASCII table tells us C = 1000011. We find this pattern (with an extra zero at the left) at the beginning of the fifth row of bits. Encouraged, we use the table in Figure 3.4 to look up the next pattern, (0)1101000, which turns out to be an "h"—we have found the message! You can verify for yourself that the subsequent bit patterns represent the remainder of the Chicken Little quip.

- DLC1 is the first of many NW projects where you must program with C pointers. A pointer is simply a variable that is used to refer to another variable using ->. For example, the function you must code is `stack::stuff(bit_frame* stuffed_frame, bit_frame* unstuffed_frame)`. Looking in nw.h, you see that bit_frame is defined as a data structure type consisting of a single array, `frame_bits[MAX_BIT_FRAME_SIZE]`. Thus, to refer to element 2 of the `bit_frame` that is passed to stuff, you would code in C: `unstuffed_frame->frame_bits[2]`. There is more information about pointers in the Helpful Hints sidebar and the sidebar at the end of Chapter 5.

- When you compile and run your code in the NW by following the directions provided for your compiler, your workbench output should show one message from the `email1` file.

Network Workbench Helpful Hints

Don't forget, you can always see the NW solution to a project by adding "//" in front of the #include in the main project module that calls in your solution module (in the case of DLC1, `stuff.cpp`).

Also, while you are debugging your bit stuffing and unstuffing routines, you may want to print out the bits your C++ function is manipulating. There is a function that does this at the beginning of module printout.cpp.

```
showbits(bit* bitdata, int length)
```

will print the data, formatted with 64 bits to a line and a blank between every eight bits for readability. For example, one function you are programming is

```
stuff(bit_frame* stuffed_frame,bit_frame* unstuffed_frame);
```

Looking up `bit_frame` in `nw.h`, you will see that the bits in a `bit_frame` are stored in `bit_frame.frame_bits`, which is of type `bit*`, just the sort of data `showbits` was built to print. So, if you want to print 150 bits of `unstuffed_frame`, you can simply include the following in your C++ code:

```
showbits(unstuffed_frame->frame_bits,150);
```

"Wait a minute," you are saying, "`bit_frame.frame_bits` is not the same thing as `bit_frame->frame_bits`." The distinction between these two is very subtle. The "dot" is used when referring to a structure using the **name** of that structure, whereas the "arrow" is used when referring to a part of a structure using a **pointer** to that structure. Because `stuff` calls for parameters of type `bit_frame*`, we are dealing with a pointer (indicated by the *). For more information about pointers, see the sidebar near the end of Chapter 5, "Data Link Control—ARQ Flow Control."

Data Link Control—Error Detection

Error Detection Methods

This chapter continues our study of the data link control (DLC) layer with an investigation of the means by which transmission errors can be detected in the DLC protocol. We will look at several methods that have been used in the DLC, and delve most deeply into the process used for the Cyclic Redundancy Check (CRC), which is used by HDLC and other important link-layer protocols today.

The basic method for checking data is to use some known characteristic to verify that the data received is probably correct. For example, if we are sending English text, and all the words received turn out to be in the English dictionary, we have an improved confidence that no character was garbled in transmission. However, it is possible for character changes to happen that do not fail this test. For example, it often happens that in typing, you may intend to type "not" but it comes out "nit," which is also acceptable to the spell-checker. This demonstrates an important principle: **We can never be 100-percent sure that any data is received as transmitted.** Even the very powerful checking method we will learn is known to miss a tiny fraction of errors.

In any event, we will not always be sending English text. Therefore, we need a method that will work regardless of the format of the data. The general approach is to send along some extra, redundant bits, derived from the data transmitted. We can derive the bits again at the receiver to determine whether it is likely that the data was garbled in transmission. The power of such an error-detecting code is measured by the probability that it will fail to detect an error.

Types of Errors

We class errors into two broad categories:

Single-bit errors, as their name implies, strike individual bits at random. Most usable transmission media have a *bit error rate (BER)* less than 10^{-3} (one in a thousand). In fact, for good media, the BER is 10^{-6} or better. Thus, the likelihood of more than one single-bit error in a data frame is miniscule.

Burst errors arise from unusual phenomena; for example, the instant when a switch is closing and is not exactly either off or on. The electric arc inside the switch lasts through many bit times, and causes electrical noise that may result in a burst of many erroneous bits. Unexpected power supply fluctuations may also cause a group of many bits to be garbled. Therefore, we need methods that can detect frames with both burst errors and single-bit errors.

Parity

One of the oldest techniques for detecting single-bit errors is to add one extra bit per group, and select that bit so that the total number of "1" bits is odd. For example, it is common to expand the seven-bit ASCII code to eight bits by adding a parity bit. Thus, the code for "D" would be 1000100 (from the table) with 1 appended (to make the number of 1 bits odd), giving 10001001. This is known as *odd parity*; if we choose instead to have an even number of 1 bits, that is *even parity*.

Parity is not a very powerful error-detecting technique. While it is guaranteed to catch a single bit error, if more than 1 bit is corrupted, on the average, 50 percent of error bursts will pass a simple parity check. We can improve the odds by using *block parity*, where there is not only a parity bit per byte, but also a parity byte at the end of a data block. The block parity bits are calculated using the *modulo two sum* so that the addition never produces a carry. A more effective variation on this arrangement is called a *checksum*, which uses normal binary addition (ignoring the carry from the high-order bit), to generate a second check byte using the data bits in reverse sequence. However, the resulting code fails to detect some burst errors that are shorter than the number of checksum bits.

Modulo Two Sum

The modulo two sum is also known in binary logic as the *exclusive or (XOR)*. We use C language notation and represent this function as "^". In adding two one-bit numbers, there are four possible combinations:

```
0 ^ 0 = 0
0 ^ 1 = 1
1 ^ 0 = 1
1 ^ 1 = 0
```

You can see that, in the first three cases, ^ behaves just like +. The difference is in the last case, where 1 ^ 1 does not produce a carry. In some cases, as in error detection, we can achieve our ends without the carry and have a simpler system. In such cases, it is common to perform binary addition modulo two. Of course, financial transactions are not such a case!

Cyclic Redundancy Check

A variety of techniques exist for error detection. They are all based on sending well-chosen redundant data. Some, such as the *Hamming code*, even allow reconstruction of the most probable value of the original transmitted data. It is a provable truth, however, that no method exists which can guarantee perfection. It is always possible to find some perverse combination of errors that any given method will fail to detect. Most data communication protocols have adopted a technique called Cyclic Redundancy Check (CRC) that has some excellent characteristics. If an additional n bits are sent, the CRC can detect:

- All single-bit errors.
- All but one error out every 2^n of any type error, so that a CRC with $n=16$ will detect all but one out of 65,536 errors. In other words, it will allow about .0015 percent of all errors to go undetected.

- All double-bit errors (when using a well-chosen coding).
- Burst errors up to n bits long, and most longer burst errors (for example, a CRC with n=16 will detect over 99.99 percent of burst errors longer than 16 bits).

CRC uses binary long division, but substitutes the modulo two sum for addition where it is used in the process. The process begins by appending to the data frame a group of n zeros, and then dividing by a specially chosen n+1 bit pattern. Mathematically this is equivalent to treating the data as a number and multiplying that number by 2^n. The reference *Data and Computer Communications* by Stallings shows the theory behind CRC calculations. When the division is complete, the remainder (also n bits long) becomes the *frame check sequence (FCS)*. The FCS is appended to the end of the original data frame when it is transmitted. Figure 4.1 shows the frame format. Figure 4.2 shows forming the FCS by long division with n=3.

One reason for the popularity of the CRC is that it is very easy to implement in digital logic. The extra n zeros are appended to the end of the data and passed serially through the logic circuit shown in Figure 4.3. The squares in the figure are storage bits; the value in each bit is shifted to its neighbor on the left, and this is done for all bits at the same time. The circles in the figure are logic gates that perform the modulo two sum function (called XOR gates). It can be shown that the logic circuit results in the long division required for the CRC. However, computers are faster than when CRC was adopted, thus the calculation is generally done in software today.

The logic circuit works because of the feedback from the output to the XOR gates. An interesting property of this circuit is shown in Figure 4.4. At the sending end, after the last data bit has been shifted through completely, the feedback path is disconnected and the FCS shifted out. Consequently, when zeros are appended to the data frame, the FCS appears in their place. At the receive end, if no data errors are detected when the frame with FCS is shifted through the circuit, the output will be 16 zeros. You can demonstrate this with the problem of Figure 4.2. Insert the calculated FCS, 111, in place of the three zeros at the end of

| FLAG | Address | Control | Data | CRC-FCS | FLAG |

Figure 4.1 Data frame format.

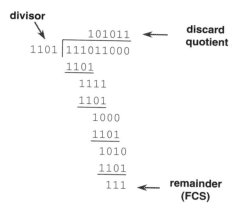

Figure 4.2   CRC calculation with n=3.

the data. The remainder will be three zeros. In practice, the CRC generator is used at the receiver by passing the entire frame through (FCS and all) and testing its output. If the output is not all zeros, an error has been detected.

Because of its excellent error-detecting characteristics, the CRC is widely used. Here are some of the more common divisors:

```
CRC-8:      100000111
CRC-16:     1100000000000101
CRC-CCITT:  10001000000100001
CRC-32:     100000100110000010001110110110111
```

The HDLC protocol uses CCITT CRC and also adds two other quirks: (1) the first 16 bits of the data are inverted before the CRC process begins; and (2) all 16 bits of the FCS are inverted at the end of the process, before it is returned.

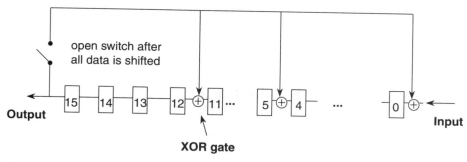

Figure 4.3   FCS generator digital logic circuit for CRC-CCITT.

SENDING END:

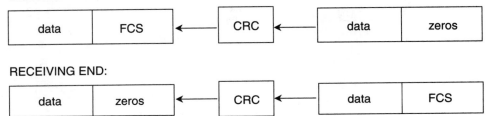

RECEIVING END:

Figure 4.4 Sending and receiving CRC-FCS generation.

Hands-On Activities

The problem and project for this chapter are designed to give you insight into how the CRC works to detect errors.

Algorithm for DLC2

The purpose here is to write a program that calculates the FCS in the same way the shift register hardware does it. Here is the algorithm to form the CRC frame check sequence:

```
NW DLC CRC Algorithm
establish an array FCS of 16 positions with initial value zero
in each position;
do for each data bit (but not for the start and end flags),
scanning the frame from left to right,
{
make a copy of the high order FCS bit, call it "feedback";
shift each FCS bit to the next higher FCS order bit;
shift one data bit into the low-order bit of the FCS;
as bits 0, 5 and 12 are shifted,
XOR them with the feedback bit;
}.
```

Problem: Calculating FCS By Hand

Given the data string: 1000011 01101000, calculate the FCS using long division with divisor 10111.

Answer: 0001

Interactive Output from the Network Workbench

So far, you have used NW in a mode where the whole program runs, and then you read the output from the screen or from file `diskout.txt`. You might prefer to see the output from your NW program one piece at a time when debugging. You can do this with NW's *interactive mode*. To turn on this mode, simply go into the main module `xxx.cpp` (for DLC2 this is `dlc2.cpp`) and uncomment the line `interactive = TRUE`. If you want to turn on interactive mode in the midst of a run, you can insert this same statement anywhere in NW code. Interactive mode will start when it is executed.

When in interactive mode, NW pauses at each `interact();` statement in the code. All of the built-in NW printout functions have this statement at the end of whatever output they are performing. The effect is to pause the console output after each output. To continue with the NW run, press Enter to continue interactive mode, "0" to continue without interaction, and "x" to stop the run.

Project: Programming the HDLC CRC

Project DLC2 requires that you complete stub function `generate_FCS` in module `crc.cpp` and run it in NW.

Controlling Network Workbench Trace Output

NW prints many details describing the data units passed from layer to layer in the stack. Trace output is produced whenever data transfer across layers in the stack, and at other key points. The selection of which messages to print is made separately for each project in the profile module `pxxxn.cpp` (for example, `pdlc2.cpp`). These messages are intended to be useful for debugging, but they do clutter the console and slow the simulation. You might want to turn some of the NW trace output off or on. The trace output function is turned off and on by the `print_at` array. The symbolic values of indexes into this array are shown near the beginning of section three in header file `nw.h`. You can change the `print_at` values either in the primary project module (for example, `dlc3.cpp`), or anywhere in any NW module. For example, to turn off the messages that show when a packet is queued, you could insert:

```
print_at[packet_queue_interface] = FALSE;
```

You might choose to do this based on the value of `sim_time` or under some other special circumstances related to the problem you are debugging.

Big End or Little End?
(Which End of the Array Is Most Significant?)

You will encounter a problem when you program `generate_FCS`: The order of the data in the FCS array is opposite from the order of the bits in Figure 4.3. This is just one example of the classic "big endian versus little endian" debate, which takes its name from an equally futile debate over cracking eggs in Swift's *Gulliver's Travels*. The problem is that one end of any data element must be "most significant"; that is, it must have the greatest weight when the data is ordered. There are good arguments for making either end most significant, so in practice the issue is settled by how the manufacturer builds the equipment.

In the NW, the bit at the left edge of the data frame occupies position zero in the data structure; that is, `bit_frame.frame_bits[0]`. This has the advantage that the frame header is always in the same place, but it also has the disadvantage that it leaves the FCS field going in the opposite direction as the bit numbers defined in the CCITT standard, so `FCS[0]` ends up holding bit 15 in terms of Figure 4.3.

What do you need to do about this? Simple: Put the incoming data into `FCS[15]`, and shift by moving `FCS[1]` to `FCS[0]`, etc. However, you need to be careful when you apply the feedback: `FCS[n+1] = feedback ^ FCS[n]` for selected bits. The "selected bits" will not be 0, 5, and 12; they will instead be 15 minus those numbers, in other words, 3, 10, and 15.

Notes

- The length of the frame has already been decoded in the stub; it is called `input_length`. Note that the *most significant bit (MSB)* of the frame is `FCS_frame->frame_bits[0]`.

- You must deal with the fact that NW treats array position zero as "most significant." This is the reverse of Figure 4.3. See the *Big End or Little End?* sidebar later in this chapter for help.

- For `generate_FCS`, the frame you receive from the Workbench will contain one of two things in the FCS field: (1) for a send frame, all zeros (in this case, these are the additional 16 zeros that are to be entered per the CRC algorithm), or (2) for a receive frame, the received FCS. Following the algorithm given previously, the FCS field will be shifted in last, with the result that the output of `generate_FCS` will be the FCS at the sending end, and zero at the receive end (assuming the CRC is passed).

- Test your code to your own satisfaction. A good approach is to showbits(FCS,16) after every shift of the data. There is an example function in the NW library that does this. To use it, add a statement CRC_example(); before print_authors(); in dlc2.cpp, run DLC2 and follow directions it produces. An example output from this function is shown in Figure 4.5.

- When finished, remove any debugging output. Your workbench output should show one message from the "email" file along with your CRC.

```
CRC-FCS Generator Example...
Enter three characters; this
program will append to them 16
trailing bits of zeros, and
print the resulting 40 bits.
This program will then calculate
the 16-bit CRC FCS.

Your three characters are:123
With 16 trailing zero bits, your
input in binary is:
00110001 00110010 00110011
00000000 00000000

Feedback    FCS Bits    Next Input

   0     00000000 00000000    0
   0     00000000 00000000    0
   0     00000000 00000000    1
   0     00000000 00000001    1
   0     00000000 00000011    0
   0     00000000 00000110    0
   0     00000000 00001100    0
   0     00000000 00011000    1
   0     00000000 00110001    0
   0     00000000 01100010    0
   0     00000000 11000100    1
   0     00000001 10001001    1
   0     00000011 00010011    0
   0     00000110 00100110    0
```

```
0    00001100 01001100    1
0    00011000 10011001    0
0    00110001 00110010    0
0    01100010 01100100    0
1    11000100 11001000    1
1    10011001 10110000    1
0    00100011 01000000    0
0    01000110 10000000    0
1    10001101 00000000    1
0    00001010 00100000    1
0    00010100 01000001    0
0    00101000 10000010    0
0    01010001 00000100    0
1    10100010 00001000    0
0    01010100 00110001    0
1    10101000 01100010    0
0    01000000 11100101    0
1    10000001 11001010    0
0    00010011 10110101    0
0    00100111 01101010    0
0    01001110 11010100    0
1    10011101 10101000    0
0    00101011 01110001    0
0    01010110 11100010    0
1    10101101 11000100    0
0    01001011 10101001    0
1    10010111 01010010

Here is the result FCS:
     10010111 01010010
```

Figure 4.5 Output of NW function CRC_example for input "123".

CHAPTER 5

Data Link Control— ARQ Flow Control

What (and Why) Is ARQ?

You should recall from Chapter 3, "Data Link Control—Framing," that the data link control (DLC) has several functions:

- **Framing.** Creating markers such that a block or *frame* of data can be identified when it arrives at the receiver.
- **Error control.** Making arrangements to detect transmission errors and, in some cases, for retransmission.
- **Flow control.** Establishing rules by which the receiver can inform the sender when it is ready to accept data.
- **Link management.** Procedures for startup and shutdown of link protocols.

This chapter will show how the second and third functions can be combined. The basic idea is that the receiving-end DLC will communicate with the sending-end DLC independently, without any supervision from the next higher layer. This is shown in Figure 5.1. It is a good example of a *peer connection*, a term that means the two are exchanging information on an equal footing—they "speak" the same protocol—but

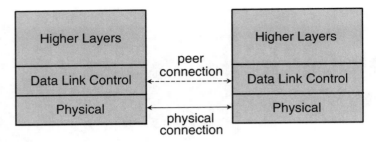

Figure 5.1 DLC peer connection.

not necessarily over a physical medium. In fact, peer connections exist at every layer of the stack. However, except at the physical layer, they are *virtual* (effectively true).

When the receiving DLC does not acknowledge receipt of a data frame after some period of time, the sending DLC sends it again. The combination of error detection, acknowledgement of frame receipt, and automatic retransmission provides a protocol feature called *automatic repeat request (ARQ)*, which also provides a form of flow control. The result is called a *reliable DLC* service. A reliable DLC is one that delivers all frames that are provided to the sender, when necessary retransmitting frames that have errors detected, and provides the frames to the next higher layer at the receiver in the order in which they were sent.

Our concern for reliability is driven by the fact that we know we can expect errors at some statistical level from the physical layer. However, the DLC could ignore errors and provide only a *best-effort* service. This is an option because providing reliability can be done at any layer above the physical layer. When we use DLC ARQ, we are tackling it head-on at the bottom of the stack. Because of the fundamental importance of reliability

Stop and Wait ARQ

The simplest form of ARQ is a positive-acknowledgement protocol. Here the sender waits after each frame for a code that we will abbreviate as ACK. This is called "stop and wait." The process is shown in Figure 5.2, where the vertical dimension corresponds to distance between sender and receiver. The transmitter (sender) is at the top, and the receiver is at the bottom. Time proceeds from left to right. The arrows represent movement of the data over time and distance. You should recall from Chapter 3 that each link has a **data rate** (number of bits it can transmit per second) and a **latency** (time for the signal to propagate

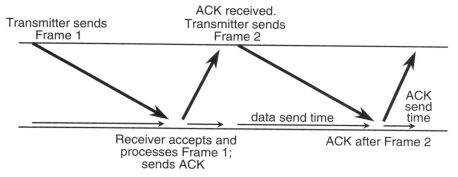

Figure 5.2   Stop and Wait ARQ for a short link.

over the link). The length of the arrows is proportional to the number of bits transmitted, because each bit requires a certain amount of time. Time to transmit is proportional to the number of bits. Latency is due to the speed of light (or other electromagnetic waves) in the medium. It is proportional to the physical length of the link.

Figure 5.2 shows the situation for a link where the time for the frame bits to pass onto the channel medium is long compared to the time for the signal to propagate from end to end (the latency of the link). Here the link is physically short, so there is almost no delay between the time the last bit is transmitted (the time of each arrow) and the time when it

Full Duplex Notes

- Because we are considering full duplex links, both ends of the link will always have the ability to send and receive. In this situation, keeping track of which end is sending and which is receiving can be a confusing process. Wherever possible, we will consider the process from one end only. That is, the examples will not include a flow of data in both directions, except for control information replies that are necessary to make the protocol work. It is important to remember that such examples are simplified. It is normal for a practical DLC to simultaneously send and receive information any time there is traffic to be passed between the two ends.

- In a full duplex link, it is normal for the transmission medium to be the same in both directions (sender to receiver and receiver to sender). In this case, the latency will also be the same in both directions.

- Full duplex protocol formats generally include a field that can be used to ACK a received frame. This saves sending a separate ACK frame because the ACK is "piggybacked" on the returning data frame.

is available at the receiver. Hence, there is little gap between the head of the first arrow (frame transmit) and the tail of the second one (ACK). The arrows indicate that the frame is moving from transmitter to receiver at a specific rate, the data rate of the link (for example, 128 kbps). We can find the amount of time this takes by the simple formula:

```
time = information_bits / link_capacity
```

For example, if we send a frame 600 bits long over a 128 kbps link, the transmit time is:

```
transmit_time = 600 / 128,000 = .00468 seconds = 4.68 ms
```

Notice that the acknowledgment also takes some time to be transmitted, but the time is shorter because the acknowledgment message is only a few bits. However, even this small amount of time reduces efficient use of the link. Ideally, we would like to have the link in use whenever there is data to be transmitted, not idly waiting for an ACK.

Now consider the case where the link is not short, as shown in Figure 5.3. Here we see that link latency is no longer negligible; in fact, it is eating into efficiency quite a lot. About half of the total time that could be used for transmitting is used instead in waiting on latency and ACK transmission. Clearly, Stop and Wait has gotten out of hand. Let's quantify link efficiency in order to understand how bad the situation is. We can define the efficiency of transmission as the fraction of total time spent actually transmitting (assuming, of course, that there is data waiting to be sent). We will neglect any time the DLC takes at either end to process the frames. In this case, we get

```
efficiency =
     transmit_time / (transmit_time + ack_time + 2*latency)
```

Units of Time

When a data channel transmits very rapidly, each bit takes a very short time. We will need to consider three such short units of time:

.001 second $= 10^{-3}$ s $= 1$ millisecond $= 1$ ms

.000001 second $= 10^{-6}$ s $= 1$ microsecond $= 1$ μs

.000000001 second $= 10^{-9}$ s $= 1$ nanosecond $= 1$ ns

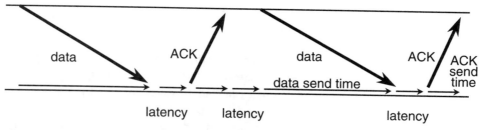

Figure 5.3 Stop and Wait ARQ for a longer link.

It is easy to see that as latency becomes large, efficiency dwindles. Consider the case of a geosynchronous satellite link with data rate 512 kbps, data frames 1000 bytes = 8000 bits long, and ACK frames 64 bits long. We know that the latency of such a link will be about .25 seconds because the signal must travel from the Earth to a 22,300 mile orbit and back. We can then calculate:

```
transmit_time = 8,000/512,000 = .0156 s
ack_time = 64/512,000 =  .000125 s
latency = .25 s
efficiency = .0156 / (.0156 + .000125 + 2*.25) = .0302
```

Thus, our expensive 512 kbps satellite link is actually performing at 15.5 kbps. Clearly, we need to find a better DLC protocol if one exists. First, however, we must consider how to keep Stop and Wait running in the presence of errors.

Timeout

When a sending DLC transmits a frame, it expects that it will not receive a reply until one round-trip time

```
(transmit_time+ack_time+2*latency)
```

What should the sender do if no reply is received? The sender must assume the frame was corrupted by errors and was considered invalid by the receiver. To deal with this, the sender creates a *timeout* interrupt, which causes the sending software to retransmit the frame. The concept of timeout is fundamental to reliable data transmission. Any reliable process needs a timeout to deal with lost data.

```
timeout =
    transmit_time + ack_time + 2*latency + processing_time
```

How Long Is a Short Link?

Figure 5.2 assumes the link is "short"—what does that mean? Let us agree that, since frames generally hold hundreds of bits (or more), any time less than the time to transmit one bit can be neglected. Now, to compare the delay in a link to one bit time, we must know how to calculate both quantities.

First: The propagation delay or latency of the link is the time for an electromagnetic signal to propagate from end to end. This is a simple calculation if we know the speed of the signal, which is the same as the speed of light (in fact, light consists of electromagnetic waves of a very high frequency). Digging back to physics, you might remember the speed of light as 186,000 miles per second (or, in a more scientific mode, 3.00×10^8 meters per second – 3E8 in C notation). What you may not have remembered is that this number represents the speed of light in a vacuum, not in a wire or a fiber optic cable. The speed of a signal in wire or glass is about 130,000 miles per second, or 2.1×10^8 meters per second. So, the latency can be calculated from the normal speed-distance relationship. If distance is measured in miles:

```
latency = distance/130,000.
```

For example, a fiber that runs directly from Washington ,DC to San Francisco, CA (about 2400 airline miles) will have a latency of 18.5 ms.

Second: The transmit time for one bit. This is simply the inverse of the data rate:

```
t_bit = 1/link_capacity
```

For example, a 1.544 Mbps link would have a bit time of 647 ns. Knowing these two formulas, with simple algebra we can compare latency to bit time to determine whether the link truly is "short" in the sense that its latency is less than one bit transmit time. For example, for the 1.544 Mbps link to have latency less than one bit time would require

```
d < 130,000*t_bit  = .0842 mile
```

So, we can say that a "short" link is less than about a tenth of a mile. Notice, however, that our definition of "short" depends on the link's data rate. The higher the data rate, the shorter "short" becomes.

Estimating `processing_time` requires information about the computers used and their workload. In this book, we will either ignore `processing_time`, or use a small constant factor as an estimate.

More Efficient ARQ

Clearly, what we need is an ARQ that lets the sender continue to transmit while the ACK process proceeds, as in Figure 5.4. This is not hard to achieve; we only need to be able to keep track of more than one

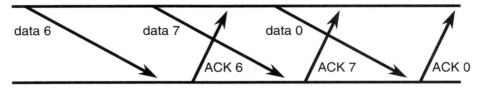

Figure 5.4 Overlapped data transmission and ACKs (3-bit field).

frame and, in case of loss, retransmit any that were lost. There are several approaches to doing this. All of them require the addition of two numbers to the protocol.

SN and RN

SN. The *sequence number* assigned to the frame that carries it.

RN. The *request number* that indicates the **next** frame the end that sent the frame expects.

A few facts about these numbers are important to remember:

- A protocol using SN and RN creates an ACK for a frame by sending back a frame with RN set to a value that is a function of the received SN. For example, the protocol we will consider in the next section uses `RN = SN + 1`. This says that the next frame expected is the one with the next value of SN.

- A protocol using SN and RN can send a *negative acknowledgement* (NACK) by sending an RN that indicates the frame was not received. For example, in the protocol to be considered in the next section, if a frame is not considered valid, the protocol just sends back a frame with RN = SN of the bad frame.

- The data fields for SN and RN in frames can only have a fixed number of bits. If too many frames are sent, the numbers will "wrap"; that is, they will go past their maximum value. The protocol must continue to work properly when this happens, so it uses a *modular number system*. Some common field sizes are three bits, which permits eight unique frame numbers (modulo 8), and 8 bits, which permits 256 numbers (modulo 256). In Figure 5.4 you can see that the three-bit field results in a maximum value of seven, so the frame number after 7 is 0.

- The number of frames that can be "in transit" at any given time is called the *window.* The general category of protocols that use windows is called *sliding window* protocols. The window cannot possibly be larger than the largest number that will fit in the SN and RN field, because there is no way to account for all of the frames not yet ACK'd.

- The window might, however, be smaller than this largest number. One reason to use a smaller window is that the sender must save or *buffer* all frames that have not been acknowledged by the receiver. The sender may not be able to allocate enough memory to buffer a large number of frames. (This was more likely to happen in years past than today. Typical computers have much larger memories today than typical computers had a few years ago.)

- For any given protocol, there will be a rule that defines how large the window can be. If the window were allowed to exceed this value, the ARQ process could associate two different frames with the same SN.

- It is very easy to get confused when you are looking at both ends of a sliding window operation. You must be careful to identify which end sent the SN and RN. There is an SN and an RN for each end.

- Remember the general rule for advancing the window: When a sender receives an ACK for the lowest frame in the window, the window can advance. Advancing means sending a new frame at the high end of the window.

- It is normal for numbers to wrap when using modular numbering. For example, with a three-bit SN field, the next SN after 7 is 0.

Figure 5.5 shows the same situation as Figure 5.4, but using SN and RN for the next protocol we will describe. Here RN is always 1 greater (modulo 8) than the SN being ACK'd.

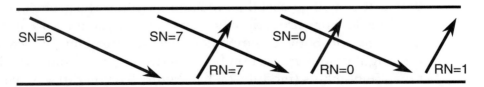

Figure 5.5   Overlapped data and ACKs with SN and RN.

Modular Arithmetic

Any time we are computing with mechanisms where the maximum size of a number is fixed, we must deal with the possibility that we will create a number larger than that size. One way to deal with this problem is to define the rules of arithmetic so that adding one to the largest possible number gives the smallest possible number. In such a system, negative numbers may be disallowed. If so, we have a *modular* system. In such a system, the quantity one greater than the maximum number is called the *modulus*, and the result of all operations is defined *modulo* the modulus. The result of a modular arithmetic operation is formed by computing the remainder when the result is divided by the modulus.

In C++, this quantity can be expressed as $n\%m$, where n is the (nonmodular) result of the calculation, m is one greater than the maximum number, and $\%$ is the C++ sign for the modulo operation. Thus, because the remainder when 11 is divided by 7 is 4,

```
11 % 7 = 4
```

For example, if we are working in a four-bit data field, we use modulo 16 and the largest possible number is $1111_2 = 15_{10}$. In this case, the result of adding 13 and 9 is

```
(13 + 9) % 16 = 6
```

Go-Back-N ARQ

Different protocol algorithms exist to solve the problem of keeping track of SN and RN for a window full of frames. The one we will consider here is called "Go-Back-N" because it deals with bad frames by retransmitting all frames in the window, beginning with the bad one. While this may seem wasteful, it works out to be satisfactory in most cases, because:

- Bad frames do not happen all that often on a practical data communication link.
- The Go-Back-N algorithm is very simple and trouble free.
- It has the advantage that good frames always show up at the receiver in order, so the buffer at the receive end only needs to be large enough for a single frame.

The rules of Go-Back-N are:

- The maximum window size is equal to the largest number the SN and RN fields can hold. This means the maximum window size is one less than the number of different SN and RN values, because SN and RN can have values from zero up to the maximum.

- At the receiver, the RN is the value of SN for the next frame expected to be received. Thus, the rule is, when a new frame is received and passes CRC, if SN = RN, set RN = SN + 1; otherwise, do nothing.

- The receiver may send an ACK containing RN, or it may wait and piggyback RN on the next data frame it sends.

- At the sender, when a frame is sent, a timer is set with timeout equal to one round trip according to the formula shown earlier. If no ACK is received by timeout, the frame is sent again.

- When the sender receives a frame with RN greater than the SN of one or more frames in the window, that is an ACK for those frames, so it deletes them from its buffer. It then sends and buffers enough new frames to keep the window full.

Figure 5.6 shows how SN and RN work in a more complicated situation, where data frames are lost due to errors. It uses a field size of two bits; thus, the possible numbers for SN and RN are 0, 1, 2, and 3. Figure 5.6 is complicated to understand, because both ends are sending at the same time. You should look carefully at the details. Note particularly the fact that the RN from either end does not increase until a new frame is successfully received from the other end. Also, note what happens when a transmission error destroys frame 1 from the bottom sender, and a NAK from the top sender shows it is still waiting on frame 1. Even though the bottom sender has already sent its frame 2, it must back up and send its frame 1 again, followed by its frame 2.

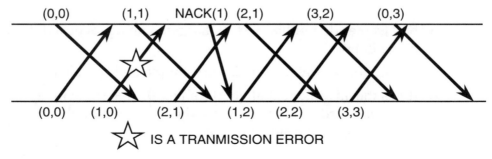

Figure 5.6   Go-Back-N in operation (SN and RN fields two bits).

Link Initialization

Now that you have learned the various techniques for ARQ, you need to understand why and how a link is initially brought into operation by the DLC. Recall from Chapter 3 on framing that it is necessary for the sender and receiver to "synchronize" so that both ends know the state of the communication process at all times. This is actually a general property of communication: The communicating processes must both be prepared for information transfer. It works this way with human communication, too. As we all know, you must have a listener's attention or you may as well not speak! We will see at every layer of the protocol stack that the two communicating processes must first arrive at a state where they are prepared to transfer information.

Link initialization is the process by which the DLC reaches a state at both ends of the link in which it is ready for information to be transferred. In the case of an ARQ link, this means SN and RN are set to zero. This can be achieved in one of two ways:

- Manually reset the software at both ends, which will start SN and RN at value zero.

- Initialize the link using a "three-way handshake" where the sender and receiver exchange messages causing reset of SN and RN (these are the first two parts of the handshake), followed by the first data frame (this is the third part).

The second method is better (if somewhat more complex) because it works without manual intervention. Figure 5.7 shows the startup three-way handshake sequence:

- Part 1. The end that wants to start the link sends a *supervisory frame* with a code that says "connect." Supervisory frames do not contain data; they provide information to manage the link.

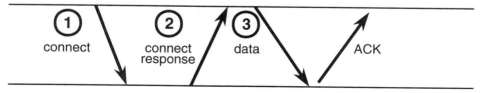

Figure 5.7 Link initialization sequence (three-way handshake).

- The supervisory frame might be lost due to errors, so the starting end also sets a timer. The timeout value is the same one we considered earlier in this chapter. If there is no response, the connect frame will be sent again after the timeout.
- Part 2. The other end responds by acknowledging the connection.
- Part 3. Now the starting end can send a data frame. The other end can also begin sending data. In the figure, it has nothing to send, so it simply replies with an ACK showing that the next expected frame will have SN=1. If the other end has data to send, it could start sending at the same time as the starting end.

The best way to shut down a link also involves a three-way handshake. It is necessary to tell the DLC at the other end to stop sending, and to complete reliable transmission of any frames still in the buffer. Either end can start the shutdown process. The three parts of the handshake are:

- The end that decides to shut down stops sending data and sends a supervisory frame with a "disconnect" code.
- The other end stops sending data, acknowledges the shutdown, and ACKs the final frame correctly received.
- The end that decided to shut down confirms with an ACK for the final frame it correctly received.

Addresses in Frames

Up to this point, we have been ignoring an important function of the DLC, *addressing*. The reason for addressing is that a link may be used in *multidrop* mode; that is, it may have several different stations with separate hardware interfaces attached. Thus, each station is assigned a unique code that the other stations use when sending frames to it. The *header* of the frame (the control information that precedes the data) includes the sending and receiving station addresses. This arrangement was popular at one time as a means of holding down circuit costs, and it still is important in local area networks. We will see it again in the chapter on Ethernet. For now, you should take a look at the frame format DLC_frame in nw.h, identify the header, and note that it includes addresses, which are called from_port_id and to_port_id.

The NW DLC State-Transition Diagram

The NW `dlc_send` function operates in one of three distinct conditions or *states*: `waiting`, `dl_sending`, and `sending_supv`. The way `dlc_send` is designed ensures that it will go back to the state it came from each time it is called, unless the program logic explicitly determines a need for change of state. This is achieved by a C case statement that causes the function to enter the logic for one of the states, based on the value of `this_iface->dl_send_state` associated with the interface in question. The value of that variable is called a *state variable* because it uniquely determines the state in which the function operates. In addition, it persists between times when the function is invoked by virtue of existing in storage that is allocated outside of `dl_send`.

A very useful way of documenting the behavior of a system with a finite number of identifiable states is a *state-transition diagram*, which shows:

- The possible states the system can take on
- What causes it to move from one state to another
- Optionally, its output when changing state

Figure 5.8 is the state-transition diagram for `dl_send`. Using this diagram, we can see that `dl_send` starts operation in state `waiting`, and

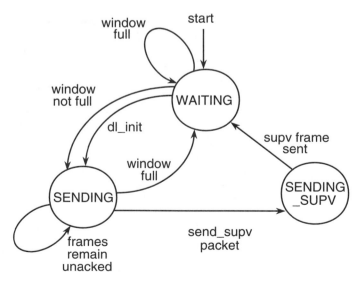

Figure 5.8   State-transition diagram for NW DLC send function.

moves to state `sending` under influence of `function dl_init` (NW's link initialization). If frames remain unACKed, it stays in sending state; if the window is full, it returns to state `waiting`, and function `send_supv_packet` can move it to state `sending_supv` (this occurs when there is no more data to send yet an ACK must be sent, which is done by a supervisory frame).

Point to Point Protocol (PPP)

Earlier in this book, we noted that DLC protocols are not truly "Internet" protocols because they are not standardized by the IETF. An exception to that rule is the *Point to Point Protocol (PPP)*, which has been standardized in order to provide a consistent way to connect between various "islands" in the Internet. PPP is used widely to provide Internet connections through dial-up links. It includes additional capabilities such as assignment of a temporary Internet Protocol (IP) address for the system that is connecting by dial-up. (Internet addresses, like frame addresses, serve to identify the sender, but the IP offers access to the broader Internet, which a DLC protocol cannot. More on this in Chapter 8 on the Internet Protocol.) PPP also provides useful options such as having a password that must be given to make the dial-up connection. The PPP frame closely resembles the HDLC frame shown in Figure 5.9; however, PPP differs from HDLC in one

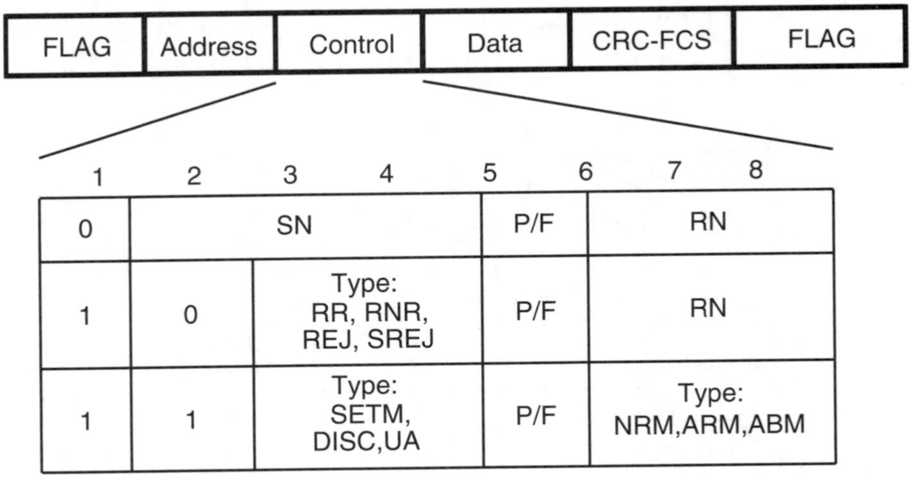

FLAG	Address	Control	Data	CRC-FCS	FLAG

1	2	3	4	5	6	7	8
0	SN			P/F	RN		
1	0	Type: RR, RNR, REJ, SREJ		P/F	RN		
1	1	Type: SETM, DISC,UA		P/F	Type: NRM,ARM,ABM		

Figure 5.9   HDLC protocol frame format.

significant aspect: It uses character stuffing rather than bit stuffing. This means that every PPP frame contains an integer number of bytes.

 # Hands-On Activities

The problem and project in this chapter are designed to give you insight into an important ARQ protocol.

The NW Go-Back-N Algorithm

All decisions in `dl_send` and `dl_receive` can be made in the context of the state contained in the structure for which `link_iface` is a pointer. Two particularly important variables for the interface (link) state in NW are the upper and lower sequence number bounds of the window associated with that interface (`link_iface`). These variables are `link_iface->SNmin` and `link_iface->SNmax`. The values of SN and RN in send and receive frames are also very important. The algorithms used by the NW DLC are:

```
NW DLC send algorithm
state waiting (in this state the DLC has been sending but has been
blocked by the fact the window is full; it wakes up here after a timeout
and takes some action):
{
  if the range between SNmin and SNmax is not smaller than the window
  (the window is full so continue with the proper actions for waiting),
  {
    send the frame in buffer position SNmin;
    after transmission continue with case waiting;
  }
  else (the range between SNmin and SNmax is smaller than the window),
   an ACK has been received so continue with case dl_sending;
}
state dl_sending (in this state the DLC expects to dequeue and send the
next frame, the first step is to dequeue and buffer the frame):
{
  if the range between SNmin and SNmax is smaller than the window,
  {
    attempt to take a frame from the input queue;
    if there is a frame available,
    {
      set SN=SNmax;
      buffer the frame in position SNmax;
```

```
        increment SNmax|mod DL_WINDOW_MAX;
    }
    else if frames remain unacked you need to continue re-sending the
    SNmin frame,
      set SN=SNmin;
    otherwise nothing remains to be sent,
    {
      set link_active to FALSE;
      set send_state to waiting;
      escape from this case;
    }
    this leaves the next frame to be sent in buffer position SN,
    finish that frame,
    {
      insert RN;
      insert CRC-FCS;
      stuff frame;
    }
    if the window becomes full with this frame,
      set dl_send_state to waiting so no more frames are sent until
      ACKs are received;
    finish by sending the frame that was just made to the physical
    layer;
  }
}
state sending_supv (in this state send a receiver_ready supervisory
frame because a send_supv packet has been received indicating dl_receive
found a need for an ACK and queued that packet):
{
  make the supervisory packet;
  send it;
}.
```

The NW DLC Send Algorithm

This algorithm is conservative in that, if it has no new data to send and frames in the buffer have not been ACKed, it simply retransmits them during idle line time. This can result in better performance in the presence of errors, in that a frame that suffered an error may be retransmitted before a NACK is received, and thus arrive sooner than it otherwise would have. This is a reasonable practice for a point-to-point link, but not for a shared link layer such as Ethernet where other senders might use the capacity instead. A consequence of this behavior is that when there are no frames to send the DLC at one end of the link will be sending the last frame sent, or a supervisory frame.

NW DLC receive algorithm
When a frame passing the CRC check is received,
{
   if RN of that frame is within the current window and above
   SNmin in the window,
      set SNmin = RN of that frame;
   if SN of that frame is equal to RN sent to other end,
   {
      release the contents to the network layer;
      increment RN using modular arithmetic;
   }
}.

Problem: Finding the Window

A very useful function will be found immediately following the initial comments in `code/dllogic.cpp`.

```
bit stack::LTwindow(byte Nmin, byte Nmax)
//  tests whether the range between two numbers is less than the
//  window size DLC_WINDOW_FRAMES, given counter range DLC_WINDOW_MAX
//  (useful in dlc_send)
//  Nmin is logically lower end of range, the lowest number not ACKed
//  Nmax is logically higher end of range, the next number to be used
//
{
  int testmax=Nmax;
  if(Nmin > Nmax) testmax = testmax+DL_WINDOW_MAX;
  return(testmax-Nmin < DL_WINDOW_FRAMES);
}
```

Your assignment is to complete a companion function, which you are likely to find useful in project DLC3. (HINT: INwindow is very similar to LTwindow.) Here is the stub for INwindow:

```
bit stack::INwindow(byte Nmin, byte Nmax)
// tests whether range between two numbers is within the
// window size DL_WINDOW_FRAMES, given DLC counter range DL_WINDOW_MAX
// (useful in dlc_receive)
{
  return FALSE; // student must replace FALSE with appropriate code
}
```

C/C++ Refresher: Pointer Variables

A very powerful feature of the C/C++ language is the ability to refer to data by the internal computer address where it resides, combined with a definition of its format. For example, at the beginning for function `dlc_send` in module `dl.cpp`, the function is defined like this:

```
bit stack::dlc_send(packet* current_packet,
                    link_interface_state* this_iface)
```

This statement says, "From this point forward in `dlc_send`, variable `current_packet` will refer to a data structure of type `packet`, and `this_iface` will refer to a data structure of type `link_interface_state`." You can see that this sort of facility improves program efficiency a great deal because the compiler can find the whole collection of data that goes by the name `this_iface` just by referring to the address that variable contains. It also improves the effectiveness of the human programmer who can remember that one variable is the key to a whole collection of data.

However, we know that powerful tools are dangerous, and this is certainly true of pointers. They manipulate machine addresses directly, and even can have their associated data format (type) changed by a feature called *typecasting* that is used in the DES functions of NW. It is very common for an addressing error (such as a protection violation or segmentation fault) to be traced to an error in working with pointers. You can steer clear of such problems simply by limiting your code to the pointers that have been set up and debugged in the NW stubs, and using them to point to the objects with which they were designed to work.

For example, to work with `this_iface`, we would first look at `nw.h` to find out what sort of information is stored in a data structure of type `link_interface_state`. By loading `nw.h` in a text editor and doing a "find," you can learn that `link_interface_state` contains all the state information about the interface, including the current values of SN and RN. Now, if you want to find the SN of the last frame sent at the interface for which `dlc_send` was called, you can use the variable `this_iface->SN`. For example, to set the SN to zero you would use:

```
this_iface->SN = 0;
```

Many of the functions you will write in NW involve state structures. The reason for this is that NW consolidates all of the state data for a particular function into a single structure. The types used for this are `host_state`, `link_interface_state`, and `mac_interface_state`. The result of treating state data in this way is that an NW stack function is entirely independent of the global state of the simulated network. It has all of the data it needs in one place!

Project: Programming Logic for Go-Back-N ARQ

Project DLC3 uses NW to create a simulation of a full duplex data link, using a link control protocol similar to HDLC to pass one sequence of frames from A to B, and another sequence from B to A. The NW software provides everything but your control logic, either in source code or from the binary library. There is a DLC module in the workbench code library, dl.cpp, that links with the other layers provided and works. Because the working of the DLC is rather complex, this project has been distilled down to its essence, which is the decision logic by which the DLC determines what to do at critical points in the protocol operation. All of the ARQ logic is held in stub dllogic.cpp. The logic for ARQ is included in the comments in dl.cpp and is the same as the algorithms provided earlier in this chapter. Therefore, you will need to analyze the dl.cpp comments and code in order to complete dllogic.cpp.

Your DLC must be able to function in the presence of transmission errors. The NW physical layer code provides an error generator so you can demonstrate that your ARQ works. As before, the simulation application is email; two files email1.txt and email2.txt are passed between nodes 1 and 2. The simulation printout is configured such that you will see the application layer in the workbench forming the email and sending it down to the data link layer.

For debugging, you will probably want to start with one email file, zero bit error rate, and possibly interactive operation. You can cause this to happen by adding statements as shown in the comments of dlc3.cpp, such as:

```
number_of_nodes_sending_email = 1;
link_bit_error_rate = 0;
interactive = TRUE;
```

At the end of the project you should remove any such statements and run with the defaults.

Notes

- If your code is working correctly, it will get all the packets exchanged eventually, even in the presence of bit errors. However, experience has shown that debugging with two files or even just with errors is difficult, so it is best to tackle the problem in pieces, like this:

- One file and no errors
- One file and errors
- Two files and no errors
- Two files and errors

- You will probably find functions LTwindow and INwindow are useful in completing the project. Many problems with this project arise from not making sliding window tests correctly.

- The ARQ algorithm provided is conservative in that, if there is no new data to send and frames in the buffer have not been ACKed, it simply retransmits a frame during idle line time. This can result in better performance in the presence of errors, in that a frame that suffered an error may be retransmitted before a NACK is received, and thus arrive sooner than it otherwise would have. A consequence of this behavior is that when there are no frames to send, the DLC will be sending the oldest frame previously sent or a supervisory frame.

- You can verify that your ARQ is working correctly checking the performance summary statistics produced by NW at the end of each run. It should look something like Figure 5.10. The "Remaining in Queue" column should be zero for DLC3. Frames sent and received are counted as they leave dlc_send and return to dlc_receive. Error frames are counted by the link error generator and CRC error detection functions. Dropped packets happen because frames with errors are detected. In Chapter 8 you will learn about the queue of packets coming from the network layer to the DLC layer. Packets also can be dropped if this queue overflows its buffer.

| Node-Interface | -Data Frames- | | ---Error Frames--- | | Packets | Remaining |
	Sent	Received	Generated	Detected	Dropped	in Queue
1 - 1	13	13	1	2	2	0
1 - 2	0	0	0	0	0	0
2 - 1	13	13	2	1	1	0
2 - 2	0	0	0	0	0	0
2 - 3	0	0	0	0	0	0

Figure 5.10   NW DLC output statistics for two nodes.

CHAPTER 6

Ethernet LANs

I n the mid-1970s, a research team at Xerox Corporation developed a way to generalize the multidrop DLC concept to an inexpensive form of interconnection that has come to be called a *local area network (LAN)*. This chapter will present concepts and a project associated with the LAN system developed at Xerox, which is known as Ethernet. In the process, you will learn how the DLC can be expanded to provide a *media access control (MAC)* sublayer that allows multiple stations to share transmission media. The next chapter will build on the MAC concept to present the other major LAN approach, token passing.

What Is Ethernet?

You should recall from Chapter 1, "The Internet Protocol Stack and the Network Workbench," that a LAN has these general characteristics:

- Spans a small distance, typically a single building, or a few buildings on a campus

- Offers high data rates (from 2 megabits per second upwards)
- Does not provide multiple (or *redundant*) paths between nodes
- Probably uses a broadcast paradigm: all stations receive every transmission
- Is relatively inexpensive
- Generally is owned by the organization that uses it

Multidrop Data Links versus LANs

This book refers to the computers attached to the LAN as *stations*, a generic word intended to convey a wide range spanning mainframes, workstations, routers, and even sales terminals. The previous chapter touched on the existence of *multidrop* links, which have several stations connected, each with its own address. The addresses are used in sending messages among the stations which, because they are all connected to the same wire, all receive every frame. With HDLC multidrop, each station's network interface and/or its system software detects which messages are intended for that station and ignores all others.

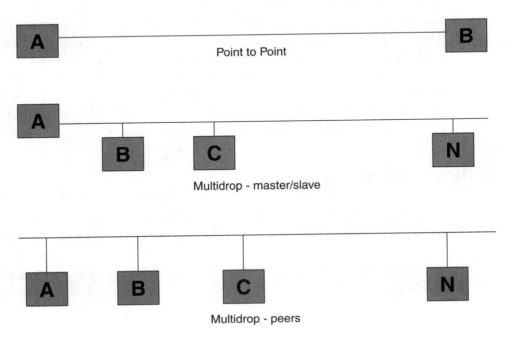

Figure 6.1   Link configurations for multidrop.

Figure 6.1 shows the development of the multidrop concept. The first serial wire links were strictly point to point, linking two stations. Then the concept of multidrop in a *master-slave* arrangement was developed. Multidrop saves on wiring costs because the wire can be strung from station to station, rather than connecting all stations to a central switch or hub. In the master-slave arrangement, the master sends a *polling* message to each slave in turn, and the slaves respond if they have data to be transmitted. This can be time-consuming if there are a lot of slaves, but it works. A refinement of this concept is the *peer multidrop* arrangement where any station can transmit to any other, using a *contention protocol* by which they contend for use of the link. We will not consider the HDLC contention protocol here. Later in this chapter, you will learn about the Ethernet contention protocol. It is very similar to HDLC contention and much more important for you to know.

From Multidrop to Ethernet, by Way of Hawaii

Ethernet can be thought of as a convergence of multidrop link technology with media access control. To understand how this happens, we must go back to the late 1960s and consider a system created to link computers among the Hawaiian Islands. Today, the islands are linked by optical fibers, but at that time the water barriers between the islands stood in the way of networking their computers. The low data rates available over submarine wires with the modems of the time were not an adequate solution, so technologists of the 50th state set out to create a radio-based network called ALOHA. The network worked like this:

- Every computer had a radio transmitter and receiver.
- Propagation time among the islands was many microseconds, because the islands are miles apart (radio waves take time to propagate, even at the speed of light).
- All frames were transmitted to a central hub. The hub would send the frame out again, to be received by its intended destination computer.
- Even if a given transmitter could receive the signals of all other transmitters, because of propagation time (the speed of light problem, again) it was not possible to know if the others had started sending; so the rule was, "if you have a frame to send, send it."

- This rule resulted in many "collisions" where two or more frames arrived at the hub at the same time.

- Thus, a second rule was needed: When you send a frame to the hub, listen for it to be retransmitted from the hub; if you don't hear it repeated, send it again.

- When retransmitting a frame, a station must wait a random amount of time to start (within some limit); otherwise, it is certain that another collision will occur when all stations start sending again at the same time.

- Due to collisions, the maximum theoretical effective use of the radio channel is about 18 percent; the rest of the capacity is unavailable.

ALOHA led to development of several other multiple-access protocols. The first was slotted ALOHA, which added to ALOHA a requirement that the stations transmit in synchronized time slots. This reduced the randomness of collisions with the result that, in theory, the maximum effective use of the channel went up to about 37 percent.

The next innovation was for the sender to listen to the channel, and not send if another station already was sending. This is called *carrier sense multiple access (CSMA)*. It works much better. In theory, it is possible for effective use of the CSMA channel to be over 99 percent. However, it has the drawback that, when two frames collide, the slot in which they collide is lost. The last step in this development was CSMA with *collision detection (CSMA/CD)*, the protocol that is used in Ethernet. In CSMA/CD, the stations listen to the medium to determine if a collision has occurred; if so, they stop sending. This has the effect of making the slots very small, on the order of maximum time for a signal to propagate across the network and back, which is the time necessary to determine that a collision has occurred. By minimizing the fraction of time used for the contention process, CSMA/CD is able to achieve a theoretical maximum utilization in excess of 99.9 percent. (Unfortunately, this theoretical result does not hold up in practice—see the description of degraded performance when Ethernet is heavily loaded, later in this chapter.)

The Xerox development of Ethernet brought together multidrop links and contention protocols, and added a third, very attractive element: much higher data rates. The higher rates were made possible by con-

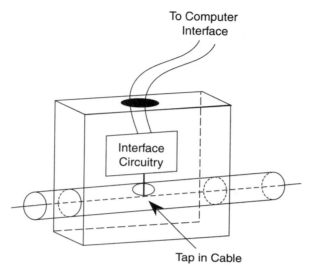

To Computer
Interface

Interface
Circuitry

Tap in Cable

Figure 6.2   Original Ethernet adapter with coaxial cable.

fining the signal to a coaxial cable. This first commercial form of Ethernet was, in retrospect, quite crude. It used a heavy coaxial cable, about half an inch thick, which had to run past every connected station and required a special terminator at both ends. Adapters were installed by cutting a hole in the cable's shield layer and inserting a tap through the internal insulation (see Figure 6.2). It is not surprising that the form of the Ethernet interface evolved rapidly. The next version was a thinner coaxial cable system, sometimes called "thinwire," which had connectors instead of cut-in taps. Later, Ethernet evolved to the system now in widespread use, which uses twisted pair wire cables and RJ-45 connectors similar to modular telephone plugs.

Why Did They Call It Ethernet?

The Xerox team that developed Ethernet thought of the coaxial cable as a medium analogous to the "ether" that was postulated by late nineteenth-century physicists to explain the transmission of light through space. A famous experiment disproved the ether theory in physics, but the notion of a fast medium for information flow suited the Xerox concept perfectly. So, the new technology came to be called Ethernet, and the name has stuck in the technical community (we will touch on the "real" name of the standard later).

How Does Ethernet Work?

What we have been calling Ethernet was formally standardized by the *Institute of Electrical and Electronics Engineers, Inc. (IEEE)* under their LAN standards, series number 802. Within this series, the standard derived from the original Xerox Ethernet is *IEEE Standard 802.3.* The types of 802.3 currently in widespread use are the 10 Mbps type, 10BASET (pronounced "ten base tee"), and the 100 Mbps type, 100BASET. The following sections consider the physical organization, protocol operation, and performance of these "Ethernet" LAN systems. This book deals with only the most common forms of 802.3. For more details, see the reference *Local Area Networks: A Client/Server Approach* by Goldman.

Open Standards

The IEEE 802 series is an excellent example of an *open standards* process. If Xerox had kept Ethernet as a proprietary standard, other manufacturers might not have been willing to risk creating new products intended to operate interconnected (or *interoperate*) with Ethernet. Xerox chose to move its work into the IEEE, which is a not-for-profit organization that describes itself as "the world's largest technical-professional society." The IEEE standards process is described as "open" because its operation is fully visible to all participants, and anybody can propose new standards features. Although only IEEE members get to vote on adoption, joining IEEE requires only a demonstration of technical credentials.

The IEEE is one of several organizations that promulgate open standards, to the benefit of the whole networking community. Some other important standards bodies for networking are

- The Internet Engineering Task Force (IETF), responsible for Internet protocol standards.
- The International Telecommunication Union-Telecommunication Standardization Sector (ITU-T), responsible for a wide range of communication standards, such as HDLC.
- The Electronic Industries Association (EIA), which provides physical interface standards such as the "RS-232" connection from workstation to modem.

Software Organization for Ethernet

In order to use a shared medium as a LAN, it is necessary to expand the DLC protocol as shown in Figure 6.3. It is important that you understand that Ethernet and other LAN protocols are expansions of the DLC, and as such are simpler in many ways than network layer protocols such as the Internet Protocol. Figure 6.3 shows that the DLC layer for a LAN has two parts:

Logical Link Control (LLC) sublayer. The protocol logic for flow control and error control, as presented in Chapter 5 on data link control. This typically is implemented in software that runs in the connected computer and is specified by protocol IEEE 802.2.

Media Access Control (MAC) sublayer. The protocol that deals with sharing the transmission media. This typically is implemented as a software driver for the network adapter interface hardware, which might be a separate box but more often takes the form of a circuit card that is plugged into the computer and also has a connector for the LAN medium. The Ethernet MAC protocol is IEEE 802.3. There are other protocols for other MAC technologies.

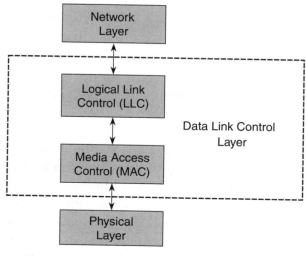

Figure 6.3 DLC for LANs.

> **Latin Lesson**
>
> The English word *medium*, meaning "in between," comes from the Latin; thus, its plural has the Latin form *media*. It is therefore appropriate to speak of "a medium" or of "several media," but not of "a media."

Physical Connections in Ethernet

The most basic LAN structure is a wire that connects all stations, as shown in Figure 1.3, and as the top model in Figure 6.4. The adapter shown in Figure 6.2 is tapped into such a wire. The same diagram applies to thinwire coaxial Ethernet LANs, which are built from coaxial cable segments plugged together to form a single long wire, or "bus." There is a limitation of 500 meters on the total length of the thickwire, and 185 meters on the thinwire. The reason for the limit will be explained later in this chapter. The thickwire system is called 10BASE5 in the IEEE standards, where the thinwire system is called 10BASE2. The 10 in these names stands for the transmit rate of 10 Mbps. These coaxial LANs have the property that a loose connection at any point in the bus can cause the network to become inoperable at all stations, due to the properties of coaxial cable transmission.

The successor system, 10BASET, is much more practical. It is assembled from twisted-pair wiring known as *unshielded twisted pair (UTP)*. This wiring is similar to standard telephone wiring, but it needs to be at least *category three* for 10BASET and *category five* for 100BASET. UTP is more flexible than coaxial cable and is interconnected with the very practical RJ-45 connector. The RJ-45 is an eight-conductor version of the standard four-conductor modular telephone RJ-11 connector. Best of all, the system is built up from hubs that serve as breakout points. A single 10BASET twisted pair can support multiple stations by using a *hub* that splits the connection several ways. If a station is disconnected from the hub, its jack is automatically disabled rather than disabling the network as in 10BASE5 and 10BASE2. (Most hubs have an indicator that illuminates when the connection is good.) The distance limitation also takes on a different form here. No 10BASET connection is allowed to be more than 100 meters from its hub, and no two stations can be more than 2500 meters apart. The lower part of Figure 6.4 shows the IEEE 10BASET layout. The same figure applies to the newer 100BASET

10BASE5 and 10BASE2:

10BASET and 100BASET:

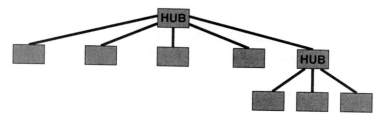

Figure 6.4 IEEE 10BASET "Ethernet" LANs.

system, which has a 100 Mbps data transfer rate with a 100 meter limitation on distance from the hub and a 210 meter overall distance, using two twisted pairs per connection. Both twisted pair standards can use multiple levels of hubs, within the overall wiring distance limitations, but 10BASET cannot have more than four hubs between any two stations, and 100BASET cannot have more than two.

Ethernet Protocol

Figure 6.5 shows the Ethernet frame format. You can see the data fields in the frame.

Preamble-SF is the synchronizing pattern and start-of-frame pattern for the Ethernet frame.

Destination is the 48-bit address on the LAN to which the frame is sent.

Source is the 48-bit address of the sending station (these addresses are wired into network adapters at the factory, and are assigned in such a way that there are no duplicates).

Length is the length of the data field.

Pad is padding, which is added to ensure that the data field is at least 368 bits long.

CRC-FCS is the cyclic redundancy code frame check sequence, as described in Chapter 4 on DLC error detection.

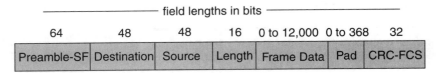

64	48	48	16	0 to 12,000	0 to 368	32
Preamble-SF	Destination	Source	Length	Frame Data	Pad	CRC-FCS

Figure 6.5   Ethernet frame format.

A key aspect of the Ethernet protocol is the CSMA/CD contention protocol, which lets independent stations share the LAN medium in a sort of "free for all" fashion. Here are the rules for the protocol:

1. If the medium is idle, transmit; otherwise, go to step 2.
2. If the medium is busy, continue to listen until the channel is idle, then transmit immediately.
3. If a collision is detected during transmission, transmit a brief jamming signal to ensure that all stations know there has been a collision; then cease transmission.
4. After transmitting the jamming signal, wait a random amount of time, then repeat from step 1.

The "random time" is derived by *binary exponential backoff*.

1. After the first collision, wait either 0 or 1 time slots (with equal probability) to transmit.
2. After the second collision, wait 0, 1, 2, or 3 time slots; after the nth collision wait 0 to 2n–1 time slots; limit n to 10 (0 to 1023 time slots).
3. After 16 collisions, report failure to the sending process.

You have just read that under CSMA/CD a station senses the carrier, and does not start sending if it senses some other station is already sending. Why then should we expect collisions at all? The answer is that, even over a distance as short as 2500 meters, it takes time for the signal to travel the length of the LAN, as illustrated in Figure 6.6. In the worst case, two stations at opposite ends of the LAN start sending at the same instant. We have to allow time for the signal to propagate to the other end of the LAN and back. The time to do this is the slot size for CSMA/CD. For example, the propagation velocity of signals in twisted pair cable is .59 times the speed of light in a vacuum, or 1.77×10^8 meters per second. So, for 10BASET:

```
slot_size_in_seconds = lan_length_in_meters * 1.77E8
```

We can also measure the slot size in bits.

```
slot_size_in_bits = LAN_data_rate * slot_size_in_seconds
```

For 10BASET:

```
slot_size_in_seconds = 51.2 microseconds
slot_size_in_bits = 512 bits
```

You can see that Ethernet relies heavily on the ability to detect collisions. If virtually all collisions are detected, transmission will be very reliable, and no time will be wasted sending whole frames that are damaged by collisions because sending will be aborted. This is the reason for the jamming frame, which is intended to make sure that all stations with colliding frames know the collision occurred so they can retransmit their frames. Collisions are detected by the interference that can be sensed when two frames are sent at the same time. Also, to avoid the possibility that a collision involving a very small frame might not be sensed, Ethernet has an established minimum frame size. Padding is added to short frames so that no frame is less than 64 bytes long.

An important characteristic of Ethernet is that it degrades significantly under heavy load. With only two stations on the LAN, it is possible to obtain nearly the full specified data rate between the two; for example, 10 Mbps for 10BASET. When multiple stations are actively contending for use of the LAN, experience shows that only about 40 percent of rated capacity is effectively usable by any station. Therefore, the practical, achievable data rate of *throughput* for a heavily loaded 10BASET

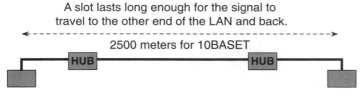

Figure 6.6 Ethernet collision timing.

LAN is about 4 Mbps. It is also important to remember that this capacity is only available in half-duplex mode. Unlike a full-duplex serial link using HDLC or a related protocol, if two stations have data to exchange, they must take turns sending frames. This leads to the surprising result that the capacity of a full-duplex 1.5 Mbps T1 link can be nearly as large as that of a 10Mbps Ethernet for some applications! To overcome this effect, 100BASET offers both half-duplex and full-duplex modes.

Switched Ethernet

In Chapter 1, you saw that there are two general models of network communication:

Broadcast networks, where each transmission goes to all stations. When it gets there, the station's network adapter or software decides whether it is addressed to the station.

Switched networks, where each transmission goes through a network of switching nodes like the one shown in Figure 1.2. The switches are responsible, collectively, for getting the transmission from sender to receiver

In general, LANs are broadcast networks, and WANs are switched networks. However, it is possible to use switching technology to obtain higher performance in a LAN. Figure 6.7 shows how a switch can interconnect four different stations without any contention or *blocking*. As long as the stations are all in pairwise communication, every pair can have a full data rate path available. (Of course, the switch can only do so much—if two stations want to communicate with the same third station, they will have to share access.)

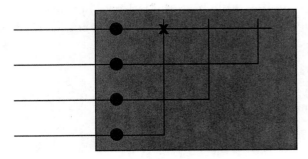

Figure 6.7   Inside a switch.

How does switching relate to Ethernet? Although Ethernet was designed as a contention protocol, it can also be used as an interface to a switch, resulting in a *switched LAN* with higher performance than would be available using contention-based hubs. There is, of course, a higher cost for the higher performance: Switches are more expensive than hubs.

 # Hands-On Activities

The problem and project in this chapter are designed to give you insight into the operation of Ethernet.

Generating Random Numbers

To implement binary exponential backoff, it is necessary to be able to deal with the requirement to wait a random period of time in order to reduce the chance of another collision. The backoff time is an integer (whole) number of slots. The integer is chosen from a range that increases with repeated collisions. All integers in the range must have equal probability of selection. The way to do this is to generate "pseudo-random numbers"; that is, numbers that are statistically random. There is a well-known method for doing this. It has been programmed and is available in NW module code/wrand.cpp. (The built-in C function rand was not used because its behavior, while always random, is different among various computer systems. NW is intended to behave the same on all systems.)

Function wrand(seed) returns an integer in the range from 0 to the largest short (16 bit) integer. It can be used to generate multiple, statistically independent sequences of random numbers by providing, as its argument seed, the previous value in the sequence. For the sequence to appear statistically independent, the starting seeds of the different sequences must be different.

NW function fwrand(seed_pointer) uses wrand to generate a floating-point random number in the range 0 to 1. fwrand automatically updates the seed to create a statistically independent sequence without the need for the invoking program to arrange for update of seeds.

Binary Exponential Backoff Algorithm

This algorithm assumes that the csma_send function that invokes backoff will create the needed initial local interface state before it starts to send a frame.

```
csma.send state initialization
{
  set max_backoff_slots to 1;
  set backoff_count to 0;
}
```

It will then invoke backoff() after each successive collision, until it is able to send the frame without a collision.

```
Algorithm for function backoff()
if max_backoff_slots is less than 1024,
  double the value of max_backoff_slots;
if backoff_count is greater than 16,
  return value -1 indicating failure;
generate a random_number between 0 and 1, using the random number
seed associated with this interface;
calculate random_backoff_slots = random_number * max_backoff_slots;
return backoff_ticks = random_backoff_slots * slot_ticks;
```

When to Multiply

A critical question in this algorithm is whether to multiply `max_backoff_slots` by 2 before or after calculating `random_backoff_slots`. Remembering that we want the outcome of calling backoff for the first time to be either 0 or 1 slots, and knowing that the starting value of `max_backoff_slots` is 1, you might think the right thing is to double it **after** using it to find the random number of slots. However, that is not right because of the way floating point numbers get converted to integers in C. The conversion involves *truncation*, meaning the fractional part of the floating-point number is discarded. If you multiply the value 1 by a random floating-point number between 0 and 1, and then convert the result to an integer, that integer will have value 0 every time because it is truncated downward from a fraction between 0 and 1. To get the right result, you must start with `max_backoff_slots` of 2; multiplying this by a random number uniformly distributed between 0 and 1 will result in 0 half of the time and 1 half of the time. See the following problem for an exercise that illustrates how this works.

Problem: Verifying *fwrand*

This problem can be done two ways. The second way takes less work on your part because it is already programmed in NW.

1. Using only a calculator, you can find the first 20 values of fwrand to understand how they are generated. Starting with seed value 101,

perform the following calculations, where % indicates the modulo or remainder function that was used in the previous chapter.

```
new_product = 1001*seed + 501
seed  = new_product%65536
fwrand = (32767-(seed%32767))/32767
```

2. Invoke function RN_example just before print_authors is invoked in lan1.cpp. This function will ask for console input to provide a seed value (try 101) and a number of test values, and will proceed to calculate that number of test values of fwrand using the seed. It will then print out how many of the values fall in each category.

```
0. < fwrand <= .1
.1 < fwrand <= .2
 .
 .
 .
.9 < fwrand <= 1.
```

You should try enough values to confirm to your own satisfaction that fwrand is uniformly distributed between 0 and 1.

Project: Programming *backoff*

In project LAN1, you will implement binary exponential backoff for the NW MAC sublayer CSMA/CD. The rules for operation of CSMA/CD (including binary exponential backoff) are as given in this chapter. A stub for the function you are to write is in backoff.cpp. The required function is

```
int stack::backoff(byte portnum)
```

This function takes a port_id (that is, an index into the interfaces[] and mac_state_data[] arrays) and generates an integer multiple of the constant SLOT_TICKS (the number of NW ticks in slot_size_in_seconds) that represents the binary exponential backoff for the interface with that port_id. This multiple is uniformly distributed from 0 to an integer that increases with number of collisions (see the protocol definition). The maximum value of the multiple is initially 1, so that backoff is either 0 or 20 if SLOT_TIME is 20. The maximum value of the multiple at any given time is stored in mac_iface->max_backoff_slots.

Notes

- To work properly, the function will require some state to persist between invocations. Appropriate variables have been established in structure type `mac_interface_state`, of which `mac_iface` represents the instance for this interface. In particular, `mac_iface->random_backoff_seed` is the seed of the `backoff` random number generator for the MAC interface. Its value will be preset by initialization functions in `init.cpp` before `backoff` is invoked.

- The function must generate a random number in the range from 0 to `max_backoff_slots`. The essence of binary exponential backoff is to double `max_backoff_slots` each time (up to 10) a collision occurs at a particular interface without an intervening successful frame transmission. The NW random number generator function is `float utility::fwrand(unsigned*)`; in other words, a function with parameter type pointer to unsigned integer, which returns a floating point number. An example of its use can be found in module `lanerrm.cpp` in the function `stack::ticks_to_next_lan_error`. However, the random number generator required for `backoff` is simpler than the one for LAN errors in that `backoff` requires only a uniform distribution of random numbers. Therefore, it is not necessary to reshape the distribution as occurs at the end of `ticks_to_next_lan_error`.

- With `SLOT_TICKS=20`, the value returned by `backoff` should be the 0 or 20 after the first collision; 0, 20, 40, or 60 after the second collision; 0, 20, 40, 60, 80, 100, 120, or 140 after the third collision, and so on. To signal failure when the backoff count exceeds 16, `backoff` should return value -1.

- The deck is stacked against CSMA/CD in LAN1. Because of the way the hosts start sending, all three of them send at once resulting in frequent collisions. This is the sort of condition for which binary exponential backoff is designed.

- When you provide a working `backoff` function, NW will execute a simulation of a CSMA/CD LAN that transmits the same email messages that were used for DLC3. With a working `backoff` function, the LAN hosts will exchange the email messages and stop.

CHAPTER 7

Token-Passing LANs and Bridging

Token Passing

In the previous chapter you saw that LANs based on contention protocols are simple and inexpensive. You also saw that contention does not lead to efficient use of transmission media. Also, Ethernet is very democratic, in that there is no provision for one station to have higher priority than another, regardless of whether one station has urgent real-time data and the other has only routine data. While in many cases these are not serious shortcomings, you should know about the existence of another group of protocols that are designed to provide more efficiency and flexibility in the LAN.

The basic approach for a contention LAN protocol is:

- Every station senses the medium continuously.
- When a station has something to send, if the medium appears idle, it transmits.
- If the medium is busy, it continues to listen until the channel is idle, then transmits immediately.

- Collisions are still possible if two stations start sending so near to the same time that the signal does not propagate between them to be sensed.

- If a collision is detected during transmission, it transmits a brief jamming signal to ensure that all stations know there has been a collision, then cease transmission.

- After transmitting the jamming signal, it waits a random amount of time, then starts over.

By contrast, a token-passing LAN is set up to ensure that collisions never occur. This is achieved by having an object called a *token* that is passed around the LAN. In a token-passing LAN, only the station that holds the token can start a new transmission. Here is the basic approach for a token-passing LAN:

- Only one node has the token.

- To send, a node must have the token.

- A specific rule is defined for giving up the token (the rule depends on the particular protocol). Often, the token is given up after sending one frame and goes to the next node in some logical succession.

- A particular advantage of token passing is that it allows for some traffic to receive higher priority by using a modified rule for passing the token, such as temporarily stopping transmission of low-priority traffic when token rotation among the nodes slows down.

- In order for the token-passing design to work, there must be some provision for maintenance functions such as creating an initial token, replacing a token lost due to transmission errors, and detecting duplicate tokens caused by transmission errors.

Token Bus

The token-passing arrangement can be used to create a LAN with a bus topology that does not suffer from the drawbacks of contention protocols. However, there is a price to be paid for the advantages of token passing. With Ethernet, adding a new station requires only plugging it into the bus or hub. With token bus, adding a new station requires a revision to the logical ordering under which the nodes pass the token around. Figure 7.1 shows a token bus network with three nodes passing a token at three successive times.

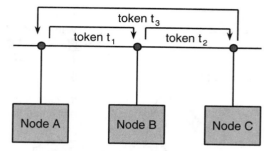

Figure 7.1   Three-node token-passing bus.

The IEEE LAN protocol 802.4 specifies a token bus that follows these rules:

- Each node has a logical predecessor and successor.

- When a node receives the token from its predecessor, it may transmit frames to any node on the bus.

- After all its frames are transmitted, or after the maximum *token holding time (THT)* is exhausted, the node passes the token to its successor.

- The current token holder is responsible for bus maintenance, including admission of new nodes to the network.

- Provisions for four classes of prioritized access are included within the standard.

Token Ring

Token passing is well suited to a LAN topology where the stations are connected in a *ring*, as shown in Figure 7.2. On a ring, the logical next node to receive the token is the next node downstream. In order for the ring to work properly, all nodes that do not have the token must set their network adapters to copy each incoming bit to the output. Each node also monitors every incoming frame to determine if the frame is addressed to that node, in which case the frame is accepted and turned over to Logical Link Control. Meanwhile, the frame continues to move around the ring.

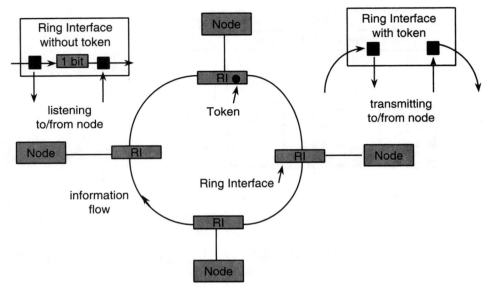

Figure 7.2   Token ring.

The rules for IEEE 802.5 Token Ring are as follows:

- Only one node has the token.
- To send, a node must have the token.
- Absent the token, a node must copy all incoming frames to its output.
- When a frame returns to the sender, the sender removes the frame from the ring.
- A node must release the token within an established THT. A typical value for THT is 10 milliseconds.
- The protocol includes provisions for prioritized reservation and distributed ring maintenance.

A particular weakness of the ring topology is that a break anywhere on a one-way ring stops all communication. This can mean tracing down the whole LAN wiring to find the break. To simplify trouble-shooting, it is common to bring the ring wiring into a hub such as the one shown in Figure 7.3. You should notice that while this hub has the same physical configuration as a 10BASET hub, its internal connections are quite different.

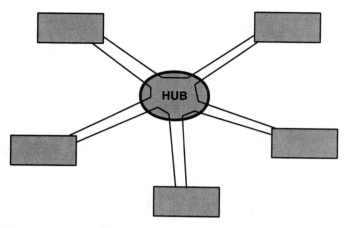

Figure 7.3 A hub simplifies token ring wiring maintenance.

FDDI

The Fiber-Distributed Data Interface (FDDI) LAN standard was established by the American National Standards Institute (ANSI), not by the IEEE. (It does, however, use IEEE 802.2 LLC.) Because it uses a fiber channel rather than a wire, FDDI has always provided for a high data rate, 100 Mbps. It also provides for an optional second fiber in the ring, on which frames rotate in the opposite direction from the first fiber. This arrangement allows an FDDI LAN with a break at the same place in both fibers to heal itself into a loop about twice as long, by looping back from the point of the break as shown in Figure 7.4.

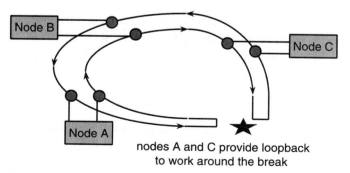

Figure 7.4 FDDI LAN continues to operate with a break in the fiber.

The rules for a FDDI LAN are as follows:

- The token is passed by appending it to a transmitted frame (no need to wait while the token comes back around the loop).

- The sending nodes must remove their packets from the ring as in a token ring.

- FDDI allows up to 500 nodes within a ring up to 200 kilometers in circumference. The distance between nodes cannot exceed 2 kilometers.

- Multiple nodes' inputs can be concentrated at one FDDI interface, so it is not necessary to make multiple fiber connections where several stations are in one place. This is important because fiber connections are more difficult to make than wire connections.

- An FDDI network may serve as a *backbone* to interconnect Ethernet LANs (you will learn more about this in the section on bridging that follows).

- In the frame header, there is a priority bit, which is used for real-time traffic. Stations with only low-priority traffic wait to send if the inter-token interval is higher than a preset number.

- The FDDI protocol can work over unshielded twisted pair (UTP) wire for a distance up to 100 meters between nodes. This system, called *copper distributed data interface (CDDI)*, saves the cost of installing fiber in physically smaller networks.

The biggest problem with FDDI is that the adapters cost roughly ten times as much as Ethernet adapters. (This is probably because they have never generated the large volume of sales needed to become a commodity item.) In the past, this meant that FDDI was used only where its higher performance was needed. Since 100BASET Ethernet has become available, FDDI has a smaller niche than before. It is used where nodes are far apart, and where traffic prioritization is necessary. Even in these applications, it is facing competition from Asynchronous Transfer Mode (ATM), which offers similar capabilities. The technology for fiber-based gigabit-per-second LANs is now being considered for standardization by the IEEE. It is likely to make FDDI obsolete when gigabit performance becomes available at competitive prices, assuming its price comes down as sales volume increases after standardization.

Broadcast in Token Rings

You learned in the previous chapter that Ethernet works by broadcasting each frame to every node. The network adapter for each node then selects those frames that are addressed to that node. Token bus uses the same model of transmission, with the additional feature that sharing of the medium is controlled by token passing rather than contention.

Token rings also fall in the category of broadcast networks, but the broadcast mechanism is different. You also have learned that a token ring works by forwarding the frame from node to node around a closed loop. During this process, each node receives every frame, but accepts only those frames that are addressed to it. Therefore, while the timing is different from a bus, the token ring does follow the broadcast paradigm.

Bridging

Before leaving the topic of LANs, you should know that it is possible to interconnect LAN segments by a method known as *bridging*. A bridge is a network component that transfers frames between LAN segments. It works by receiving a frame from one LAN in a buffer, then sending that frame on a second LAN, as shown in Figure 7.5. In the next chapter, you will learn about a much more powerful way to interconnect LAN segments, using Internet routers. However, many LANs have been installed with bridges and are still using them rather than converting to routers. Also, some non-Internet protocols are not capable of being routed. For these protocols, bridges are the only way to expand the LAN.

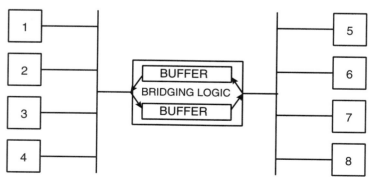

Figure 7.5 LAN bridge.

The type of bridge that has widest applicability is the *transparent bridge*, which features internal logic able to learn the addresses of stations on both sides of the bridge and use this information to forward frames. For example, the bridge in Figure 7.5 would learn that stations 1 through 4 were on one side of the bridge, and 5 through 8 on the other side. If it received a frame from 1 addressed to 5, it would forward that frame; if it received a frame from 1 to 4, it would do nothing.

Bridging has three main advantages:

- On a heavily loaded LAN, bridging may be able to reduce loading by isolating traffic within segments. This works only where the LAN can be segmented in such a way that much of the traffic on each segment is between stations on that segment, with relatively smaller amounts of traffic bridged across segments.

- When a single LAN must extend over a distance greater than its protocol allows (for example, 2500 meters for 10BASET), a bridge can link two or more segments together. Because it buffers the frames that pass through, it behaves like a station on each LAN. As a result the slot time is kept within the protocol specification for each segment.

- Bridges are available to interconnect different LAN types. For example, with an FDDI-to-Ethernet bridge in each building, an FDDI backbone can be used to interconnect buildings on a campus as shown in Figure 7.6. (In this sense, "campus" is not limited to institutions of higher learning, but can include any area with multiple buildings that are close together.)

 ## Hands-On Activities

The problem and project in this chapter are designed to give you insight into the operation of a token-passing LAN.

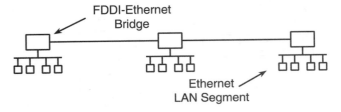

Figure 7.6 FDDI backbone bridging Ethernet LAN segments.

NW Token-Passing Protocol

The timeout necessary to implement the token LAN is implemented as a special code that is sent to token_receive when a timeout occurs.

The token interface hardware automatically forwards all frames except those that contain a token or are addressed from this host.

```
When a frame is received, it is a timeout, token, or data;
if the frame contains a timeout code,
{
  if the frame's timeout_SN matches mac_buffer->timeout_SN,
  {
    send the frame in mac_buffer again;
    start timeout again;
  }
  return;
}
if the frame contains a token,
  look at mac_buffer->current_frame, if there is a frame waiting in
  current_frame,
  {
    send it;
    start a timer to call token_receive back in case the frame is
    lost;
    return;
  }
  else (i.e. no frame waiting),
  {
    forward the token to next host;
    return;
  }
unstuff the received frame so its contents can be inspected;
at this point the frame must contain data,
if data is from this host (indicates a completed transmission),
{
  increment mac_buffer->timeout_SN;
  pass the token forward;
  return;
}
else (i.e. data is not from this host),
{
  the data must be addressed to this host (including multicast and
  broadcast) or the interface would not have delivered it,
  pass the data to dlc_receive;
  return;
}.
```

Problem: Predicting Token Ring Performance

In this problem you will use what you have learned about token LANs to predict the performance that will be simulated by the NW LAN. The times in this problem are in NW simulation ticks (10^{-7} seconds each). Where necessary, you should round to the nearest full tick.

a. Project LAN2 simulates a token ring LAN with five hosts (nodes). The data rate on the LAN is 100 Mbps, and the average frame length is 100 bytes. Find the number of ticks to transmit an average frame. (HINT: `transmit_time` is given by the formula in Chapter 5 on DLC ARQ.)

b. The latency of each segment in the NW token ring is 2 microseconds (20 ticks), and the delay in the network adapter to forward the frame is 2 ticks. The time from start of sending until the frame has rotated back to its sending host is transmit time plus the number of segments, five, times the sum of link latency and network adapter delay. Find this number of ticks, which is the length of time an average frame has dedicated use of the LAN.

c. Passing tokens also takes time. Token frames must enter every host without being bypassed in the interface. On the average, a token must be sent through half of the five hosts before it finds a new message waiting to be sent. Token transmission delay, consisting of processing delay, link latency, and transmit time, requires a total of 67 ticks. Find the average token-passing delay in ticks.

d. There are nine messages in the email files for project LAN2, but one of them does not cross the LAN because it is delivered to the host that sends it. Using your answers to b and c, predict how long the token LAN will be occupied from the start to end of sending the other eight messages. Do not consider time in the higher layers of the stack (most of this time is overlapped with LAN operation in any case). *Answer: 2,864 ticks.*

Project: Programming *token_receive*

Project LAN2 requires you to program at a higher level by invoking the NW functions that support token LANs. You are to complete the function `stack::token_receive` in stub module `token.cpp` to make the Workbench token LAN work. The algorithm to be implemented in this function is the one given previously, and also is provided as comments in `token.cpp`. It embodies the primary logic of a token-passing LAN. In addition, `mac.cpp` contains several functions that implement the primitive operations necessary for `token_receive`. You will be able to complete the function by providing control logic to invoke these functions in the proper sequence.

Notes

The Workbench token LAN is always connected physically in order of hostnum; thus, if there are three hosts, the token moves from host 1 to host 2 to host 3 to host 1 and so on.

- The timeout necessary to implement the token LAN is implemented as a special code that is sent to `token_receive` when a timeout occurs.

- The NW token is a variation on the start-of-frame flag. The token pattern is `11111110`, in place of `01111110` that we have been using.

- It is important to make the tests for timeout, token, and data frame in the order given in the algorithm.

- The token interface hardware automatically forwards all frames except those that contain a token or are addressed from the host to which the interface is attached.

- The Workbench produces a lot of output in LAN2 because it prints a trace output each time the token moves to a new host.

- By its nature, the token will never stop moving around the LAN; therefore, project LAN2 will never run out of events. The NW run will always stop when `sim_time` exceeds `max_DES_ticks`.

- The `token_send` function is not invoked in the same way as in the NW `dlc_send` and `csma_send`. Instead, a frame to be sent is placed in the send queue by the NW network layer send function. When the token comes to `token_receive` for a particular host, if there is a frame waiting in the queue, that frame will be sent. If not, the token will be forwarded to the next station in the ring.

- There are functions in `mac.cpp` that are intended to be useful in programming `token_receive`. These include `forward_token`, `start_token_timeout`, `token_present`, `mac_buffer_contains_frame`, `timeout_code_present`, `timeout_matches_mac_buffer`, `fromport`, and `token_send`. Function `mac_to_dl` in module `intrlyr.cpp` is used to invoke `dl_receive` with a received frame.

- When a data frame is received at a token LAN host, a curious thing happens. The frame starts through the token LAN adapter for that host, and then through another, and possibly through one more, before the frame is received in the host! The reason for this becomes clear on close inspection of Figure 7.2. As described earlier, every frame passes completely around the token ring and stops when it gets back to the host that sent it. Although each interface in the NW token LAN buffers 24 bits rather than only one bit as in Figure 7.2, the first part of a frame passes through the interface and on to the next interface or two before the complete frame has been received by the host.

More on Network Workbench Output for Debugging

You already know about NW function `output`, which prints up to six character strings to the console and also to file `diskout.txt`. There are several other output functions in NW, all of which use `output` so their results also go to the same two places. Here are some functions that you may find helpful in printing data when debugging your `token` function:

`outputn(int)` prints an integer as a six-digit number

`show3(char*,byte,byte,byte)` prints a character string label and three bytes (such as `netnum`, `hostnum`, `ifacenum,` or `portnum`)

`showbits(bit*,int)` prints the bits contained in the first argument; the second argument is the number of bits to be printed.

CHAPTER 8

Network Layer:
The Internet Protocol

Up to this point, we have been concerned with the technology of individual links, which comes under the general heading of data communication. This chapter introduces a new area with larger horizons, the one that makes the Internet possible.

It may seem strange that we have just now come to the network layer, when the previous chapters deal with "local area networks" of two different kinds. This is due to an inconsistency in networking terminology. Under the definition used in the stack model, a LAN is not a network at all because it works by broadcast and therefore does not provide for selective delivery of messages. Another way of saying this is that the network layer provides two functions: addressing and routing. Addressing in LANs is achieved by brute force: Every network adapter is manufactured with a unique address, which is used to send frames to the node that uses the adapter. Routing does not happen at all in a LAN, unless we count the filtering used by bridges to pass frames selectively between LAN segments. You will learn in this chapter how simple but sophisticated addressing and routing mechanisms make possible the network of networks we call the Internet. The key functions provided by these mechanisms are:

Addressing. Assigning a unique code to each node that makes it possible to send data to that node from any computer connected to the Internet.

Routing. Providing a way for each router in the Internet to determine which one path, among the paths it has available, is likely to be the best one to reach a particular address.

Internet Addresses

How does the Internet solve the addressing problem?

IP Packet Format

Every computer attached to the Internet must have a unique number called an Internet address assigned to it. These addresses are assigned in blocks, much like telephone numbers. Your home or office telephone number is probably the same in the first six digits (including the area code) as your immediate neighbors' numbers. They are all part of the same block of numbers. This makes it possible for the telephone system to find and connect to your telephone easily from phones all over North America and in many other parts of the world. The Internet uses a similar arrangement, with blocks of numbers assigned by the Internet Addressing and Naming Authority (IANA).

The basic data unit at the network layer is called a *packet*. Figure 8.1 shows the format of an Internet protocol (IP) packet. The data part is the payload provided higher layers. In this chapter, our focus is on the packet header.

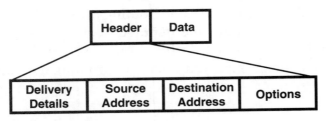

Figure 8.1 Overview of the IPv4 packet format.

Figure 8.2 shows some details of the IPv4 packet header. You can see from the number of fields it contains that IP is considerably more complex than Ethernet. Three of the fields are worth special attention:

Fragment offset is needed because IPv4 allows a packet to be broken up into smaller packets if it passes through a network with a *maximum transfer unit (MTU)* limitation that is smaller than size of the entering packet. Such fragmented packets are reassembled at the destination host.

Time to live is a misleading name; the "time" really is a count of *hops* or routers through which the packet must pass. The idea here is to let the sender limit how far through the Internet the packet is intended to go. Each router subtracts one from the number in the field; when it reaches zero, the packet is discarded in the router. This avoids having stray packets hang around the Internet for indefinite periods of time.

Protocol is a code showing the protocol of the next higher layer (most often this is TCP).

You may be wondering how the packet header relates to the frame header of the HDLC or Ethernet protocol at the DLC layer. The answer to this question is that the packet, header and all, is carried in the data field of the DLC layer. This arrangement is true at every layer: The entire *protocol data unit* of one layer is the data for the next

0	4	8	16	19	24	31
VERS	HLEN	SERVICE TYPE	TOTAL LENGTH			
IDENTIFICATION			FLAGS	FRAGMENT OFFSET		
TIME TO LIVE		PROTOCOL	HEADER CHEKSUM			
SOURCE IP ADDRESS						
DESTINATION IP ADDRESS						
IP OPTIONS (IF ANY)				PADDING		
DATA						
...						

VERS—protocol version
HLEN—header length in 32-bit words
SERVICE TYPE—precedence and handling options
TOTAL LENGTH—packet length in bytes
IDENTIFICATION, FLAGS, FRAGMENT OFFSET—used in fragmentation
TIME TO LIVE (TTL)—max number of routers to forward
PROTOCOL—code for transport protocol
HEADER CHEKSUM—error check for header

Figure 8.2 Details of the IPv4 header.

Versions of the Internet Protocol

The particular protocol described here is IP version 4 (IPv4), which is the one now used in the Internet. The IETF has developed a new version, IPv6, which may replace IPv4 in a few years (see Appendix E for more information). IPv6 has a larger address field to allow the Internet to expand and differs in some other details. Its basic operation matches the description of IPv4 here.

layer down. Figure 8.3 illustrates this concept for the transport layer, network layer, and data link layer.

IP Address Format

The source and destination addresses in the IP packet are 32 bits long. The range of addresses possible within the 32-bit format is called the *address space*. Each IP address field is divided into three parts: a *network prefix* plus a *host address*, both preceded by a code that defines the network *class*. (Today the class is of historical interest only.) The network prefix identifies a particular subnetwork or *subnet*, a concept fundamental to the Internet architecture. A subnet is a network (most often, a LAN) that provides a mechanism to reach individual computers, which are called *hosts*.

Figure 8.4 shows the way Internet addresses were originally organized in *classes.* With the exception of class D (multicast), every class con-

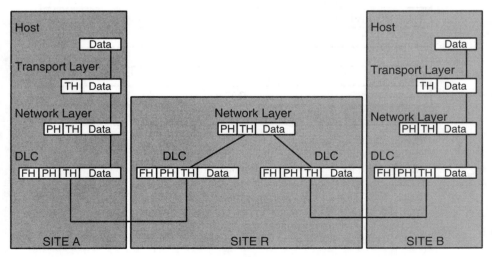

Figure 8.3 Nesting of frame headers, packet headers, and transport headers.

```
Class A—128 nets with 16M hosts each
   0nnnnnnn hhhhhhhh hhhhhhhh hhhhhhhh
Class B—16K nets with 64K hosts each
   10nnnnnn nnnnnnnn hhhhhhhh hhhhhhhh
Class C—2M nets with 256 hosts each
   110nnnnn nnnnnnnn nnnnnnnn hhhhhhhh
Class D—Multicast, 256M groups
   1110gggg gggggggg gggggggg gggggggg
Classless—split in some other way,
          for example:
   110nnnnn nnnnnnnh hhhhhhhh hhhhhhhh
```
NOTE: (K = 2^{10} = 1024, M = 2^{20} = 1048576)

Figure 8.4   Historic IP address formats.

tains a subnet address (depicted by the letter n) and a host address (depicted by the letter h). The class code identifies the format used. The designers of IPv4 laid out these classes as a way of organizing large, medium, and small networks, and Internet multicast. Today Internet addresses are a scarce resource, so they are allocated in a "classless" way that is more efficient in its use of addresses.

IP Address Notation

Keeping track of IP addresses in binary would be quite cumbersome, as every address would require 32 characters. A traditional computer technique for dealing with this problem is to use hexadecimal numbers, where each digit corresponds exactly to four bits. In fact, a lot of Internet software will accept this format. However, the Internet has a different convention that you need to know. The convention is to convert each group of eight bits into a decimal number, using normal rules for binary-to-decimal conversion. Thus, for example, a NETLAB server:

```
10000001 10110110 01000001 000001012 = 129.174.65.5
```

Subnetting

A *subnet* is a network that is part of a larger network. In principle, every network attached to the Internet is a subnet of the Internet. Here is how subnetting works:

- The first part of the address (the nnnn part) is used to deliver the packet to the subnet.

- The second part of the address (the hhhh part) is used by the subnet to deliver the packet to a particular host.

- The subnet mask is a bit pattern that has ones in the nnnn part and zeros in the hhhh part. For example, the subnet mask used in NETLAB is 11111111 11111111 11111111 00000000_2 = $255.255.255.0$

- The best way to describe the division between n and h is to provide the count of n bits after the network address, separated by a slash. For example, 129.174.65/24 is another way of saying the NETLAB subnet addresses have 24 n bits and 8 h bits. This is called *prefix notation*.

The idea of creating a network of networks has turned out to be very *scalable* over the past few years as the Internet has grown from tens of networks to tens of thousands. This sort of scale would not be possible if every subnet had to be dealt with individually. Part of the way the Internet works is that the subnets themselves have subnets. For example, George Mason University was assigned a sixteen bit network prefix, but that address is actually used as 256 sub-subnets with 24 n bits. The NETLAB subnet is one of these. The Internet sees GMU as a 129.174/16, and delivers all packets with destination starting 129.174 to the main GMU router. The university then sends the packets to individual subnets, so that any packet destined for 129.174.65.x goes to my laboratory. There the packet is delivered based on the last eight bits of the address, using subnet mask 255.255.255.0. The relationship is illustrated in Figure 8.5.

The way IP addresses are organized into network prefix and host address (often with sub-prefixes) is a powerful feature of the Internet architecture, but it does suffer from one limitation. Because prefixes must be assigned as a continuous group of bits at the beginning of the

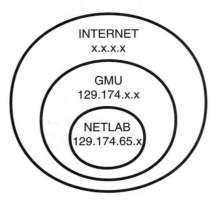

Figure 8.5   Subnet relationships for GMU NETLAB example.

IP address, the number of addresses grouped under the prefix must be a power of two. This means addresses always are assigned to using organizations in blocks containing a number of host addresses such as 128, 256, 512, 1024, etc.

Another example showing how subnets and masks work is the way *Classless InterDomain Routing (CIDR)* groups addresses. Suppose a company has a CIDR block of 2048 addresses, for example 10.218.168.0 to 10.218.175.255. These could be combined under a mask of

```
11111111 11111111 11111100 00000000₂ = 255.255.252.0.
```

Thus, any packets containing the block address defined by the first 21 bits would be routed together to the company's gateway. From there, they would be routed to different subnets. It is common for CIDR addresses to use prefix notation as a more compact way of representing the mask; thus, our example company's CIDR block might be 10.218.168/21.

Internet Domain Names

When you use the Internet, it is unlikely that you specify the address of the host you are accessing in numeric format. That does work, but most people prefer to remember NETLAB.GMU.EDU rather than 129.174.65.1. The system that converts symbolic names to Internet addresses is called the *domain name system (DNS)*. Another clever idea of the Internet designers was to decouple DNS from the organization of physical addresses. Thus, DNS servers are organized in a hierarchy of names: NETLAB is part of GMU is part of EDU, the domain assigned to institutions of higher learning. A DNS query on a name within the domain GMU.EDU probably will return an address from GMU's assigned class B network, but you can't be sure about that because it is not a requirement. You will find more information on DNS in Chapter 12 on servers and clients. At this point, it is sufficient to say that a distributed system of servers exists in the Internet, and these servers are able to translate any valid DNS name into an IP address.

Linking Network and DLC Layers

You may be wondering how Internet addresses relate to LAN addresses such as those used in Ethernet. The answer is that, within a subnet, there must be a one-to-one mapping between the two types of addresses. That is, every Internet address on the subnet must be associated with a known LAN address that is used at the DLC layer to reach that Internet address. Because of this, there is a need for three protocols that are used within the LAN to deal with addresses.

- The *Address Resolution Protocol (ARP)* is used by the router to build a table of Ethernet addresses with matching IP addresses. The router broadcasts an ARP request, and the host with a matching IP address replies with its Ethernet address.
- The *Reverse Address Resolution Protocol (RARP)* is used by a host that needs to be told what its IP address is (usually this will be a terminal with no hard disk on which to record the IP address). The host broadcasts a RARP request and some other host that has the responsibility to answer RARP replies with a matching IP address.
- The *Dynamic Host Configuration Protocol (DHCP)* is one step beyond RARP. The idea is to assign an IP address "on the fly," to save having to manually configure an IP address. Some host on the subnet (often, the router) is assigned a pool of IP addresses that it can pass out for temporary use, in response to broadcast DHCP requests.

Other Network Protocols

Many network-layer protocols are not part of the Internet protocol suite. Here are the names of three protocol families that you may hear about. These largely have been eclipsed by the Internet Protocols in recent years.

Open Systems Interconnect (OSI) protocols were developed by the ITU-T to be worldwide open standards for networking. The *seven-layer OSI model* associated with these protocols is still widely used (see the reference by *Data and Computer Communications* by Stallings).The OSI network layer protocol is *X.25.*

Systems Network Architecture (SNA) is proprietary to International Business Machines (IBM) Corporation.

Internetwork Packet Exchange (IPX) is a proprietary to Novell, Inc., a major provider of system software for LANs, known as NetWare.

How Do You Say That Word?

Does routing rhyme with booting or touting? The answer is, you can pronounce it either way; neither pronunciation is "preferred."

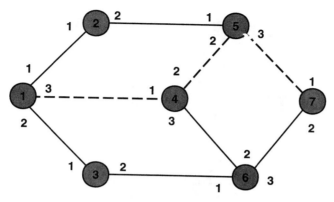

Figure 8.6 WAN with links in route 1-4-5-7 shown as dashed lines.

Routing in the Internet

Routing is the process whereby a set of paths to Internet addresses is found and prepared for use by a router. Consider the network in Figure 8.6, which has a route from node 1 to node 7 shown as dashed lines.

The information needed by a router in this WAN is simple: For any node, it only needs to know which interface the packet will use. For example, when node 1 sends a packet to node 7, it only needs to know that its route to node 7 goes through its neighbor node 4. You might think the whole path 1-4-5-7 should be considered, but that is not necessary. Node 1 counts on nodes 4 and 5 to do the right thing when the packet gets there. Therefore, the only information node 1 needs to send a packet to node 7 is to use interface 3. (Even if node 4 has a different route to reach node 7, such as 4-6-7, the packet will still be delivered.)

Figure 8.7 makes it clear that our WAN is an Internet, with a two-host LAN at every node. This is, in fact, the sort of simplified Internet model used by NW. In this simple model, the number on the router is also the subnet number, and the address of a host is n.h; for example, 1.2 is host 2 on the LAN connected to router 1. Now we can see how Internet routing works. Any packet from subnet 1 that is addressed to subnet 7 follows the same path; they all go to router 4, because that is the path router 1 is using to get to router 7. Here again, the only information router 1 needs to send a packet to subnet 7 is to use interface 3.

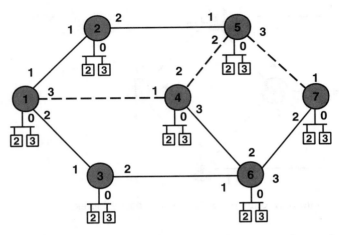

Figure 8.7 Internet with route from subnet 1 to subnet 7 in dashes.

Optimal Routing

The remainder of this chapter is devoted to the question: How does a router decide which route is best? Because the LANs don't add anything to the discussion, only the routers will be shown in the remaining diagrams of this chapter.

The way routes are determined is to optimize some measurement along the path that will be taken. This is called a *cost* function, even though it usually is not priced in dollars. The most common cost functions for routing are hop count and delay.

Hops. The number of links a packet must cross from source to destination may be the only information we have available for routing. For example, in Figure 8.7 the minimum distance from node 7 to node 1 is three hops. This is described as a *distance vector* approach to routing, which means the measurement for any destination is obtained by adding the local hops to that obtained from neighboring routers (which add their hops to those obtained from their neighbors, etc.). While it is possible for the distance vector approach to use a cost measurement other than hops, the method most often used is to count hops.

Delay. You have already seen one aspect of delay, the link latency plus transmit time described in Chapter 5 on DLC ARQ. Another (and potentially larger) source of delay is queueing. If a packet is routed to an outgoing interface while another packet is already being transmitted, the new packet goes into a buffer in a *first-come, first-served queue.* If many packets arrive in a short time, this queue can build up to the point where there is a significant wait in the queue for the packets to be transmitted. Using the total delay (including queueing), or some other cost metric that measures the status of each outgoing link, is described as *link state* routing.

The way a router learns the cost associated with paths is the subject of the next chapter. In this chapter, you can assume the cost information is somehow known. Figure 8.8 shows a WAN that has costs associated with the links. In the general case, there will be a different cost associated with each end of a link, because the traffic crossing the link probably is not the same in both directions. Here, to simplify matters, the costs in Figure 8.8 are those seen from node 1. The goal then is to find the path that minimizes the cost for node 1 to reach any other node. We are treating node 1 as the *source* node. To have a complete routing solution we would have to repeat this process using each node as the source.

Given the costs shown in Figure 8.8, we can now see why 1-4-5-7 is the optimal path from 1 to 7. However, this is only the path to one node. To complete the routing process, you must consider all nodes. Here is the complete list of routes from node 1:

```
1-2
1-4-6-3
1-4
1-4-5
1-4-6
1-4-5-7
```

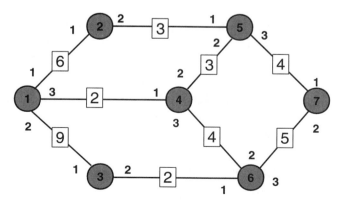

Figure 8.8   WAN with link costs as seen from node 1.

You should notice particularly the path from node 1 to node 3. On this path the distance vector approach would give the simple route 1-3. However, the cost of that route is higher than the route selected, 1-4-6-3.

Routing Table

The router must be able to forward packets with a minimum of processing. To support this, the results of routing are organized into a table that shows what the next-hop node is for any destination router. Each next-hop router must be a node that is connected by a direct link to the router for which the table is built. If the interface is already occupied sending a packet, the packet is placed in a *first-in, first-out (FIFO) queue* to wait its turn for transmission. Here is the routing table for node 1 that is equivalent to the paths shown earlier. You should notice that, because no shortest path goes from node 1 to node 3, interface 2 is not used.

DESTINATION	INTERFACE
2	1
3	3
4	3
5	3
6	3
7	3

Dijkstra's Algorithm

There is a famous algorithm, invented by the Dutch computer scientist Edsgar Dijkstra (pronounced dike-stra), that will find the optimal route very efficiently. This algorithm finds the shortest path from a given node to all other nodes by constructing the path in order of increasing path length h. No other algorithm can find optimal routes more efficiently. Here is a formal description of the algorithm, where N is the set of all nodes, s is the source node (node 1, for our example), R is the set of nodes incorporated by the algorithm, C_n is the cost of the least-cost path from node n to node s, and D_{ij} is the cost of the link from node i to node j. You should study this elegant algorithm until you understand it. If you find the set-theoretic notation hard to follow, try the alternate format used in the NW version in the next section.

- Initialize: $R = \{s\}$ and $C_n = D_{ns}$ (if unreachable, the delay is infinite)
- Add to **R** the node with the least-cost path from node s

  Find h not in **R** such that $C_h = \min C_n$

  Add h to **R**
- Update the least-cost paths: $C_n = \min [C_n, C_h + D_{hn}]$ for all n not in R
- Repeat preceding two steps until $\mathbf{R} = \mathbf{N}$

Hands-On Activities

The problem and project in this chapter are designed to give you insight into computing optimal network routing.

NW Form of Dijkstra's Algorithm

Here is a version of Dijkstra's algorithm that lends itself to the NW project for this chapter. In this version, the set of all nodes **N** is {1..nnets}. This version assumes the existence of NW function cost(i,j,k) that returns a floating point number representing the cost, as seen by node i, to send a packet across the link from node j to node k, or a very large number if there is no direct link from node j to node k. The nodes in the NW network are called routers and are identified by the netnum of the LAN connected to them. The optimize_routes NW function has input parameter source (the source router) and returns a data structure forward_routers, where forward_routers.router[n] is the optimal next-hop node to reach node n from node s. This function is a direct mapping into NW of Dijkstra's algorithm as defined previously in this chapter, with the addition of capturing the forward_routers data structure.

```
Dijkstra's route optimization algorithm for NW
required storage:
  array R that will represent Dijkstra's set R;
  array C of costs associated with route from n to source;

initialization:
initialize R[0] to source;
do for all n from 1 to nnets,
{
  initialize C[n] to cost, as seen from source of the link,
  from source to n;
```

```
      initialize forward_routers.router[n] to n;
}
do for all h from 1 to nnets,
{
   add to R the router with the least-cost path to source:
   set cost_of_h to a very large number;
   do for all n from 1 to nnets,
   {
     do for all j from 0 to h-1,
       if any R[j] contains n, skip this n;
     if C[n] is less than cost_of_h,
     {
       set cost_of_h to C[n]
       set R[h] to n;
     }
   }

   update the least-cost paths:
   do for all n from 1 to nnets,
   {
     find cost_of_h_to_n, as seen from source,
     of link from R[h] to n;
     if C[R[h]] plus cost_of_h_to_n is less than C[n],
     {
       set C[n] to C[R[h]] plus cost_of_h_to_n;
       set forward_routers.router[n] to
       forward_routers.router[R[h]];
     }
   }

   stopping rule- quit when all routers are in R:
   do for all n from 1 to nnets,
     do for all j for 0 to h,
       look for an n that is not in some R[j];
   if no such n is found, break out of this (do for h) loop;
}.
```

Packet Forwarding Algorithm for NW

```
Look in the this_net->routing table for the next_hop network
number;
Look in the exit_interfaces matrix to find the interface that
goes from this network router to that network;
Return that value.
```

Problem: Calculating Routes Using Dijkstra's Algorithm

Carry out Dijkstra's algorithm by hand, using Figure 8.8 with node 5 as the source. *Answer: 5-4-1, 5-2, 5-4-6-3, 5-4, 5-4-6, 5-7.*

Project: Programming *optimize_routes and forward_iface*

In project WAN2, you make routing work for a node.

a. Add a function to compute the optimal routing before the network simulation begins. This will mean adding to the stub function `stack::optimize_routes` that is provided in `fwdopt.cpp`. This function is invoked by `main` to compute the optimal static routing before the simulation starts. In later projects, it will also be invoked for dynamic routing. Your function will obtain the cost metric from the function in module `cost.cpp`. `float network::cost(thisrouter, fromrouter, torouter)` will return the cost of the link between `fromrouter` and `torouter` when invoked. In WAN2, this cost is `1,544,000/link_data_rate`, regardless of the value of `thisrouter`. In a later project, the value will be dependent on dynamic routing information, so it will be dependent on the value of `thisnode`.

b. Forward packets using the routing table you have calculated. This requires that you complete stub function `stack::forward_iface (subnet_state* this_net, destnet)`. This function needs only a small amount of code to provide the forwarding logic.

Notes

- There is a constant HUGEFLOAT in `nw.h` that can be used for the "large number." `cost` returns this number for any pair (`fromrouter, torouter`) that do not have a link between them.

- You should run project WAN2 without link bit errors (the profile `pwan2.cpp` is already set up for this). As before, you can debug with a variable number of email files. For your final run you should use the default for WAN2 (zero bit errors, three email files).

- Remember, arrays for net and host do not use array position 0. Interface 0 is reserved for the LAN interface and is not used in the WAN2 project.

- You can verify that your packet forwarding is working by checking the network layer performance summary statistics that NW prints at the end of each run. It should look something like Figure 8.9. No matter how many nodes your network has, you should see that total packets sent plus total packets forwarded equals total packets received.

```
Host        -----Unicast Packets-----
            Sent    Received Forwarded

1.1         1          8         2
2.1         5          3         2
3.1         3          0         0
4.1         0          0         0
5.1         0          0         0
6.1         0          2         0

Totals:     9          13        4
```

Figure 8.9 Network layer statistics from NW.

CHAPTER 9

Network Layer: Routing Protocols

Now that you understand the concepts of packet forwarding and optimal routing, you may wonder how the data needed for routing gets to the router in the first place. This chapter answers that question.

What Is a Routing Protocol?

You might think from its name that a *routing protocol* "does" Internet routing, but it does not. As you learned in the previous chapter, routers use whatever information about the network they have available to deal with arriving packets by:

Forwarding each packet as soon as possible after it arrives. This means picking the interface by which the packet should leave the router (one of the serial links or a LAN connection) and getting it on to its way in microseconds or, at most, milliseconds.

Calculating routes that are optimal in light of the information available. This is done less frequently, perhaps every 10 minutes.

By contrast, routing protocols exist to **transfer routing information among routers**. There are two general cases for routing:

Static routing is set up one time and does not change. Usually, a human operator sets it up. This is entirely appropriate when only one path exists. It is also appropriate when policies of the network(s) involved define only one path for packets based on some characteristic(s) (most often, the source and destination addresses). Under this circumstance, most packets will follow a *default route* that applies to any packet that does not have an explicit route in the static *routing table*. However, static routing may not be such a good idea if there is more than one possible route to reach the packet's destination, because the static route may be the one that is congested or it may be out of operation.

Dynamic routing is calculated periodically based on information provided from other routers by way of a routing protocol.

Basic Categories of Routing Protocols

Three broad categories of routing protocols are used in the Internet today.

Distance-vector routing protocols communicate the number of intervening routers to a particular destination. To get from one router to the next, the packet passes through a link, which could be either a point-to-point circuit or a multi-access LAN. Moving from one router to the next in this way is called a *hop*. Figure 9.1 shows our familiar WAN example with some new link costs. Using a distance-vector approach, the best path from node 1 to node 6 would be either 1-3-6 or 1-4-6. We have selected 1-3-6.

Link-state routing protocols, as you would expect from the name, communicate the state of each link in some part of the network in terms of some cost metric. Delay in queue is the cost metric used most often. Figure 9.1 shows the costs associated with each link. You can see that, from a link-state standpoint, the optimal path from node 1 to node 6 is 1-2-5-7-6, twice as many hops as the distance-vector method would have chosen.

Border gateway or *exterior gateway* routing protocols are used between networks managed by different groups. Such a separate management domain is called an *autonomous system* (AS). Node 1 in Figure 9.1 is connected to a neighboring AS by a border router, also called a

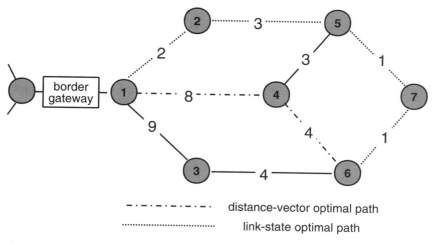

Figure 9.1 Network with three possible routing protocol types.

border gateway. The idea is that each AS determines its own routing, but they all must cooperate to make the Internet work. Such *inter-domain* routing is not sophisticated enough that multi-network paths through the Internet can be optimized by a calculation like Dijkstra's algorithm. Instead, the border gateways *advertise* the network numbers they are able to reach. If a particular AS has more than one neighbor that can provide a path to some distant subnet, the choice among paths is made by a *routing policy* that is set up by human operators. This is almost the same as a static route, but it does have the feature that, when the path through one neighboring AS fails totally, a path through a different AS will be used.

Other Router-Router Communication

There is another protocol that is used for communication among routers. Routers need to exchange control information such as error statistics, clock synchronization, congestion control, and reachability tests. The *IP Control Message Protocol (ICMP)* is used by routers to exchange this sort of information. The last category, reachability testing, is the basis of two Internet features you might experience on any workstation/host.

■ A host may receive a message "ICMP unreachable" as a response when it sends its router a packet with a destination address for which the router has no path.

Continues

Other Router-Router Communication *(Continued)*

■ A host may send an *ICMP Echo* request. This is a packet that is addressed to a host or router, which when received is supposed to be answered with an echo reply to the sender. This is the basis of the *ping* application that is available on many systems. When in doubt as to whether some host is reachable through the Internet, you can execute the ping program with a simple command. For example, "ping netlab.gmu.edu" will receive a response (or not) depending on whether there is a usable path to netlab.gmu.edu from the sending point. On computers with a version of the Microsoft Windows operating system, the command "ping" must be run from a MS-DOS command window.

A related application that you might find useful is the *traceroute* program, which shows the actual route that packets are currently following from your host to the Internet address you give it, along with the times for three trial packets. For example, "traceroute 129.174.65.1" would show you to route from your computer to netlab. You can also use the DNS name, so "traceroute netlab.gmu.edu" would work as well. On computers with a version of the Microsoft Windows operating system, the command is "tracert" and it must be run from an MS-DOS command window.

Internet Routing Protocols

Routing protocols operate either within an AS, or in the case of the border gateway, between two AS. Because no one routing protocol needs to work across the whole Internet, there is no one "standard" Internet routing protocol. There are, however, three routing protocols that are used most widely, one for each of the routing protocol types described in the previous section.

Distance-Vector Routing Protocol: RIP

The *Routing Information Protocol (RIP)* is an old standby. It was developed by the University of California at Berkeley early in the history of the Internet and is supported by virtually every router manufacturer. It works by sending out routing packets on a best-effort basis. These packets contain an entry for every reachable subnet and the number of hops associated. A router that receives a RIP packet from its neighbor can take all reachable subnets from the packet, add one (for the hop to the neighbor), and include them in its own tables. RIP updates are simple and need not happen very often, as the routing changes only when links are added, deleted, or fail.

Link-State Routing Protocol: OSPF

The *Open Shortest Path First (OSPF)* routing protocol was developed to provide the advantages of link-state routing in an open standard (see the sidebar on open standards in Chapter 6). The path it finds is the one with the minimum value of the cost metric, optimized using the Dijkstra algorithm. OSPF is used within an AS and is scoped to cover limited areas because routing data exchange among routers can become a significant load on the network if too may routers participate. OSPF offers a network operator a number of features that we will not consider here, beyond noting that the protocol has facilities for *load balancing* to make most effective use of all network resources. Here we will consider only its basic operation, to understand how link-state routing works.

A cornerstone technique in OSPF is *flooding*, where a router sends out routing packets to all of its neighbors, which in turn send them to their neighbors. Clearly, it is important to limit flooding somehow; otherwise, one flooding operation could generate packets that circulate around the network forever! One way flooding is limited is that it stops at the AS boundary. Another technique to limit flooding traffic, which is used in NW, is to use the TTL field in the IP packet header. You should recall from the previous chapter that the contents of this field are reduced by one every time a router forwards a packet. When the TTL reaches zero, the packet is dropped. In OSPF, flooding is not continued for routing packets that are found to match an entry that is already in the routing database.

Another very important concept in OSPF is the Link-State Advertisement (LSA) database. An LSA packet contains the link states for a router or summarizes the link states for a collection of routers. For example, an OSPF router LSA packet contains all of the states for the links associated with the router that sends it. Each router collects all of the LSAs it receives into a database that it uses for the Dijkstra calculation.

Border Router Protocol: BGP4

The sheer size of the Internet today results in huge reachability tables in the border gateways between autonomous systems. Where an AS has only one path to the Internet, these tables are less important because the default route for all packets leaving the AS must be that one path. In the more general case, an AS may have an interconnection known as a *peering* with several other autonomous systems. In this case, the border routers are configured to favor a particular path if more than one neighboring AS advertises a route to some destination.

Stability of Dynamic Routing

A potential problem with dynamic routing protocols such as OSPF is *instability* due to routing updates. A routing update may show that path A is overloaded while path B is lightly loaded. The result can be that most of the traffic shifts from A to B, and now B is overloaded! OSPF provides for load balancing to avoid this problem. Stability is also increased by longer routing update intervals, which tend to smooth out oscillations in routing. Most routers in the Internet use an update cycle of at least several minutes.

 # Hands-On Activities

The problem and project in this chapter are designed to give you insight into the operation of a link-state routing protocol.

Network Workbench LSA Update Algorithm

```
copy ifacenum into the updated LSA entry;
increment the routing_SN in the router host port corresponding
to ifacenum and copy it into the updated LSA entry;
copy the queue_depth in the router port.
```

Problem: Generating Load-balanced Routing by Hand

The problem with assigning routing based purely on link capacity is that it ignores the traffic patterns among nodes. From the previous chapter, you know the NW routing matrix generated by that approach. As it turns out, about two-thirds of all the frames transmitted in project WAN3 pass over the link between nodes 1 and 2. (To be more accurate, about one-third go from 1 to 2, and one-third go from 2 to 1.) The link capacities in the project WAN are shown in Figure 9.2 by the thickness of the lines. Based on these capacities and the heavy loading of the link from node 1 to 2, derive an alternate routing table for node 1 that

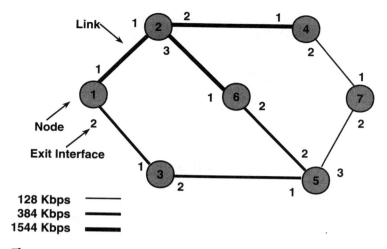

Figure 9.2 Seven-node project network.

balances the load better among its links. *Answer (destination net, next node): (2,2); (3,3); (4,2); (5,3); (6,2); (7,2).*

Project: Programming *update_LSA*

Project WAN3 is a study of dynamic routing. The idea behind dynamic routing is that, by knowing where the network is heavily loaded, it is possible to route some packets by other paths and achieve better overall performance. But we must be careful in this because sending link-state information also consumes network capacity. In this project you will:

1. Complete function `stack::update_LSA`, found in `rteupdt.cpp`, which collects router state data for NW's dynamic routing protocol. This protocol is patterned after the Internet routing protocol OSPF, but with much more limited function. It follows the general paradigm of shortest path first (SPF) routing by distributing the LSAs of each router to all other routers. Here is how it works:

   a. When the NW simulation starts, function `stack::startup_routing` in module `init.cpp` builds a static routing table using function `optimize_routes`, which you programmed in project WAN2. This creates a forwarding table showing, for any destination router, which interface is used to pass the packet to the neighbor router that will receive the packet next. `start_routing` also initializes each router's local LSA database with the initial values of the cost function. The cost function for `compute_routes` is `network::cost` in module `cost.cpp`.

b. After each `routing_update_interval` passes, each router node updates its own local routing database from its link-state data. This is done by invoking `stack::update_LSA` to create an updated `SPF_LSA` consisting of the link's interface number, the sequence number (`SN`) of this LSA (which first must be incremented in the link-state storage), and the queue depth at the link's interface. The router then uses flooding (broadcast) to send a copy of its new LSA to all other routers in the WAN. The code for this is in function `stack::routing_send` in module `routing.cpp`. The flooding uses network-level broadcast that is provided in `nl.cpp` and `mcsend.cpp`. A flooding packet is broadcast from a node only if the packet contains new information that is not in the node's routing database.

c. After the second `routing_update_interval` and all subsequent ones, the router updates its forwarding table using its local LSA database, which will have been updated by receipt of other routers' LSAs. This also is accomplished in `routing_send`, and happens only when `DYNAMIC_ROUTING=TRUE`.

d. The updated LSAs are received by function `stack::routing_receive` in module `routing.cpp`, and are used to update the router's local LSA database.

2. After you complete `stack::update_LSA`, you should experiment with routing protocol behavior by selecting a new value of `routing_update_interval`. If this interval is too short, too much of the network's capacity will be consumed in propagating routing, and routing may be unstable, resulting in "route flapping." If it is too long, "hot spots" in the network may persist when better routing could help them. You should select a `routing_update_interval` value and insert it before the line `print_authors` in `wan3.cpp`. If you choose a good value, you will see that the number of routing packets is a smaller fraction of overall traffic at active routers, and fewer packets will be dropped

due to buffer (queue) overflow. You can see these statistics in the summary at the end of the NW output.

Notes

- WAN3 uses NW's unreliable DLC layer and transport layer, so the effects of packet loss are made evident in that some email messages that are sent are never received because the packets are dropped. None of the loss is due to link errors because the bit error rate is set to zero in the WAN3 profile. All of the losses come from packet queues overflowing. A small fraction of the messages shown as sent but not received in the final NW statistics are not lost; rather, they are still sitting in router queues when the simulation ends so they are never received. We will see in project TRN1 how the Internet is able to deliver messages reliably, even when packets can be lost.

- While rerouting will help traffic overload at some routers, it cannot solve the problem if a router is receiving more traffic than it has capacity to send. You should be sure to distinguish between the two cases.

- For WAN3, the simulation stopping point (`max_DES_ticks`) is set to a larger number than in previous projects, so the routing has a chance to stabilize.

- The data transmitted in WAN3 comes from the same email files that are used in DLC3 and WAN2. However, the email application is set to send the same messages over and over in order to create a heavy traffic load because link state routing is most beneficial under heavy loading. For this reason, WAN3 will always terminate due to DES tick limit exceeded as it will never run out of email messages.

- The profile in `pwan3.cpp` does not call for NW to print the data being transmitted. To see the data you could set some of the profile values at the point indicated by comments in the `wan3.cpp`:
  `print_at[umessage_send_interface] = TRUE;` or
  `print_at[usegment_receive_interface] = TRUE;`

- On the other hand, you might want to turn off printing for faster runs during the tuning process:

```
print_at[packet_drop] = FALSE;
print_at[routing_send_interface] = FALSE;
print_at[routing_receive_interface] = FALSE;
```

- The profile in pwan3.cpp includes interactive = TRUE; so you can test your code by stepping through the routing packets sent. Just press Enter for the simulation to move forward one step. To leave interactive mode, you can compile with interactive = FALSE where indicated by comments in stack::simulation, or you can type a zero before "return."

Transport Layer: TCP

O ur progress upward through the protocol stack has been slow but steady. We have come to the "first name" of the well-known TCP/IP protocols. TCP is the *Transmission Control Protocol,* and it is the *reliable transport protocol* for the Internet.

What Does a Transport Protocol Do?

The most important thing to understand about transport protocols is that they work *end to end* within the network. This means that they operate only in the hosts with the application software. The routers that perform the network layer's packet switching do not examine the transport header. This was shown previously in Figure 8.3. Another way of looking at the situation is shown in Figure 10.1, which shows that, even though the router probably has TCP in its stack to support its own applications, its transport layer does not participate in the TCP connection between hosts A and B. Transport is an *end-to-end* function, and as such it communicates with the network layer only in the end-point hosts. Figure 10.1 also shows that the data unit of the most important transport layer protocol (TCP) is called a *segment.* Each segment gets wrapped into a packet by the network layer. In turn, the packet is carried within a frame by the DLC layer.

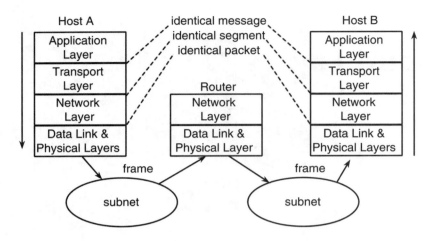

Figure 10.1 Transport layer locations.

There are two major categories of transport protocols.

Reliable transport protocols ensure that messages provided by the application at the sending host are delivered to the application at the receiving host, uncorrupted, in the order in which they are sent. These techniques are much like those described in Chapter 5, "Data Link Control—ARQ Flow Control."

Best-effort transport protocols do not attempt to provide any reliability— if lower layers do not deliver the message, the message will be lost.

In the Internet, the *Transmission Control Protocol (TCP)* provides reliable transport, while the *User Datagram Protocol (UDP)* provides best-effort protocol. Both TCP and UDP perform common transport layer functions.

- TCP and UDP provide a consistent service interface to the application layer (you should remember that a "service" is what a protocol offers to the next higher layer), so that changing between them is not difficult.

- TCP and UDP provide the ability to identify the processes that are communicating, by means of a *port* number that is identified with a process on the host. Thus, any instance of communication using TCP/IP or UDP/IP can be identified on a host by a 48-bit endpoint number, as shown in Figure 10.2. This endpoint is called a *socket* in many implementations of TCP/IP.

socket = IP address + port number

48 bits   32 bits   16 bits

Figure 10.2   Socket: the Internet end-to-end communication identifier.

UDP is a simple protocol. Its only real function is to tag the data segment with a port identifier. Any relationship among multiple UDP segments transmitted to the same socket must be established by the application layer. TCP is much more interesting. It will occupy our attention for the remainder of this chapter.

Functions of TCP

The first function of TCP is to establish a connection between the two ends. A TCP connection is defined by the sockets used on both hosts involved. At this point, it becomes necessary to drop the terminology "sending host" and "receiving host" because TCP assumes a full-duplex data flow, where either host can send to the other. In fact, both must do some sending for the connection to work. From this point forward, we will instead describe "host A" and "host B," in cases where TCP is communicating between A and B

You may have heard that the Internet uses a *connectionless* protocol. The term "connectionless" means that, when an IP packet is transmitted, there is no predetermined path (*virtual circuit*) the packet will take. It does not mean that it is practical to transmit a long stream of information between two Internet hosts without some "hookup" procedure. The way this is done is reminiscent of the way a DLC link is established because it has the same function: to ensure that the two ends get into a proper state to transfer information effectively. For this reason, a three-way-handshake is used by both DLC and reliable transport in creating a connection to transfer information. TCP also uses a similar procedure again to disconnect at the end of transmission. Figure 10.3 shows how the three-way handshake works. Because the connection request could be lost in transmission, the source must set a timer when it issues the request and try again if a timeout occurs. You should notice that the range of TCP sequence numbers (SN) is much larger that than available for HDLC, and also

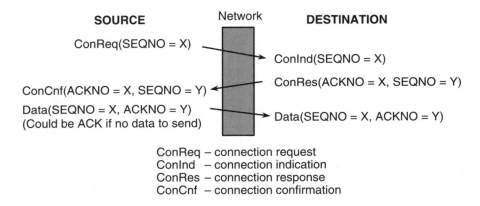

Figure 10.3   TCP connection message sequence.

that the TCP three-way handshake involves exchanging an initial sequence number for both ends that is chosen at random. The large range of sequence numbers provides a high confidence that the sending end can try multiple times if necessary to establish a connection, with no concern that delayed packets from any false starts might trigger a connection where the two ends are not synchronized. Each new start has a new sequence number, so unsynchronized connections will not happen.

In order for a connection to occur, both ends must execute an *open*.

- First, one end must execute a *passive open*, which means it must be in a "listening" mode, ready to receive a connection. This action usually is associated with a server that is prepared to offer some network-based service.

- Second, the other end must execute an *active open* where it sends a connection request (identifiable by having its "SYN" bit set) to the waiting server. At this point, the three-way handshake ensues, and the connection is made.

Fragmenting and Reassembling Data

TCP treats the data provided by the application layer as one long, continuous stream. Unless told otherwise, TCP collects the bytes of this stream into long segments sent from A to B, while at the same time another stream may be moving from B to A. It is important to remember that everything TCP does happens end to end, between two hosts.

The goal is to get the stream from A to B as quickly as possible within the rules of the network, **in the order in which it was sent and with no losses**. To do this over a packet network, TCP must break down the stream provided by the application into *segments* no longer than one network MTU. It does this by assigning a number to each byte in the stream of data. The numbers are 32 bits long and can "wrap around" and start over (like the DLC SN) if necessary.

Figure 10.4 shows how TCP packages the data for transmission. After your study of the DLC frames and network layer packets in previous chapters, it should come as no surprise that the transport layer adds a header to the data segment. It is not important that you understand every field in this header. There are a few of the most important ones:

Source port and destination port are the 16-bit port numbers that, together with the source and destination IP address, form the socket numbers at the sender and receiver. (Remember, either A or B can be the sender. Within a given connection, if one is sending, the other must be receiving, but both can be sending and receiving at the same time.)

Sequence number (SEQNO) works like the DLC SN, but it is a 32-bit number (within the overall stream) of the first byte in the data stream flowing from sender to receiver.

Acknowledgment number works like RN in the DLC. It, too, is a number within the stream being sent from sender to receiver. It represents the number of a first byte in the data stream coming from the receiver to the sender. The byte number is the first one following those that have been received correctly.

HLEN is the header length in words.

0	4	10	16	24	31
SOURCE PORT			DESTINATION PORT		
SEQUENCE NUMBER					
ACKNOWLEDGMENT NUMBER					
HLEN	RESERVED	CODE BITS	WINDOW		
CHECKSUM			URGENT POINTER		
OPTIONS (IF ANY)				PADDING	
DATA					
...					

Figure 10.4 TCP segment format.

Control bits affect how the segment is dealt with. Examples are SYN, ACK, and FIN, which are used for connect and disconnect, and PSH, which indicates TCP is sending a partial segment at the request of the application. A typical reason for a push is to support remote interactive applications that respond to small amounts of input; for example, telnet needs to "push" individual keystrokes.

Window tells how many bytes the sender is willing to receive in the stream coming back from receiver to sender.

Checksum is used for header error detection.

Well-Known Ports

Most of the TCP port numbers are available for whatever application needs to use them. However, some of the low port numbers are pre-assigned to specific applications or functions. Each application connects to the *well-known port* that is reserved for it. For example, the hypertext transfer protocol (http) associated with the World Wide Web is assigned to port 80. Therefore, a Web browser that is directed to a particular URL, for example //netlab.gmu.edu/NW, will open a TCP connection using port 80. Figure 10.5 shows some of the well-known port assignments.

Multiplexing Data Streams

TCP is capable of providing multiple streams of data between two computers at the same time. Sometimes this feature is used to support more than one application simultaneously. For example, when working from home, a user can open a remote terminal (telnet) window on a home computer to access an office computer, while at the same time transferring files back and forth using ftp. Moreover, it is also possible to have multiple connections open at the same time for the same application. Web browsers routinely open several simultaneous connections to fetch the multiple files of a complex Web page. How is this achieved?

Multiple instances of the same application are able to use TCP simultaneously because the well-known ports are not actually used on the client end. Instead, each of them serves as a "meeting place" at the server end for a particular application. The application client connects to the server's well-known port and uses this connection to identify a free port on the client's host. The free ports have values of 1024 or

Port	Keyword	Description
11	USERS	Active Users
13	DAYTIME	Daytime
15	NETSTAT	Network status program
17	QUOTE	Quote of the Day
20	FTP-DATA	File Transfer Protocol (data)
21	FTP	File Transfer Protocol
23	TELNET	network terminal emulator
25	SMTP	Simple Mail Transfer Protocol
37	TIME	Time
42	NAMESERVER	Host Name Server
43	NICNAME	Who Is
53	DOMAIN	Domain Name Server
80	WWW-HTTP	World Wide Web HTTP

Figure 10.5   Some TCP well-known ports.

higher. The server sends data to the free port number on the client's host. At the time of connection, the exchange of initial SEQNO and ACKNO values shown in Figure 10.3 takes place.

Full-Duplex Transmission

When host A is sending to host B, it is possible that B sends to A only the ACKs that tell A to send the next segment of data. It is also possible that B has some other data coming to A. The TCP connection is truly full duplex, in the sense that B can be sending data to A while A is sending to B. If this is the case, TCP does the same clever thing you saw in the DLC ARQ: It piggybacks ACK and NACK codes on the data that is flowing in the reverse direction.

End-to-End Error and Flow Control

This brings us to the part of TCP that makes it "reliable" transport. TCP uses a sliding window that is similar in purpose to the DLC sliding window. However, where the DLC window establishes the number of frames that can be sent before an ACK is received, the TCP window establishes the maximum number of bytes sent in the data stream before an ACK is received. As you saw in the TCP header, the acknowledgment number points to the specific byte in the stream that the receiver is expecting to receive next.

Another thing TCP has in common with the DLC is the need to establish a timer in case the ACK never arrives and in cases where the data gets lost somewhere between A and B. The timeout value must reflect the *round-trip time (RTT)* from A to B through the network, and then back from B to A. The initial estimate of RTT is obtained during the exchange of connection information. Thereafter, TCP maintains a running estimate of RTT that continuously averages past values with the most recent ones. Because there may be significant variation in the RTT from one segment transmission to the next, TCP also maintains a running estimate of the deviation in RTT and factors the deviation into the timeout.

TCP Startup and Congestion Avoidance

We are nearing the end of the list of TCP's functions. Before we wrap things up with a description of the disconnect, you need to know about a TCP function that is absolutely critical to keeping the Internet usable. Because most packets in the Internet have a TCP segment as a payload, it is possible to tailor much of the Internet's behavior by specifying how TCP will work. For this reason, the IETF has defined TCP in such a way that it responds to indications of congestion by slowing down transmission.

Congestion occurs when the senders collectively try to send more than the Internet can handle, even though dynamic routing causes traffic to use all available paths. In Chapter 8 on the network layer you learned that packets are placed in a queue, awaiting their turn to be transmitted. The more congested the network becomes, the longer the packets must wait. In extreme cases, the queue overflows the buffer and packets are dropped. Therefore, TCP is able to sense network congestion when the RTT increases, and when there are timeouts due to dropped packets. IETF standards require that the size of the TCP window must be used to avoid congestion as much as possible.

TCP starts sending with a small window that is increased during a *slow start* process until either congestion is sensed in the form of increased RTT or dropped packets, or the receiver's maximum window size is reached. After transmission reaches its full rate, the sender is required to respond to an indication of congestion by reducing the size of its window. Because no more segments can be sent when the window is full, a reduced window has the effect of slowing down transmission by all senders and, as a result, reducing congestion. When all senders cooperate in reducing their traffic to a workable total, the Internet's capacity is shared more fairly.

The feedback involved in TCP congestion avoidance has a possible drawback: Just as with dynamic routing, it could become unstable. If all senders reduce their transmission rate, the RTT may get better quickly. If the senders respond to the improvement by increasing their windows quickly, the result will be another round of congestion. If you have ever driven on a high-speed highway that was running at full load, probably you have experienced this phenomenon. Traffic races along for a bit, then slows to a standstill. The solution to this problem is for TCP to be fast on the brakes, but easy on the gas pedal. This is done by reducing the window size by half each time congestion is sensed, but increasing it only by adding increments when the RTT gets shorter.

Disconnect

When a TCP connection is terminated, the three-way handshake again becomes important for graceful shutdown of the connection. Figure 10.6 shows the disconnect process. Either end of the connection can decide to disconnect, so both ends must deal with the possibility that the disconnect may not go as it should. In a proper disconnect, both ends receive an ACK for all segments they have sent. But, of course, it is always possible that the host on the other end crashes or the network path to

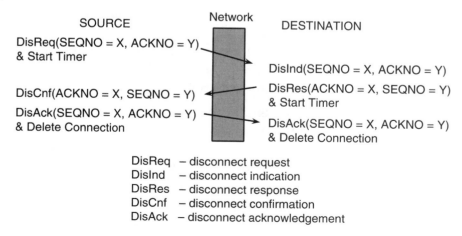

Figure 10.6   TCP disconnect message sequence.

that host becomes unusable. In this case, the host on each end starts a timer when it issues a disconnect or replies to a disconnect. When the timer expires, the TCP software continues with the disconnect.

 # Hands-On Activities

The problem and project in this chapter are designed to give you insight into the operation of a reliable protocol similar to TCP.

NW Reliable Transport Algorithm

Here is how the NW TL works:

- Connection is established using the normal three-way handshake. In the process, the receiving end sends a window size to the sending end (default value is 60 bytes = 3 segments). The window size is the number of bytes the receiving end TL is prepared to buffer at one time (not counting the message buffer). In general, the bytes being transported could be part of a very long stream of data. It happens that the application in NW is short email messages.

- Initially the sending end transmits a window full of segments (if the data to be sent is that long), then it waits for ACKs (some of which may arrive before the full window has been sent).

- Each time a segment is received, the receive end ACKs the last byte of contiguous data received (which may not include the segment just received, if some intervening segment has gotten lost). If some data has been received so that the full window is not needed, it closes down the window to cover only the data that is needed. Unlike TCP, the ACK is not piggybacked on data going in the other direction; it is sent as a segment with no message payload.

- Each time the sending end receives an ACK, it looks to see (a) if the window shown in the ACK has room for more data to be sent, and (b) if the ACK implies a need to retransmit some segment that has been sent previously. If either a or b is true, it schedules a call to the send_seg module in its host, to send the appropriate segment.

- When the sending end transmits a segment, it sets a timer. If that data has not been ACKed when the timer expires, it re-sends the segment.

- When the sending end receives the ACK for the last data, it sends a FIN segment, sets a timer, and waits for a FIN ACK. If the acknowledgment is not received, it repeats the process until a FIN ACK is received, and then shuts down.

■ While a connection is open to a receive end, that receive end will not accept any other connections. It ignores attempts to connect, but it will accept ACK segments for its own send side. Also, only one connection is established per send side at a time. You may find the state-transition diagram in Figure 10.7 to be useful in understanding how the NW reliable transport send and receive processes interact with each other.

```
NW rtl send algorithm
state closed (tl_send is inactive at this host, this is the call
from appl_send):
{
  copy the message to outgoing_message;
  send a segment with ack=0, syn=1, fin=0;
  set timer for net_rtt_timeout;
  set tl_send_state to syn_sent;
  initialize state for send side of connection;
}
```

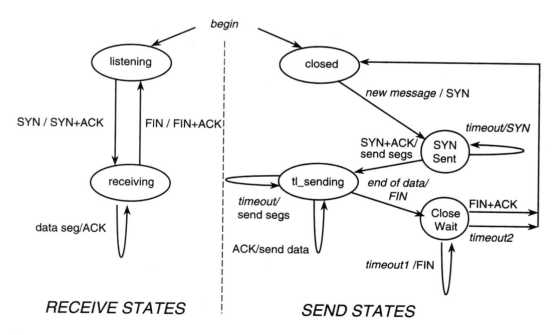

Figure 10.7 NW reliable transport states and transitions.

```
state syn_sent (a SYN has been sent to open connection; either an
ACK has been received or the timer has expired):
{
  if ACK has not been received
  {
    send the connection request SYN again;
    set timer for net_rtt_timeout;
    send the SYN again;
  }
  else
  {
    set tl_send_state to tl_sending;
    start transmit;
  }

state tl_sending (connection has been established and tl is send-
ing the message in outgoing_message, when any segment is sent,
save a copy in tl_buffer and set a timer to call trans_send back
after net_rtt_timeout time units; send_seg does this):
{
  use any segment that has been received from other end to
  clean out tl_buffer;
  update send_window_start;
  update send_window_size;
  send to NL any TL segments that need sent;
  schedule timeout;
  escape from this case;
}

state close_wait (tl has sent all the data, received ACKs for all
of it, and sent off a FIN; either another segment has been
received, or the timer has expired):
{
  if another segment has been received with ack=1, syn=0, fin=1
  (FIN-ACK)
  {
    set tl_send_state to closed;
    schedule read of another email;
  }
  else
  {
    send the FIN twice;
    set a timer for net_rtt_timeout;
  }
  set tl_send_state to closed.
```

NWrtl receive algorithm
state listening (tl_receive is listening at this host; only a SYN
should be received:ack=0, syn=1, fin=0):
if a SYN is received,
{
  reply with an ACK-SYN (ack=1, syn=1, fin=0,ackno=seqno+1);
  set tl_receiving_from_net and tl_receiving_from_host;
  set tl_receive_state to receiving;
  escape from this state;
}
if a FIN is received (because FIN-ACK from this host gets lost),
 reply with FIN-ACK;
break;

state receiving(tl_receive has received a SYN and replied ACK-SYN
at some point, now it is accepting data segments):
{
  if a SYN (ack=0, syn=1, fin=0) arrives from the connected
  net host (this means the SYN-ACK previously sent had not reached
  the sending end before timeout, so it is necessary to repeat
  the response to SYN above),
  {
    reply with an ACK-SYN (ack=1, syn=1, fin=0,ackno=seqno+1);
    set tl_receiving_from_net and tl_receiving_from_host;
    set tl_receive_state to receiving;
    escape from this case;
  }
  if it is not a FIN (ack=0, syn=0, fin=1),
  {
    create an ACK segment (ack=1,syn=0, fin=0, ackno=highest
    contiguous segmtno received +1);
    place the ACK segment in the incoming_message buffer;
    escape from this case;
  }
  if it is a fin (ack=0, syn=0, fin=1) (all data has been sent
  and ACKed),
  {
    send a FIN-ACK segment (ack=1,syn=0,fin=1);
    pass the message to the application layer;
    set tl_receive_state back to listening;
    escape from this case;
  }
  if a segment is received from a net-host other than data from the
  one that is connected and sending (probably it is a SYN segment
  from another host that is trying to connect, but this transport
  layer does not allow connections to multiple hosts at the same
  time),

```
      if it is a FIN,
        reply with a FIN-ACK;
      else (the other host will keep trying, when the current
      connection is finished it will get its chance to connect),
        ignore it;


algorithm for sending NW TL segments (function send_rt1_segments)
if reply_seg contains an ackno indicating that a previously sent
segment has not been received (ackno<last_char_sent),
  do for all segments in the buffer (the number is
  TL_MAX_BUFFER_SEGS),
    if that segment has had time to reach its destination
    (sim_time minus segment sent_time is greater than
    net_rtt_timeout),
      send that segment again from the tl_buffer;
calculate window_end as the smaller of
(send_window_start+send_window_size-1)
and (sending_message.size-1);
while last_char_sent is less than window_end,
{
  make another segment from the message;
  send the segment;
}
for each segment in tl_buffer,
  if segment has timed out waiting for ACK (sim_time minus
  segment sent_time is greater than net_rtt_timeout),
    retransmit the segment in tl_buffer;
if send_window_start is greater than or equal to size of message
being sent (all data has been sent and ACKed),
{
  send FIN;
  set tl_send_state to close_wait;
}.
```

Problem: Tracing Transport Layer Delivery of a Message

Run the NW solution to TRN1 by commenting out the line #include
"tlsend.cpp" in trn1.cpp, then compiling and running trn1.cpp.
Find the first "email" message sent by the application layer, note the
source and destination net/hosts, and trace the flow of TL segments
between the sender and receiver. Make a table with an entry for each
segment, to show how the message is built up from segments at the
receive end. Be sure to follow the process all the way through to the
last FIN-ACK. The data structure segment can be found in nw.h.

TIME SENT	SEQNO	ACKNO	WINDOW	ACK	SYN	FIN	DATA SIZE	DATA

What Is Really Happening Between Layers in NW?

If you read the code in the NW stack modules (`class stack`) carefully, you will see that something more is happening than is shown in a typical stack such as Figure 1.5. If the stack modules worked like Figure 1.5, the transport-layer send function would invoke the network-layer send function. Instead, the last step in a `utl_send` invokes something called `utl_to_nl`. What's happening here?

The answer is shown in Figure 10.8. The NW stack layers must participate in the discrete event simulation (DES) process. So, instead of calling the network-layer send function, the transport-layer send module must call a function that interfaces to the DES. There is a whole collection of such functions in module `interlyr.cpp`. They have several important roles in NW.

- They provide a consistent interface between functions in `class stack` and the DES modules, which are in `class network`.
- Depending on the values in the `print_at` array, they may print the value of the data unit being transferred between layers; for example, the segment sent from the transport layer.
- They capture the statistics that are printed at the end of the NW run.
- They provide each stack function with a pointer to its appropriate state data structure; for example, `host_state* this_host` for transport and network layers. This state structure contains all information local to the host that is needed by the stack function. As a result, one copy of a stack function is able to represent its assigned layer for every host in the simulated network.

Figure 10.8 describes the process between layers. The stack function invokes an `interlyr` function, which collects simulation statistics. It also invokes the DES `schedule_event` function, which places an entry on the DES event list, indexed to the number of ticks from the current simulated time when the event will "happen." After the other events waiting to happen have been cleared from the list, the event is removed from the list by the DES `next_event` function. This in turn invokes the next stack function down; in this case, the network-layer send function.

Delay between layers is only a few ticks, representing processing time at the transport layer, but the same DES mechanism is used for any delay. For example, at the physical layer, the delay due to transmit time plus latency is calculated and used to determine how many ticks later the last bit of the data frame will be received at the other end of the link.

Project: Programming send_rtl_segments

In project TRN1 you will complete a working reliable transport for the NW. The transport layer `tl.cpp` contains both a best-effort transport

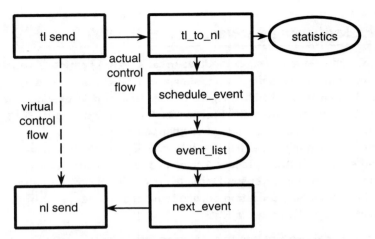

Figure 10.8 Control flow for discrete event simulation in NW.

protocol and a reliable transport protocol. The reliable protocol has two major modules: rtrans_send and rtrans_receive. An important part of the code for the send module has been broken out into a separate function, send_rtl_segments, which contains the logic that determines when segments get transmitted.

In project TRN1, the DLC does not use ARQ; thus, the data is not delivered reliably by the datalink layer. Instead, the transport layer must provide reliability on an end-to-end basis, in the presence of lost frames and packets lost due to queue overflow in the network layer. The reliable transport layer deals with all forms of packet loss, as long as the network succeeds in delivering some fraction of the packets sent.

rtrans_send has four parts corresponding to the four states a sending host can have: closed, syn_sent, tl_sending, close_wait.

The code provided is complete for all of these but sending. All of the code you must write goes in one function, which implements the tl_send state processing. The function is called send_rtl_segments and is contained in module tlsend.cpp. There is a stub version in the code directory.

Notes

- Before beginning to implement tlsend.cpp, you should study the RTL send and receive algorithms carefully to understand how the reliable transport layer works. Figure 10.7 probably will prove helpful.

- The default conditions for project TRN1 are one error in 10,000 bits and three email files. As with other projects, you may find debugging easier with only one email file and no errors.

- The profile function provided is set to suppress simulation details below the transport layer; however, you can add statements to trn1.cpp that change the print_at[ ] values to different values if you wish, as described in the sidebar in Chapter 4. You may also want to set interactive=TRUE to step through the protocol operation.

- A good way to check whether a segment in the tl_buffer holds data is to check sent_seg.size. If this variable is greater than zero, the segment holds data.

- In programming tlsend.cpp, you will need to use function make_segment. The parameters of make_segment are as follows:

  current_msg   Application layer message being sent.

  start_offset   First character of that message to be
                     placed in this segment.

CHAPTER 11

Multicasting and Multimedia

This chapter will introduce you to a powerful new type of networking called *multicasting*, which is useful when the same information is to be delivered to more than one destination in the Internet. Use of multiple human interface media (*multimedia*) is covered in this chapter as well because of the close association between multicasting networks and multimedia applications.

What Is Multicasting?

The examples up to this point in the book have been for *unicasting*, which is the process by which a packet gets delivered to a single destination address. This is fine for one or two destinations, but it quickly becomes inefficient if there are more destinations. A multicast-capable network can deliver the same packet to a whole group of addresses. The packet crosses the network only once. It is copied at every router serving a host that is a member of the multicast group to which it is addressed. Figure 11.1 shows how multicasting works. The WAN routers keep track of which LANs have a host participating in each multicast group. The overall arrangement resembles a tree, with its

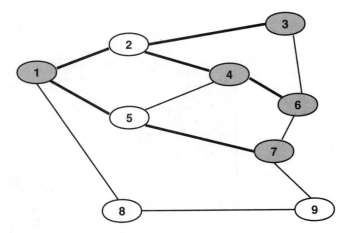

darker links form multicast tree
shaded router nodes support multicasting hosts

Figure 11.1 Network with multicast tree.

root at the router that first started the current session in the group. This is called a *multicast tree*.

The routers in the tree all must be multicast capable. What if some of the routers are not? Where multicasting "islands" need to communicate across the unicast Internet, it is possible to connect the islands with *tunnels* created by carrying the multicast packets as the payload of unicast packets. Figure 11.2 shows a case where a multicast router has no multicast neighbors and therefore must exchange multicast packets through a unicast tunnel.

Why Multicasting?

Much of the traffic in today's Internet is appropriate for delivery by unicast. Traditional applications such as remote terminal (telnet), file transfer (ftp), World Wide Web (http), and person-to-person electronic mail call for point-to-point delivery of packets. However, for almost any point-to-point application, there exists a group equivalent. Some of these involve groups of computers (for example, distribution of data files or software updates to groups of hosts). However, in many cases, delivery to a group of addresses is needed because the application is supporting a group of people who are collaborating in some way.

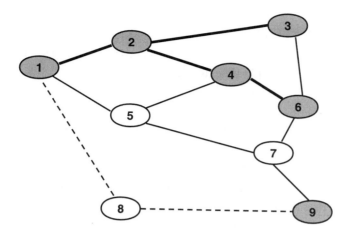

dashed links form multicast tunnel
shaded router nodes support multicast routing

Figure 11.2 Multicasting through unicast tunnels.

- Group text windows (often called "chat") support communication within an online group of people.
- Group Web browsing is a good way for online teachers to show slides.
- Group email delivery is a great way to distribute news.

Real-Time Multicasting

Another important use for multicasting is a class of multimedia applications that have human interfaces for audio, video, and still images in addition to text.

- The telephone system is already largely digital. Normal telephone sets communicate *analog* signals (voltages that are proportional to sound pressure) to the nearest telephone office, where they are converted to digital form, continuous streams of bits. The telephone network transmits these streams of bits to other telephone offices worldwide. By breaking such streams into packets, they can be delivered over the Internet. As a result, Internet *telephony* is a growing unicast application. The same software that is used for the point-to-point calls can also be used for applications such as Internet teaching. My GMU networking classes are available over the Internet while I am teaching, and afterward from a server.

- Video also is rapidly becoming a digital commodity in both High Definition Television (HDTV) and the Digital Video Disk (DVD). The most immediate use of video in the Internet is for *teleconferencing*, but many people envision that in the future the Internet also will be used for commercial distribution of motion pictures for entertainment.

- Computer-generated graphics can be used to create a "virtual environment" where people can interact through the network. This is already being done for military group training. The required graphics for a commercial version already exist in computer games; the next step is to distribute them over the Internet.

Multimedia applications are very often used in a *real-time* or *synchronous* mode, where all members of the group participate at the same time. That requires the network delay (latency) for delivery to be very small. This is true for any application where the people involved must be able to interact with each other. If the application does not call for immediate interaction, it can work in *asynchronous* mode, where the data is delivered after a significant delay.

For real-time delivery, the network must be able to provide a *quality of service (QoS)*. To achieve acceptable QoS for real-time multimedia applications, the network's packet loss, latency, and the variation of latency (known as *jitter*) must meet a defined level. That level must be sufficient to produce audio that has no gaps in the sound, and video that has an acceptable smoothness of motion. Today's Internet has no mechanisms for guaranteeing QoS; thus, real-time multimedia applications are generally confined to those subnetworks where capacity is adequate to meet the requirements.

Internet QoS Developments

The Internet effectively has only one QoS class at present. It is called *best effort*, which means the network makes no commitments other than "I'll do what I can to deliver each packet." Two other service qualities have been defined, but are not generally available. Both of them are based on the idea of supporting a point-to-point flow of packets between two hosts in the Internet, or a multicast flow among a group of hosts.

Guaranteed QoS ensures that every packet is delivered within a specified latency and jitter, unless the network breaks, no matter what the overall network loading may be. This QoS is achieved by reserving sufficient network resources (link and router capacity) to meet the guarantee, without ever exceeding the limits of installed network capabilities.

Controlled Load QoS behaves like the best-effort service of a lightly loaded network. Packets are dropped only rarely, and the statistical performance of the network can be characterized accurately, as long as the specified load in bits per second and packets per second is not exceeded. This is true even though the network actually may be heavily loaded. For example, a controlled load specification might call for at least 98 percent of all packets to be delivered within 100 ms, and no more than 1 percent of all packets to be dropped. Unlike Guaranteed QoS, Controlled Load allows the network to drop packets within the specification. This means the network can take advantage of bursty traffic to offer significantly more Controlled Load capacity than it can guarantee absolutely. Overall, the bursts average out so all of the commitments are met, on a statistical basis.

Two major mechanisms have been developed to support improved QoS, but neither has been deployed widely. The first major thrust by the IETF was the *Integrated Service (IntServ)* model, which envisions the Internet providing a powerful, pervasive communication system with goals similar to those of ISDN: a unified capability for voice, video, images, and other formats in addition to traditional data. One mechanism that has received considerable focus within the IntServ model is the *Resource reSerVation Protocol (RSVP)*. RSVP provides a way of communicating QoS requirements throughout the network on an individual flow basis. Although RSVP has been implemented by major router vendors, it turns out that the requirement to keep track of the details of a large number of flows is very difficult to meet. Thus, RSVP has been successful only for moderate numbers of flows.

Demand for real-time, multimedia communication has continued to grow. As a result, the IETF has begun to consider another model called *Differentiated Services (DiffServ)*. In this model, individual flows do not require reservations because they are allocated from bulk capacity that is set aside for QoS traffic. These bulk allocations are established by agreements among ISPs. The actual data rate introduced by users is policed by an ISP's router at the entry point to the network (often called the *edge*). Some vendor-unique versions of DiffServ are already in place. As standardized versions are defined, it seems likely that this model will be deployed widely as a way of supporting real-time multimedia communications in the Internet.

Both IntServ and DiffServ assume that a significant portion (perhaps 50 percent) of network capacity remains committed to best-effort packets. This makes it easier to meet the resource reservation commitments and also ensures that users who do not have reservations can still get some level of service, however poor.

The MBone

Currently, the only part of the Internet that supports multicasting with wide availability is the Internet Multicast BackBone (MBone), which is available at many laboratories and institutions of higher learning in the United States, and to a lesser extent at similar facilities internationally. The MBone provides a working demonstration of the power of real-time multimedia. Meetings and conferences are distributed locally, regionally, and worldwide via multicast. A popular suite of tools used for MBone meetings includes tools that distribute audio, video, text, and a graphic computer-screen "whiteboard" to multiple sites simultaneously. Unfortunately, the MBone also provides an excellent example of the need for QoS, because it provides only best-effort service. When too many multimedia sources send across the MBone at the same time, the quality of all ongoing meetings becomes unacceptable due to lost packets. Audio quality becomes unacceptable when as few as 5 percent of packets are lost. The situation further illustrates the difficulty of managing a free-for-all, shared environment. The lessons of MBone need to be taken very seriously by ISPs who support real-time multimedia communications.

Multimedia Protocols

Electronic mail was one of the earliest applications to make widespread use of multimedia, and therefore it had a major influence on multimedia standards. You need to start with this nonreal-time application in order to understand current multimedia protocols.

MIME

The Internet mail standard is the *Simple Mail Transfer Protocol (SMTP)*. SMTP has the attractive property that the protocol control fields are human-readable text labels such as FROM: and REPLY-TO:. The *multimedia Internet mail extensions (MIME)* provide a standard way to include multimedia objects within SMTP mail. Some of the basic MIME object types are as follows:

- **Text.** Plain old ASCII characters are the bedrock of SMTP mail.

- *Hypertext.* This is text that can have properties of font, size, bold, italic, underline, and color. Even more important, it can have embedded links to other hypertext, as is commonly done in Web pages.

- **Audio clips.** These are digitally recorded sound files. Thus email using MIME can hold spoken messages or recording of music.

- *Graphic image format (gif).* This is a format where each individual picture element (*pixel*) is represented. This requires very large files; for example, the lowest common full-screen resolution is 640 by 480 pixels, a total of 307,200 pixels, which if stored in a common color format requires 24 bits (8 bytes) for each pixel, a total of 921,600 bytes.

- **Still images.** The *Joint Photographic Experts Group (JPEG)* standard provides a way to *compress* the image to a smaller number of bytes than a gif, based on the fact that large portions of most useful images contain the same information repeated over and over (otherwise, there would be no recognizable objects).

- **Moving images** (possibly including sound). The *Motion Picture Experts Group (MPEG)* standard provides a way to compress the images based on the fact that most video that is useful consists of a sequence of frames with much the same content from frame to frame (otherwise, it would be seen mostly as moving blurs).

HTML and HTTP

The *World Wide Web* has generated another set of standards that have influenced multimedia significantly. The Web is mostly used in asynchronous mode where pages are prepared in advance and then displayed in near real time through *browser* software that displays the pages on demand as they are accessed over the Internet.

- *Hypertext Markup Language (HTML).* Provides for coding a document containing any of the MIME-types.

- *Hypertext Transfer Protocol (HTTP).* Provides for dynamic Internet access of files encoded in HTML or any MIME type, using TCP for transport. A fundamental rule is that the TCP connection is kept open only long enough to transfer one HTML file.

- *Common Gateway Interface (CGI).* This specification provides for generating HTML documents interactively at the HTTP server-based on Web page input.

- *Java.* This is a programming language used to create programs called *applets* that run locally with the Web browser and can interact with the user (interaction with other Internet sites and/or with local files is also possible, if permitted by local security policy).

- *Streaming audio and video.* Custom Web clients such as RealAudio and RealVideo use a very high level of compression. They work over best-effort QoS by buffering enough data to give a high confidence that Internet "stalls" in delivery will not disrupt the multimedia flow, and start playback only after a significant amount of the stream has been received, which precludes real-time operation. Thereafter, they play back the multimedia while a stream of data continues to be delivered and use TCP flow control to avoid over-running the receiver's buffer.

RTP

All of the nonreal-time multimedia formats can be delivered in real time, given adequate QoS. The *real-time transfer protocol (RTP)* provides packaging for real-time multimedia data for Internet transfer. RTP provides a generic transport framework for real-time data *streams* (continuous flows of packets). It runs "over" UDP (that is, RTP receives service from UDP, which in turn receives service from IP). The data formats supported are recognized MIME types. There is an *RTP Control Protocol (RTCP)* that supports monitoring of RTP data delivery in a manner intended to be scalable to large multicast networks. At present, the principal use of RTP is to support audio and video, but other applications such as distributed *virtual reality* are possible in the future. The MBone audio and video tools use RTP.

Multicast Protocols

Here we consider the protocols that make multicasting work at the network layer.

IP Multicast

Internet Protocol—multicast (IPmc) is exactly the same Internet protocol you learned about in Chapter 8, "Network Layer: The Internet Protocol." It is distinguished only by the fact that a multicast address, as shown in Figure 8.4, is used in the packet's destination address field.

IGMP

One key to making IPmc work is the ability for hosts to join and leave multicast groups on the LAN. This function is accomplished using the *Internet Group Management Protocol (IGMP)*, which defines how a host tells its router it needs to send and receive packets addressed to a particular group. It is not used between routers, only between hosts and their supporting routers.

Multicast Routing Protocols

Because multicast addresses refer to groups of hosts, they cannot be used to identify individual routers in the multicast tree. Therefore, multicast routing uses unicast IP addresses to select the best path for the tree. Multicast group information is exchanged among routers using one of three multicast routing protocols that are available at present. Two of them are equivalent to the more common unicast protocols that you should recall from Chapter 9, "Network Layer: Routing Protocols."

- *Distance Vector Multicast Routing Protocol (DVMRP)* is the multicast equivalent of RIP and distributes cost in terms of the number of hops to a particular router.
- *Multicast Open Shortest Path First (MOSPF)* is the multicast equivalent of OSPF and distributes cost in terms of link states in the same way as OSPF.

- *Protocol Independent Multicast (PIM)* routing is related to DVMRP but also contains facilities for optimizing locations of tunnels because experience shows that human-configured tunnels tend to proliferate in ways that waste network capacity.

In addition to these, the IETF is working on a multicast version of the border gateway protocol (BGP) for interdomain multicast routing.

 # Hands-On Activities

The problem and project in this chapter are designed to give you insight into multicast networking.

Multicast in NW

NW contains a network layer that supports a single multicast group (netnum=254) and includes support for a file mc.txt containing, for every netnum, the number of multicast hosts on the subnet (0 if none). The participating hosts start with 1 and end with this number (if only the router participates, the number will be 1). This file is read into this_net->mhosts_in_mc_group by read_net, where this_net is of type subnet_state* and is stored in array net_state_data[netnum]. Also, the number of hosts in the group is available as this_net->mc_grp_size, and the root of the multicast tree is available as mc_tree_root. Function create_multicast_topology generates the NW static multicast tree as entries in the array this_net->mc_iface[ifacenum], value TRUE for any interface that supports the multicast group.

```
NW Multicast Topology Algorithm

set m to 1;

fill up the mc_group matrix:
do for all n from 1 to nnets,
{
  if net_state_data[n]->hosts_in_mc_group is greater than zero,
  {
    set mc_group[m] = n;
    increment m;
  }
}
```

```
use the unicast routing table to trace each mcnet and turn on
mciface bits in the path:
do for all m from 1 to mc_grp_size,
{
    search down a new path from mctree_root to this m,
    flagging interfaces in the tree:
    set k to mc_tree_root;
    while k is not equal to mc_group[m]
    {
        set next_k to net_state_data[k]->routes.router[mc_group[m]];
        set mc_iface to TRUE at both ends of the link from k to
        next_k;
        set k to next_k;
    }
}
.
```

Problem: Drawing a Multicast Tree

Figure 11.3 shows a multicasting network with the multicast tree high-lighted. Only the router hosts participate in the multicast group. Draw the equivalent multicast tree for your NW network. Do it this way:

1. Run the Workbench solution to WAN4. It will print out the multi-cast router interfaces matrix, which contains a 1 for each interface that participates in the multicast tree.

2. Use the matrix to superimpose the multicast tree on your solution to the problem for WAN1.

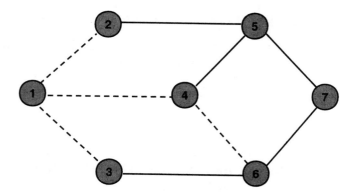

multicast tree shown as dashed lines

Figure 11.3   Network with multicast tree.

Now, assuming one multicast packet is sent from each host 1.1, 2.1, and 3.1, predict the number of multicast packets that will be received at each host in your network. *Answer: For seven-mode networks: routers 1, 2, and 3 receive 2 packets; routers 5 and 6 receive 3 packets; routers 4 and 7 receive no packets.*

Project: Programming *create_multicast_topology*

In project WAN4, you will create a multicast topology module for NW. In order for the multicasting to work, you must program a function `create_multicast_topology` that computes the contents of two global arrays for static multicast.

`mc_group` contains only the values of netnum in the multicast group, a total of `mc_grp_size` entries.

The variable that tells whether an interface supports multicast is

```
net_state_data[netnum]->mc_iface[interface]
```

This variable is initialized by NW to FALSE; your function is to insert 1 in the entry for each interface that is required to replicate multicast packets. That means you must first determine the multicast tree. This becomes simple when you use the routing matrix (which has already been computed before `create_multicast_topology` is called), and flag the interfaces in the path from `mctree_root` to every host in `mcgroup`.

The multicast network layer uses the presence of these flags on the interfaces to determine where to replicate and send multicast packets.

NW is set to send one multicast packet containing 30 "@" from each host 1.1, 2.1, and 3.1, to represent multimedia stream traffic.

Notes

- It is important that your flagged interfaces define a tree, with no closed paths; otherwise, the multicast packets will continue to circulate around the network until their TTL expires.
- The information needed to set the `mc_iface` flags is contained in two sources: the network topology arrays created in project WAN1

and the forwarding logic created in project WAN2. Your solution will be correct when `mcgroup` and `mc_iface` match the Workbench output, and one copy of each multicast packet sent by any host participating in the NW multicast group is delivered to all other participating hosts.

- You should first understand the multicast matrices and why the packets are delivered where they are before developing your own solution. As before, you can comment the line `#include mtopo.cpp` in `wan4.cpp` to see the NW solution. You may find it instructive to set `packet_ttl=2` in `wan4.cpp` and observe the result.

- In the profile for project WAN4, `lan=FALSE;`, meaning no LAN hosts will participate in multicast packet delivery (that is, only the routers will generate and receive multicast packets). However, `internet=True;` so the NW internet notation (such as 2.1 for the network 2 router) is used.

- The default setting for WAN4 is `interactive=TRUE`, so the run will stop after every output. To advance one step, press Return or Enter; to run without stopping, enter 0; to kill the simulation, enter x.

CHAPTER 12

Application Layer: Servers and Clients

M any of the protocols that make the Internet work for us are at the top layer of the stack. These *application-level protocols* provide a standard way to implement common network functions. The process of standardizing started with the classic Internet applications: email, file transfer (*FTP*), and remote terminal emulation (*telnet*). It continues today with a wide range of increasingly powerful applications, including *hypertext transfer protocol (HTTP)* for the Web and the *Simple Network Management Protocol (SNMP)* that helps network operators manage the Internet. This chapter will begin by looking at the *client-server* model that is used in many of these protocols, describe some of the more common application protocols, and end with a project motivated by an Internet mail list server.

The Client-Server Model

Figure 12.1 shows the client-server environment. The network (shown as a "cloud") often is a LAN, but can be a WAN subnet or the whole Internet. The idea is that a server is offering some service that is used at other stations on the network, while a client is the software through

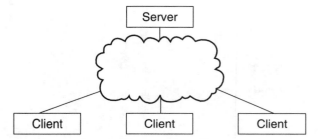

Figure 12.1   Client-server environment.

which a user receives that service. The range of possible services extends to anything that can be done at the remote station. For example:

- Database operations (an important special case of this is the *domain name system* server *(DNS)* that provides mappings of DNS names to IP addresses)
- Intensive computation
- Multimedia file storage (this includes the *Web servers* that provide HTML files using HTTP, as well as servers of recorded audio and video)
- Making recordings of real-time traffic for later playback
- Print service to produce paper documents from network files
- Providing security keys on demand
- Electronic mail services: sending, receiving, and storing

The distinction between client and server is based on where the service is performed. This is reflected in the computer itself only to the extent that higher performance is needed to provide some services. A workstation may double as a server, and a computer that supports a client for one function may also support a server for that same function or for a different function. Also, one computer may support server software for several functions.

Typically, the client program is less complex than the server and demands fewer resources of its host computer. The latest trend is toward *thin clients* that exhibit this simplicity near its logical extreme. The goal of the thin client approach is to have as much as possible of the total system processing in the server. This makes it possible to run the client on an inexpensive workstation or as a Java program in a Web browser.

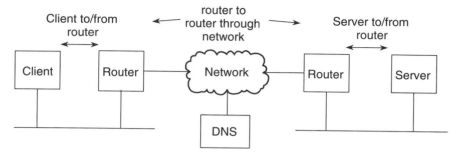

Figure 12.2 General case for Internet client-server message flow.

Figure 12.2 shows the general case for message flow between client and server. Of course, the client and server can both be on the same LAN, an arrangement that is likely to provide better performance. Also, they may use different DNS servers (or no DNS server at all, should the users be willing to provide numeric IP addresses).

Most Internet client-server operations use TCP. You should recall from Chapter 10 on transport protocols that TCP provides for delivery of a stream of data that arrives in the order sent, with no missing data and no detectable errors. The alternative to TCP is UDP, which provides only best-effort delivery. Most client-server applications need the reliability provided by TCP. The general logic for a typical client-server operation is shown in Figure 12.3.

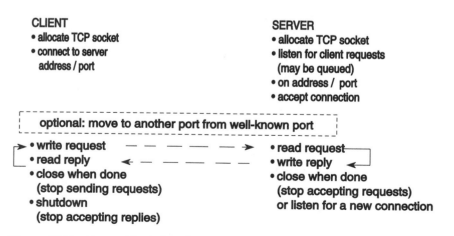

Figure 12.3 General logic for client-server operation.

The general logic of Figure 12.3 goes like this:

1. The server prepares to accept a TCP connection (you should recall from Chapter 10 on transport protocols that one end of the connection must be opened first; this "passive open" happens at the server end).

2. The client-end port is drawn from a pool of free ports available on the client host; it need not match the server port.

3. The client makes a TCP connection to the server (most Internet services are associated with a "well-known" port, to which the client connects).

4. If the server is able to support more than one client simultaneously, and requires a separate port on its host computer to do this, client and server may move the connection to new port numbers.

5. At this point, the client sends one or more requests in messages to the server, to which the server replies with messages providing the service.

6. Normally, the session terminates when the client's requirements are satisfied and it disconnects. If the server must shut down for some reason it can simply stop accepting requests and close the connection.

7. After the client disconnects, it is normal for the server to go back to passive open status, ready for a new connection.

Some Important Internet Services

This section will provide an overview of some of the more important services available in the Internet. In general, each of these services has an associated protocol that is used by its clients to communicate with its servers. Many of these protocols are described in detail in the reference *Internetworking with TCP/IP* by Comer. The message formats are similar to those shown for frames, packets, and segments in previous chapters. They are not reproduced here.

Domain Name System (DNS)

You should recall from previous chapters that the DNS provides a host name directory service for the Internet. Virtually every Internet host has a DNS client that can send a request containing an Internet name such as "NETLAB.GMU.EDU" to a DNS server and receive a reply containing the IP address corresponding to that name, such as 129.174.65.1. DNS is quite a sophisticated system. Here are some of its important characteristics:

- The DNS servers form a *distributed system*; that is, a system of cooperating processes on computers interconnected by networks. DNS is designed in such a way that the servers cooperate to keep up-to-date name-to-address mappings available throughout the Internet.

- The *root domain* servers, for example COM (U.S. commercial), MIL (U.S. military), GOV (other U.S government), and EDU (U.S. higher education) are known by all other servers and are responsible for providing the location of the next-level domain when queried. Thus, EDU would respond that GMU.EDU has its primary nameserver at 129.174.1.8. There are many other root domains, including national servers (our local elementary school is at a VA.US address).

- Every domain at any level is expected to have at least one *secondary nameserver* that maintains a full copy of the primary's name-to-address database, usually on a different subnet from the primary. The secondaries' addresses also are returned from a query to the root server, so the secondary can be queried in case the primary does not respond. Each secondary nameserver periodically receives automatic updates from its primary nameserver.

- Each DNS server maintains a *cache* storage of name-to-address mappings it has received recently. These are automatically deleted in a few hours. Many subnets designate a local nameserver even if they do not have their own domain because with this arrangement they will receive quick response on commonly used names from the local server's cache. Except at the root domains, the nameserver usually does not require a separate computer; it runs as an additional software subsystem on a host that provides other services.

- Most nameservers will respond to any query. Although you should use a nameserver as few hops away from your host as possible for good performance, in a pinch you can configure your computer to use any nameserver. You can also make an explicit query on a nameserver using the command *nslookup*, which is available on Unix and Windows operating systems.

- DNS also provides for *inverse DNS* lookup, where the server is sent an IP address and returns the DNS name associated with that address. In order for this service to work, the root nameservers must hold tables showing the associated DNS domain for each block of IP addresses. If properly configured, the server for that domain will reply with the appropriate name, given the IP address. However, some organizations do not maintain inverse tables in their DNS servers, so an inverse query is less likely than forward DNS to produce a usable response.

- There is growing incentive to maintain the reverse tables: Many organizations have begun configuring their Internet servers of all types (even Web servers) to refuse service in cases where the client's IP address does not generate a valid inverse response. This policy is motivated by the fact that people trying to do something underhanded in the Internet often use unregistered IP addresses so they will be more difficult to trace.

Terminal Emulation (telnet) and File Transfer Protocol (FTP)

Both telnet and FTP operate over TCP.

- The telnet protocol allows any host to provide a text window equivalent to a command-line console on a remote computer.
- The file transfer protocol (FTP) provides facilities to copy files to a distant computer that runs an FTP server. It includes related capabilities such as the ability to create new directories.

Telnet and ITP servers are widely supported by Unix systems and are available on Windows NT systems as an add-on. Clients are available on all Unix and Windows systems.

Normally, users of telnet and FTP must have accounts with associated passwords and privileges on the remote computers they are using. However, for FTP there is a variation that can be useful if you don't care who reads your files. Called *anonymous FTP*, it works by connecting anyone who supplies the username "anonymous." The user is then asked as a courtesy to provide an email address, on the honor system. This feature allows distribution of information to the public without the bother of creating accounts. (Of course, only documents selected for public availability are made accessible.) For example, anonymous FTP is used by the IETF to make its open standards documents widely available. However, its use has been reduced recently because its function is duplicated by the Web, which also exists to transfer files.

Simple Mail Transfer Protocol

Transferring files is a function common to several major Internet applications. In the case of electronic mail, what is really being sent is a *mailfile* representing the user's message, plus any attachments. Per the *Simple Mail Transfer Protocol (SMTP)* standard (RFC822), email itself is encoded in an ingenious way: The fields such as TO:, FROM:, and so forth are encoded in just the way you read them on your screen. Thus, it is possible to read an email file on any text screen and understand the message.

Understanding the attachments may not be so easy. Unless they are text attachments, they must be encoded in some way to deal with the fact that ASCII has only 128 characters, while a byte has 256 different possible values. Several different encodings are available; a good mail client should be able to handle the full variety. Encoding the attachments is a function of the SMTP mail client. By the time the email reaches the server, it is just character data, with a group of formatted labels at the front that are both human and computer recognizable to allow the email to be delivered.

The role of the SMTP server is to accept email files from clients, store them, and open TCP connections to transfer the mailfiles to the servers for the addressees. Just as with other client-server systems, an SMTP mailserver need not reside on the same LAN as its clients. However, performance will be best if there is minimal network delay between client and server. The basic idea is this: The SMTP email client packages the mail with standard labels so it can be delivered and transfers it to the SMTP server. Within a brief period of time (minutes to hours), the server transfers the file to the addressee's server, where it waits until the addressee uses an SMTP client to read it. The most common arrangement is shown in Figure 12.4. Here again, it is possible for the whole arrangement to exist on a single LAN, and possible for more than one DNS server (or no DNS server at all) to be used.

The email situation is complicated somewhat if the client needs to be connected intermittently. This could happen for reasons of economy (the cost of occasional dial-up is less than that of a leased line) or for reasons of convenience (connecting to email from home or when

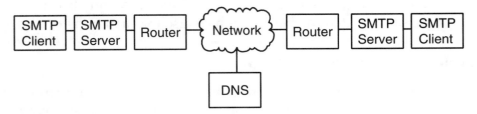

Figure 12.4 SMTP message flow.

travelling). In this case, a protocol is needed that can exchange user identification and control information between client and mailserver. Two common protocols used for this purpose are the Post Office Protocol (POP) and Interactive Mail Access Protocol (IMAP).

List Servers

An offshoot of email is the need for a program that sends an email to a list of addresses, known as a *list server, mail reflector*, or in its simplest form, a *mail alias*. Although considerable complexity is possible, the basic function here is very simple: receive an email and send a copy of it to a list of addresses contained in a file. More sophisticated list servers include features oriented toward controlling access to this powerful capability, which can literally turn one email into thousands with very little effort on the part of the user. The Internet equivalent of junk mail, known as *spam*, is sent by parties who wish to use the services paid for by others to gain free advertising or attention of some sort. Here are a few of the features that might be provided in a list server.

- A *moderated list* that requires a human to release each email sent to the list.

- A *closed list* that is available only to a community of users who are registered some way in advance.

- A list that requires *subscription* or *enrollment* before it will accept email for distribution to the list. Most commonly, subscription is achieved by sending an email to the server. For such a list, it is common to require that any party receiving email distribution service (sender as well as receiver) must be a member of the list. To gain membership, it is necessary, at the very least, for the user to send a request from a host that is registered for inverse DNS so that the source of the email can be traced.

Network News

Network news is a logical extension of list service; in fact, some of the smaller *news groups* it serves are implemented as mailing lists. However, the volume of news is such that a more selective distribution mechanism is needed. The news articles are contributed from a wide variety of sources and are organized in a hierarchy with top-level categories such as "comp" (computing), "sci" (science), "rec" (recreation), "soc" (society), "k12" (pre-college schools), and the infamous "alt" (a wide variety of topics, some of them very kinky). An example of the hierarchical group structure is "comp.lang.c," a group devoted to the C programming language. Some significant attributes of the News system are as follows:

- News is distributed in the same format as email (SMTP), but with a special header defined in RFC1036. Thus it is human readable as text.

- It is distributed through a "newsfeed" from another site that receives News. The sites collectively are known as *USENET* and form a virtual network that runs (mostly) over the Internet. The news articles are automatically placed in files keyed to their group names.

- Users receive News through a special client, which (again, like email) may either reside online collecting incoming news or connect periodically for reading. There is a *Network News Transfer Protocol (NNTP)*, defined in RFC977, that allows the client to download News articles selectively, either wholesale based on the user's group interests or selectively based on the user's selection of subject lines.

- The client/server relationship can work either by *pull*, where the client takes articles selectively, or *push*, where the server offers articles as they become available, and the client accepts or declines. The protocol for this works by stop and wait, as described in Chapter 5, "Data Link Control-ARQ Flow Control."

World Wide Web Servers

You should recall from Chapter 11 on multimedia that Web documents use the HTTP/HTML format. HTTP is quite similar to FTP, with the limitation that each Web file accessed requires a separate TCP connection. Because of this constraint, some Web servers open multiple connections to deliver the multiple files that are common in today's complex Web pages more quickly. You should recall from Chapter 10, "Transport Layer: TCP," that TCP begins each connection with a "slow-start" transmission that increases the window size slowly to avoid congestion. Based on this, you might conclude that opening many short TCP connections would not result in the best possible performance. (This conclusion is consistent with my experience!)

Because of the many small connections involved, plus normal Internet connection delays, response of Web browsers can be quite slow at times. One way to speed up service for frequently accessed Web sites and to reduce Internet traffic is to install a *proxy server*, as shown in Figure 12.5. The proxy server holds a cache of recently accessed Web pages and serves them to clients on the LAN. The pages are delivered quickly because they don't have to be fetched across the WAN. The proxy server has a cache aging policy so its contents are deleted after some period (typically 24 hours). It also plays a role in network security that will be described in Chapter 13.

In addition to ordinary HTML and related multimedia formats (graphic images plus audio and video clips), HTTP increasingly is associated with interactive operation (CGI, Java, and security dialogs) and with streaming audio and video. Also, there has been a move recently to integrate various Internet services under a family of clients launched from the Web browser, with the Web server at the core of a system of servers. This in turn increases the complexity of the Web server and its associated protocols.

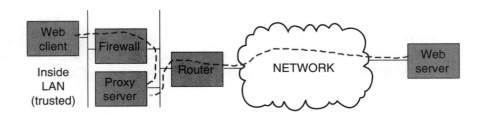

- Untrustworthy remote servers deal with only trusted proxy server
- Web client accesses proxy server through trusted port in firewall
- Proxy server fetches Web pages from remote Web server
- Proxy server serves pages to client, may also cache them to reduce future access time

Figure 12.5   Proxy Web server architecture.

Simple Network Management Protocol (SNMP)

This book consistently represents LANs and WANs as simple structures, with small numbers of nodes. Alas, the truth is far from that. Experience says that any organization installing a network should expect to find a multitude of useful ways to use it. Every new application seems to bring more complexity, and with it, more management headaches. However, network engineers are clever: They have found a way to make the network help manage itself! They do this by setting up network resources so they are able to report on their status using a standard protocol. Commercial network management software is then able to use that protocol to determine the status of the network and display it in a form that enables network operators to keep track of what is happening and take appropriate action. The network resources managed can be anything—circuits, routers, multiplexers, servers, power management systems—on any device that can have its status reported by a computer.

The protocol enabling this important function is the *Simple Network Management Protocol (SNMP)*. SNMP does not follow the client-server model exactly. Because a major part of its role is collecting data from machines, it uses an *agent* instead of a client to capture the data. The function of an agent is to do what a person would do if present: Keep track of how the network device is working. The agent maintains a collection of data in a defined format called a *management information base (MIB)* and transmits it over the network to a management program on request. The data is divided into three categories:

- Status data that is available to anyone on the network that queries the agent (you could think of this as "public" data)

- Status data that is available only under authenticated access ("private" data)

- Control information sent to the agent over the network (which also requires authentication, of course!)

Working with these three categories of information, an SNMP agent becomes the remote eyes and hands of a network manager. Commercial network management software packages such as Hewlett-Packard's OpenView allow remote operators to monitor continually the status of all network resources and control their behavior.

Hands-On Activities

The problem and project in this chapter are designed to give you insight into the operation of a list server. This is the first project that uses the NW "internet" model with both WAN and LANs.

NW Listserver Algorithm

```
If incoming_message.text contains "subscribe",
{
  if the list contains less than LIST_SERVER_CAPACITY entries,
  {
    add the source_net and source_host from the message at the
    end of the array of list_server_addresses;
    increment server_list_count;
  }
  return;
}
otherwise replicate email copies to the list:
do for server_list_count,
{
  copy incoming_message to outgoing_message;
  insert net number and host number from list_server_addresses
  in outgoing_message;
  invoke send_email using outgoing_message with message coded
  for best-effort transport;
}.
```

Problem: Predicting List Server Traffic Levels

An email list server is supporting a list containing 800 addresses.

a. If 10 percent of the email traffic on the server's host goes to the list server, and the host receives 1500 messages per day, what percentage of the outgoing email traffic is generated by the list server? (Assume that, on the average, each incoming email not destined for the server results in one outgoing email.) *Answer: 99 percent.*

b. If the average email contains 300 bytes, and the outgoing link capacity from the router serving the host is 64 kbps, what fraction of the link's capacity is being used to support email traffic? (Assume that the link has no losses and that overhead from headers, ACKs, etc., adds 20 percent to the email traffic.) *Answer: 6.3 percent.*

Project: Programming *list_server*

In project INT1, you will program the logic for the NW email list server. It is a very simple list server and operates as follows:

- When the global variable `run_list_server` is `TRUE`, host 2.1 acts as a list server rather than as a normal email host. All email arriving at this host is assumed to be intended for the list server.

- When an email with the word `SUBSCRIBE` in the beginning of its text field is received by the list server, the server adds the source address of that host (`netnum` and `hostnum`) to the server address list, if there is space remaining in the list. It does not acknowledge the subscription back to the sender.

- When the list server receives any other email, it sends a copy of that email to each host in its address list.

Notes

- There is a stub function for the list server in module `lstserv.cpp`.

- Email to and from the list server uses the NW best-effort transport protocol `utp`, not the NW reliable transport protocol. The reason for this is that the NW reliable transport protocol `rtp` is not capable of accepting connections from multiple hosts at the same time.

- To avoid having regular NW email mixed in with the list server email, `number_of_hosts_sending_email` is set to one in the INT1 profile module `pint1.cpp`.

- The INT1 profile for NW is set up so three hosts subscribe to the server at the beginning of the run. After 50,000 ticks, host 1.1 starts sending its email. The test file for host 1.1 contains only one message, so the traffic you will see in your test consists of three subscription messages, one email to the list server, and three email messages replicated by the list server to its three subscribed hosts.

CHAPTER 13

Network Layer: Security and Firewalls

The Internet grew up as an open, academic research environment. Originally, there was little concern for security because the Internet community was more like an extended family than a business environment. The situation has changed dramatically with the introduction of commerce to the Internet. In this chapter, you will learn basic principles of network security and how firewalls make it possible to be connected to the Internet and still trust the data in your computer.

Security Principles

Before we begin to look at Internet security technologies, you will need some basic terminology and concepts.

Definitions

The first principle of security is that security must be designed into a system when the system is developed and must be part of every design decision. Otherwise, the system is likely to have some weak point that can be exploited to break the security in spite of all other measures.

A related principle is that it is possible to provide for security at any layer in the protocol stack. The important thing is to find the right place(s) to secure the system.

Here are some basic definitions we will need in this chapter:

- *Confidentiality* exists when information is disclosed only to those intended to receive it.

- *Integrity* exists when information cannot be modified without the modification being detected.

- *Physical security* means locking things up. In general, you can expect that information stored in your home and office will stay secure. Also, you must expect that information sent over the public Internet may come into the hands of someone who might abuse the information. Network security is about making sure the abusers can't get at information you want to keep confidential or destroy the integrity of information that is important to you.

- *Authentication* is a process designed to ensure that communicating parties are who they say they are.

- *Access control* is a process designed to ensure that authenticated users are given access only to appropriate information.

- *Nonrepudiation* exists when a party involved in some communication cannot later claim noninvolvement.

Encryption Concepts

Sending coded messages may bring to mind spies and military secrets, but it turns out that some form of encryption is basic to almost every aspect of network security. The basic idea is pretty simple. Suppose we took our CRC algorithm (the one derived from the diagram in Figure 4.3), changed the positions of the bits that are XOR'd with the feedback, and kept those bit positions secret, as in Figure 13.1. This time we would actually transmit the "scrambled" output of the encoder, not just use it to create the FCS. Just as it did in FCS formation, it turns out the same logic can be used by the receiver to "undo" the resulting scrambling if the same feedback bit positions are used. If we did this, we would have created a simple encryption scheme such that the transmitted data would be meaningless to anybody who did not know the feedback bit positions. However, just as with the CRC, today we

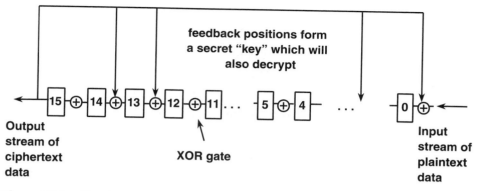

Figure 13.1 Simple encryption system similar to FCS calculation.

would be more likely to use software than hardware to perform this manipulation.

Here is the basic terminology for encryption.

- *Encryption* (sometimes called "scrambling") is a process that renders data unintelligible to parties who do not know how it was encrypted.
- *Decryption* is the process of rendering the data intelligible again.
- *Plaintext* is the data before it is encrypted, and *ciphertext* is the encrypted data.
- An *encryption algorithm* is a process that encrypts data. Normally, the algorithm is known to all parties, but the data cannot be decrypted without a special code called a *key*.
- The *key* has a value that is very hard to guess. Parties who want to keep their data confidential need to protect the key.
- Given a knowledge of the encryption algorithm, a lot of encrypted data, and a powerful computer, it is possible to *crack* the key. Doing this relies on a knowledge of the data; for example, knowing that in English text "e" is the most common letter.
- *Weak encryption* is relatively easy to break, but also easy to perform. *Strong encryption* is hard to break. In the interest of national security, the U.S. government has placed limits on the use of strong encryption. In general, encryption is stronger when the key is longer, and when the data unit used by the algorithm is longer. However, for most commercial applications, weak encryption is good enough

because commercial competitors are not willing to invest the resources required to crack it.

- *Cracking* a code is a lot easier if you have a sample of the data both encrypted and unencrypted, so it is important never to expose any encrypted data for which the plain text has been exposed.

- If the key or the confidential data become known somehow, they are said to be *compromised*.

- It is a good idea to change the key periodically, to limit the amount of data available to the cracker. *Key distribution* is a process designed to make this easy. It establishes session keys between communicating parties. The session keys themselves are encrypted for distribution, using a different key. Because the keys themselves are random numbers that are sent only once per session, it is possible to use the distribution key for a long time with a very low risk of compromise.

- In *symmetric encryption,* the same key is used both to encrypt and decrypt the data.

- In *public-key encryption,* the key to encrypt is different from the key to decrypt; in other words, the system is asymmetric. The encryption key is called a *private key* and must be kept secret; the public key is made available to the world. This means the system is built such that the private key is very difficult to deduce given the public key and the encrypted data. It is possible also to encrypt using the private key and decrypt using the associated public key. However, public-key encryption is very intensive computationally and therefore is generally used for distribution of session keys, not for encrypting large amounts of data.

Ways to Use Encryption

Enough basic terminology. Let's turn to some diagrams that show ways to secure the data in a system. One of the oldest approaches, link encryption, is shown in Figure 13.2. The idea here is to provide physical security for everything but the data crossing the communication link, and to use encryption for that.

Link encryption is a great way to go if the source and destination don't need to interact with the Internet at all. In essence, it creates a separate, private network. However, it rules out using the Internet, because it assumes no packet network, only a circuit network, between the

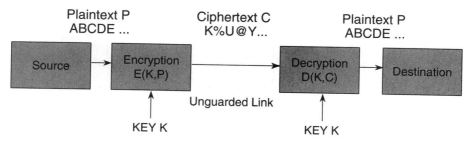

Figure 13.2 Link encryption.

encryption and decryption. Figure 13.3 shows a more Internet-friendly type of encryption.

Figure 13.3 shows packet encryption. The packet headers are purposely left in plaintext, while the rest of the packet is encrypted. This lets the routers pass the packet around the network, without knowing what its contents mean (which is how they are supposed to work). Here again, the end systems must be physically secured. The network is shown as a *cloud* in Figure 13.3, a symbolism meaning "it is just there, we don't know what is inside."

There are other ways to use encryption and related calculations. Figure 13.4 shows a related calculation used to generate an authentication code that can be sent with a packet to show that it is from the sender it claims to be from. A related technique, known as a *message digest*, is used at the application layer to authenticate electronic mail and other messages. An example of a message digest standard is MD5.

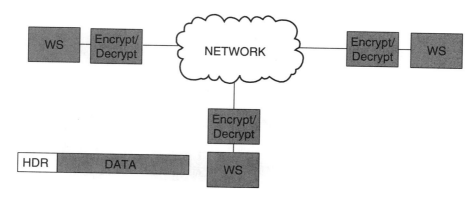

• Body of packet encrypted, header in clear
• Community of sites all have the same key

Figure 13.3 Packet network encryption.

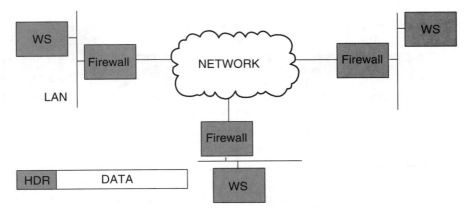

- Body of packet in clear, header in clear or substituted by firewall
- Community of sites established by tables in firewalls
- Packet may contain authentication or be encrypted by firewall

Figure 13.4 Packet authentication.

Another use of encryption at the application layer is *privacy-enhanced mail (PEM)*, shown in Figure 13.5. PEM often uses public-key encryption to send the session key (in this case the symmetric key for a particular message). The public-key arrangement offers a lot of flexibility. For example:

Authentication. Since the encryption and decryption are inverses, given that A encodes her identity with her private key, the fact that B can decode A's identity with her public key proves that A sent the

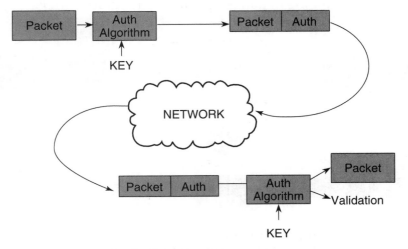

Figure 13.5 Application-layer encryption.

message. This provides non-repudiation, which in general is only possible with public-key encryption.

Confidentiality. If A encrypts data with B's public key before encrypting the same data with A's private key, then only B can decrypt the data and only B can find out that the data was from A.

Key Distribution. If the data A encrypts this way is a private symmetric encryption key, then only A and B will be able to decrypt data encrypted with that private symmetric encryption key.

Figure 13.6 shows a firewall system, which has the same topology as packet encryption but treats the packets much differently. Where network encryption achieves both confidentiality and authentication, the firewall system achieves only a weak form of authentication. Firewalls were developed to keep out insidious people (sometimes called "hackers" or "crackers") who tamper with networked computers for what seems to be the pure joy of destruction. Using a firewall also provides a form of authentication because you know that packets allowed in are from people who should have access to the data behind the firewall. However, you can only have limited confidence in this because one hacker trick is "spoofing" packets to fake their origin.

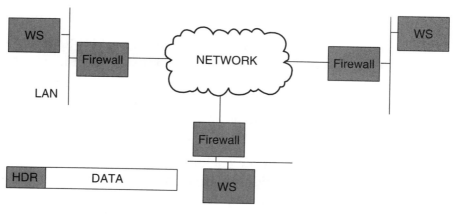

- Body of packet in clear; header in clear or substituted by firewall
- Community of sites established by tables in firewalls
- Packet may contain authentication and/or be encrypted by firewall

Figure 13.6   Firewall security.

How Firewalls Work

The *firewall* takes its name from a safety barrier such as the one between the engine compartment and passenger compartment in motor vehicles, which is designed to keep those on one side safe from dangers such as fires on the other side. An Internet firewall is intended to keep systems on a LAN (or even a whole intranet) safe from the attacks that could come from the Internet. The basic role of a firewall is to allow only packets from trusted IP addresses. Beyond this, many alternatives exist. For example:

- The basic firewall is just a packet filter; if your IP address is not on its list to be passed, your packet doesn't get in.

- Using the IP Security (IPSEC) protocols, a firewall can encrypt the packets, in which case it is really acting as a network encryption system. It also can authenticate them to defeat spoofing. This provides much stronger network security.

- Using one form of IPSEC, a firewall substitutes the IP address of the firewall for that of the host (workstation) being protected. This means the block labeled "data" in Figure 13.6 is actually the whole packet to or from the host. The firewall then interacts only with other firewalls. It performs authentication on packets that pass through the network, so its partner firewalls can have a high confidence that the packets are from within their trusted community.

- A firewall may allow certain categories of packets to pass through, based on values of the packet data. For example, it is possible to allow packets from different Internet applications selectively, based on the port number in the transport-layer header matching the well-known port for a particular application. This is called an *application-level gateway*.

- It is also possible to allow packets to come in from the network if they are part of a session established by a host behind the firewall. This arrangement is sometimes combined with the proxy server arrangement (Figure 12.5) described in Chapter 12, "Application Layer: Servers and Clients." Web browsers behind the firewall receive service from the proxy server, which has a TCP port number that is allowed to pass through the firewall.

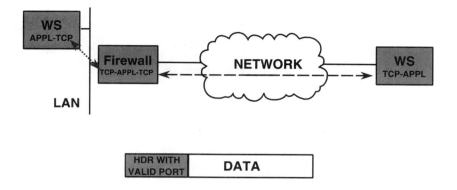

- Header contains TCP well-known port for some applications
- Firewall has separate TCP connections to local and remote WS
- Firewall passes valid data for this application only
- May also limit access to a community of sites

Figure 13.7 Circuit-level firewall security.

- The most sophisticated and powerful type of firewall, called a *circuit-level gateway*, uses a lightweight application layer to provide a path that appears to be a "circuit" (as in a wire) that will pass through the firewall only packets destined to a particular TCP connection. The application may be configured not to accept incoming connections. Thus, only packets containing valid data and participating in a specific TCP connection are allowed through the firewall. Figure 13.7 shows how this works.

Hands-On Activities

The problem and project in this chapter are designed to give you insight into the operation of a basic packet filter firewall.

```
NW Firewall Algorithm

For all values of index up to number_of_trusted_nets,
   compare source_net in current_packet to trusted_nets[index],
      if there is a match, return TRUE;
if no match is found, return FALSE.
```

Problem: Predicting Firewall Traffic

A particular network has six subnets. Of these, subnets 1, 3, and 6 form a community of trust. They can send packets to other subnets,

Subnet	Number of Hosts	Multicasting Hosts
1	5	1
2	3	2
3	4	3
4	1	0
5	1	1
6	3	1

Figure 13.8   Network for problem.

but their firewalls are set to allow only packets from the community to enter their subnets. The subnets support hosts as shown in Figure 13.8. The problem is to predict the number of packets received at each host with the email and multicast traffic in the time period described next, assuming no packets are lost to errors or queue overflow.

a. Hosts 1.1, 2.2, and 3.3 are sending email. 1.1 sends one message, 2.2 sends five messages, and 3.3 sends three messages.

b. Hosts 1.1, 2.2, and 3.3 also are sending multicast traffic. Each sends one packet. (Remember, the firewall also stops multicast packets.)

Answer: Received packets at 1.1: 10; 1.2: 1; 2.1: 11; 2.2: 3; 3.1: 6; 3.2: 2; 3.1: 1;5.1: 3; 6.1: 5; 6.2: 1; all others: 0.

Project: Programming *allow_packet*

Project INT2 involves the firewall in NW, which is a simple packet filter. By studying network-layer code modules nl.cpp and mcsend.cpp, you can see how it works.

- There is a single community of trust within NW. It consists of a group of subnets specified in array trusted_nets. The number is held in number_of_trusted_nets.

- The router for each subnet doubles as a firewall. If global variable firewall is TRUE, routers serving the trusted_nets will allow packets to enter only if the packet's source_net matches the number of a subnet in trusted_nets.

- The determination as to whether a packet qualifies to pass the firewall is made by function `stack::allow_packet(packet*)`. The parameter is a pointer to the packet being considered for admission. The project consists of completing the stub for function `allow_packet`.

Notes

This is an internetting project, involving both WAN and LANs.

- INT2 is set up to pass the familiar set of email messages, along with a single multicast packet. The best-effort transport protocol utp is used, so that each email message occupies just one packet.

- As in other projects, you may find it is easier to debug your program if you start with a simpler set of traffic. Setting `number_of_hosts_sending_email=1` and `MULTICAST=FALSE` may help.

- You should review your output to be sure the correct number of packets is passing through each firewall.

CHAPTER 14

Putting It All Together: Internetting

Congratulations! You have worked your way through 13 chapters. At this point you should have working code similar to a selection of key Internet protocols. You may have noticed that each of our NW protocols was tested in a purposely limited scope. As a result, you have yet to see real internetting behavior, where a message transmitted by a host on one LAN is received correctly at a host on a different LAN, with all activity such as routing updates, dropped packets, and frame errors rendered transparent to the user.

This chapter contains no new protocols or technology. Your only purpose here is to show that the stack you have painstakingly constructed in the Network Workbench (NW) works. This is "where the rubber meets the road!" Project INT3 exercises the full internetting capability of the Workbench. Email is exchanged among hosts on different LAN subnets, and multicast traffic is passed over both the WAN and LANs.

Your Own Mini-Internet

As with other aspects, internetting in NW represents a simplified version of the Internet protocol suite. For example, it uses only one address per host, rather than one per interface. Also, it limits each subnet to one router, which is always host 1 and always has application and transport functions present.

NW multicast traffic is modeled as a repeated sequence of best-effort frames, each containing 30 "@" characters. These are transmitted with exponentially distributed intersegment time. Because its multicast traffic represents a continuing stream of data, in INT3 the Workbench will not stop until terminated by the value of `max_DES_ticks`. To generate only one message per multicast sender, set `al_msg_intervals[][].mal_msg_delay` to a negative value.

More significantly, the internetwork represented in NW is tiny by comparison to the real Internet. Nevertheless, a lot of Internet-like behavior is captured in this project. If your protocol code has been faithful to the algorithms provided, you will have the satisfaction of seeing all of your "email" words of wisdom delivered to the right addresses using your stack.

Moreover, you are now in a position to act as your own Internet Engineering Task Force. If you have an idea for a new protocol feature, the facilities to try it out are all there in NW. In fact, many of the current NW protocols were first introduced as NW experiments by my students at George Mason University. I would be very pleased to consider any contributions you may make to the NW project. Send them to mpullen@gmu.edu. I will acknowledge your contribution if it is used in a future version of NW. Of course, I will also verify the code by programming a version myself. A lot of student time goes into NW projects, and making good use of student time is important to me—that is how NW got started in the first place!

Hands-On Activities

The problem and project in this chapter are designed to give you insight into the operation of LANs and a WAN working together as an internet. This could represent an intranet or one small corner of the Internet.

Problem: Predicting Internet Traffic Levels

In project INT3 the hosts send a combination of traffic:

1. The same nine messages of email that occur in most other NW projects; however, in INT3 this email goes between nodes on different LANs. In the general case it must cross two LANs in addition to the WAN, so the average message goes three hops. The average number of packets sent to transmit a single email (including opening and closing the connection) is about 13.

2. A stream representing real-time data, sent using NW multicast. The multicast traffic comes from host 2.2. About 10 packets are sent during the simulation. This traffic is delivered to the each of 8 hosts in the NW multicast group, except the sender.

3. Routing packets from the NW link-state routing protocol, which are generated by every `routing_update_interval=600000 ticks`. Every router (host 1 on the subnet) will broadcast one routing packet from every interface at this interval. The average broadcast routing update packet is repeated three times before it is terminated, and every broadcast packet received by an average of 3.4 nodes.

The profile for INT3 includes a value of `max_DES_ticks=2000000` as the endpoint for the simulation. The time value of one tick is 10^{-7} seconds (100 nanoseconds).

Using the facts provided above, for an 18-host, 7-router network estimate within 10% the total number of packets received at all NW hosts during an INT3 run, in each category: unicast, multicast, and broadcast. Don't forget that any packet forwarded by a router is received before it is forwarded. You should compare your answers with actual NW results. *Answer: 351 unicast; 63 multicast; 214 broadcast.*

Project: Integrating Your Stack

Project INT3 is a challenge to the quality of your programming. All of your solutions for the other NW projects will be run as an integrated stack. If your stack is correct, it will yield the same application-layer statistics as the Workbench code. Lower-layer statistics may differ because of minor differences in protocol implementation.

Notes

- To investigate project INT3 incrementally, you can start with `number_of_hosts_sending_messages=1` and `multicast=TRUE`. This will let you observe a single email message passing across WAN and LAN.

- You can then either increase the number of hosts sending, or set `multicast=TRUE` to observe one host sending to the multicast group (you should also set `max_DES_ticks=100000` because the multicast traffic generator will keep running until max ticks expires).

- Finally, you can run three hosts generating both email traffic and multicast. This case begins to approximate the sort of activity that is normal on real internetted systems.

- While it is possible to run the listserver and firewall modules under INT3, it is not recommended. The listserver's use of best-effort transport can produce strange results when combined with reliable-transport email. The firewall blocks reliable transport connections from untrusted subnets, with the result that those hosts freeze up and are not able to send the remainder of their email.

Network Workbench versus the Real Protocol

You may wonder what price we are paying for the abstractions that make Network Workbench (NW) easier to work with than a real Internet stack. A general answer to this question is that the more complex the protocol, the more it had to be simplified for NW. Simple bit stuffing is done the same in NW as in the real stack, whereas the NW routing protocol and reliable transport protocol represent considerable simplifications of OSPF and TCP, respectively. In this appendix, you will find a description of how the protocol for each project differs from the "real thing."

DLC1

The DLC protocol used in many real networks is *High-Level Data Link Control (HDLC)*, or one of its close relatives. With regard to bit stuffing, the NW DLC is identical to HDLC. HDLC was standardized by the *International Standards Organization (ISO)*.

DLC2

As in DLC1, the CRC technique we are using here was taken from HDLC as standardized by the ISO. The particular choice of divisor was established by the International Telegraph and Telephone Consultative

Committee (*CCITT*—an acronym derived from the French form of the name), which is now known as the International Telecommunication Union–Telecommunication Standardization Sector (*ITU-T*).

NW omits one aspect of the HDLC CRC. HDLC inverts the first 16 bits of data when forming the FCS and inverts the resulting FCS. The reason for the inversions is to eliminate the possibility that a string of zeros added to the beginning or end of the frame might form a valid FCS. This is important because it is common for communications links to fail in such a way that they generate zeros as output.

DLC3

The Go-Back-N in NW is motivated by the HDLC protocol but is not identical. In particular, we are using a very small window size (two frames). This is done to make debugging easier; the NW DLC will work with any window size DL_WINDOW_FRAMES that is not larger than DL_WINDOW_MAX (which represents the largest number the SN and RN fields will hold, and therefore the modulus of ARQ computations). Figure 5.9 shows the frame format for HDLC, which you will see is considerably more complex than the DLC_frame described in nw.h. For a detailed description of the control codes, see *Data and Computer Communications* by Stallings.

INT1

Real listservers use SMTP email over the reliable transport TCP, whereas the NW listserver is constrained to use a best-effort transport protocol because the NW reliable transport protocol does not support multiplexed operation. As explained under project TRN1, this is necessary in order that the NW transport project has reasonable scope. Also, real listservers acknowledge subscriptions with email replies, and they offer other services, the most basic of which is the ability to unsubscribe. Moreover, NW email is considerably less sophisticated than SMTP email.

INT2

The NW firewall is the very simplest type of firewall. Most real Internet routers provide a more sophisticated set of filtering options; for example, they might allow selective filtering depending on application or transport protocol. The other types of firewall described in Chapter 13 provide more complex functions. Also the use of the NW best-effort transport protocol for email is unusual for two reasons: (1) real email is sent using a reliable transport protocol (TCP), and (2) many firewalls refuse to accept the Internet best-effort transport protocol UDP because they rely on having a TCP connection initiated by a trusted party inside the firewall. UDP is connectionless, so that requires TCP.

INT3

Please see the discussion in the section "Your Own Mini Internet" in Chapter 14.

LAN1

The backoff function in NW is identical to the one in Ethernet.

LAN2

The NW protocol behaves like token ring, in that a frame must complete rotation around the ring before the token is forwarded. It is simpler than a real token ring protocol in that it assumes the stations are arranged around the ring in order of their assigned addresses. Also, it uses a 24-bit buffer at each node in the ring, whereas some real token ring adapters forward frames with only a one-bit delay. However, like FDDI, NW uses a link data rate of 100 Mbps for its token protocol. This will allow you to observe the effect of a very fast data channel on LAN operation.

TRN1

NW contains a TCP-like protocol that breaks a message into segments and transmits a window's worth of segments. However, the NW reliable transport layer (rtl) omits many of the sophisticated features of TCP:

- It sends very short segments (20 bytes payload), in order that you will get a chance to work with a sliding window using the "email" traffic provided in NW.

- It uses a simplex data stream with only control information flowing back from receiver to sender. This means if A is sending to B, there is no returning stream on which to piggyback ACKs and NACKs, so they are sent as segments with no data.

- It does not multiplex data streams between hosts. In fact, under the NW reliable transport protocol, a host will not accept more than one transport connection at any given time, so it does not even use port numbers. It will, however, send one stream and receive one steam concurrently (this means the receive part of the protocol must accept ACKs and NACKs for the sending part in between receiving data from some other node).

- It does not do anything to avoid network congestion. Congestion avoidance is a key function of the real TCP in the Internet.

- TCP allows the application to provide new sending data continuously through the period of connection, with optional indication to "push" new data as it is provided, whereas NW requires that the whole outgoing message is provided at the time the application layer invokes the `rtl_send` service.

Because of these simplifications, the states and possible transitions in the NW reliable transport layer are significantly simpler than those for TCP (see Figure 10.7). For those who want to delve deeper, the reference by Comer includes the more complex state-transition diagram for TCP.

WAN1

Network topology is the same, wherever you find it. However, the matrices in WAN1 are unique to NW. There is no identical implementation in the Internet.

WAN2

The NW routing problem is the same problem that must be solved in Internet link-state routing protocols such as Open Shortest Path First (OSPF). OSPF also uses Dijkstra's algorithm.

WAN3

NW contains a routing protocol inspired by OSPF. It includes flooding and LSAs. However, the NW routing protocol does not contain any of the advanced features of OSPF. An NW LSA is an entry for a single interface only, although the NW SPF routing packet does contain entries for all interfaces to one router. Like OSPF, NW uses a new SN with every routing update. However, NW uses a very short routing update interval, 20 ms, in order that the behavior of the routing protocol can be seen in a relatively short simulation.

WAN4

NW multicast uses a static multicast tree, whereas IP multicast builds the multicast tree dynamically using multicast routing protocols and IGMP.

Installing the Network Workbench

Two different phases are required to install NW:

- **Install** moves the NW software from the CD-ROM or network download to your computer's hard disk.
- **Setup** creates a **working** directory where you will edit and run your programs and places all the files you need in that directory. The setup you run determines the size of the network NW will simulate.

Also there is an important difference between the way NW runs under different operating systems:

- On **Windows** systems NW is set up to support only one user, so the working directory comes under the main NW directory.
- On **Unix** systems NW is set up for multiple users, and the working directory comes under the user's home directory.

Before running setup or installing, you should first be familiar with the makeup of NW. The NW files are organized into directories:

code. C++ code for Network Workbench

data. Data for networks and email files

bcb. Files for Borland C++ Builder

linux. Files for Linux Unix with Gnu g++

mvc. Files for Microsoft Visual C++ Version 6

redhat. Files for the Red Hat 6.0 distribution of Linux Unix with Gnu g++

sun. Files for Sun Solaris Unix Version 2.7 with Sun C++

Also in the NW top-level directory are several files that provide background information on the development, organization, and operation of NW.

Input files to NW are `nnets.txt`, `wan.txt`, and `emailn.txt` (where n is 1, 2, or 3, and various project parts use differing numbers of files from 0 to 3). Some parts also use `mc.txt` and `lan.txt`. Output comes on the screen, and in file `diskout.txt`.

Each project has a main module `xxxn.cpp` and a profile module `pxxxn.cpp`, where `xxxn` is a project code such as `wan1`. Although all NW program code except solution modules is available in directory `code`, you will not normally compile all of NW in every run. Only the main module, profile module, and your solution code are compiled in each run. The rest of NW comes from a precompiled library. This library also is the **only** source of NW solution modules.

To see the Workbench solution to any assignment, just comment out the `#include` in `xxxn.cpp` that otherwise would select your module, then run the Workbench. If your module is not `#included`, the Workbench version will load from the library. The library files are different depending on the compiler you are using, but there are exactly two libraries for each compiler: one with a reliable DLC (`rd` in the name), the other with a best-effort DLC (`ud` in the name).

To ensure you are off to a good start with correct C function interfaces, NW provides stub modules as a framework for your solution code. These stubs also have an `author` function where you should insert your name. This is used for printing out module authors at the beginning of NW execution.

In the remainder of this appendix, the notation `nw*` stands for the top-level directory (folder) in the NW software as loaded on your computer's hard disk. For example, as this is going to press, the latest version of NW is 4.0, which uses top-level directory nw40, so you would use nw* for that version wherever you see nw* in the directions that follow this.

Downloads

Future updates of NW will be distributed through Web site http://netlab.gmu.edu/NW.

Microsoft Windows

NW is available under two different compilers for Windows: Borland C++ Builder Version 4, and Microsoft Visual C++ Version 6.

Borland C++ Builder

Before loading NW, load Borland C++ Builder 4 per directions from Borland.

Installing

If you do not have a distribution CD-ROM

{

- download the NW distribution nw*.bcbdist.exe to c:\temp

- double click on the file you have downloaded to unzip it to c:\temp

- click "OK", then "Unzip", then "OK" again and the software will unzip and install

}

else (you do have the CD-ROM)

{

- change to the top-level directory on the CD-ROM

- double-click on install-bcb.bat to install the software

}

The software will install in directory c:\nw*.

Setup

Go to folder c:\nw*\bcb and run setup6, setup7, etc. as appropriate to the network you need. This will copy the files you need into folder c:\nw*\working. You can edit and run the .cpp files there while keeping clean copies in the original directories.

The files are:

From nw*\.bcb, the .mak files and compiler.h.

From nw*\data, the network data files nnets.txt, wan.txt, lan.txt, and mc.txt, and email files email1 to email3.

From nw*\code, all main programs xxxn*.cpp, profile modules pxxxn.cpp, and code stub files backoff.cpp, crcstuf.cpp, dllogic.cpp, firewal.cpp, fwdopt.cpp, lstserv.cpp, nlroute.cpp, rteupdt.cpp, setparms.cpp, token.cpp, tlsend.cpp, topo.cpp, and wtopo.cpp.

Running

1. Now, in folder nw*\working, click on xxxn.mak (for example, for wan1 click on wan1.mak). BCB will open with a xxxn.cpp project window. (If you already have BCB running, you can click on File -> Open Project, but you will need to select *.mak under Files of type.)

2. Use file->open to load the module you want to work on into BCB (for wan1, nw*\working\topo.cpp). Add your code to solve the project assignment. Be sure to add your name to the first line in the place provided. If you need to see a clean copy of the .cpp file, it is in nw*\code.

3. When you click on the Run icon "green triangle," both xxxn.cpp and the function you are writing should compile. If your code compiles successfully, BCB will also link and run it. The output will be shown on the screen and written to file diskout.txt in folder nw*\working. You can observe it using the BCB editor or other editor such as Windows Notepad.

4. To see the Workbench solution to the assignment, just comment out the `#include` in `xxxn.cpp` that brings in your module and run the Workbench. If your module is not #included, the Workbench version will load from the library `nw*\bcb\libbcbud.lib`. (For `dlc3`, this will be `libbcbrd.lib`. For `nwmain` and `int3` you can choose either library.)

Microsoft Visual C++

Before loading NW, load Visual C++ per directions from Microsoft.

Installing

If you do not have a distribution CD-ROM

{

- download the NW distribution `nw*.mvcdist.exe` to `c:\temp`

- double click on the file you have downloaded to unzip it to `c:\temp`

- click "OK", then "Unzip", then "OK" again and the software will unzip and install

}

else (you do have the CD-ROM)

{

- change to the top-level directory on the CD-ROM

- double-click on `install-mvc.bat` to install the software

}

The software will install in directory `c:\nw*`.

Setup

1. Run MVC and click `Tools -> Options -> Directories`.
2. Select "`Include files`" and add, **IN THIS ORDER**: `c:\nw*\working`, then `c:\nw*\code`. Once configured, these should persist between MVC sessions.

3. Go to folder `c:\nw*\mvc` and run `setup6`, `setup7`, etc. as appropriate to the network you want. This will copy the files you need into folder `c:\nw*\working`. You can edit and run the `.cpp` files there while keeping clean copies in the original directories.

The files are:

- From `nw*\mvc`, the project folders for all of the various NW projects, each containing several files.
- From `nw*\data`, the network data files `nnets.txt`, `wan.txt`, `lan.txt` and `mc.txt`, and email files `email1` to `email3`.
- From `nw*\code`, all main programs `xxxn.cpp`, profile modules `pxxxn.cpp`, and code stub files `backoff.cpp`, `crcstuf.cpp`, `dllogic.cpp`, `firewal.cpp`, `fwdopt.cpp`, `lstserv.cpp`, `nlroute.cpp`, `rteupdt.cpp`, `setparms.cpp`, `token.cpp`, `tlsend.cpp`, `topo.cpp`, and `wtopo.cpp`.

Running

1. In folder `nw*\working`, click on folder `xxxn` (for example, for wan1, click on wan1). Then click on file `xxxn.dsw`. MVC will open with a `xxxn.cpp` project window.

2. Use `File->Open` to load the module you want to work on into MVC (for wan1, `nw*\working\topo.cpp`). Add your code to solve the project assignment. Be sure to add your name to the first line in the place provided. If you need to see a clean copy of the `.cpp` file, it is in `nw*\code`.

3. To compile your code into NW, click on `Build -> Build xxxn.exe`. If your code compiles successfully, MVC will compile it and also link it.

4. To run NW, click on the red exclamation point (!).The output will be shown on the screen, and written to file `diskout.txt` in folder `nw*\working`. You can observe it using the MVC editor or other editor such as Windows Notepad.

5. To see the Workbench solution to the assignment, just comment out the `#include` in `xxxn.cpp` that brings in your module and run the Workbench. If your module is not `#included`, the Workbench version will load from the library `nw*\mvc\libmvcud` (for dlc3, this will be `libmvcrd`. For `nwmain` and `int3`, you can choose

either library by changing the library to be used: click on `Project->Settings->Link` and edit `libmvcxx.lib` in the `Object/library` window, making `xx` either `ud` or `rd`, twice in the line).

Unix

NW originally was developed in the Unix environment. It uses no vendor-specific functions and thus should be portable to any Unix. Currently libraries are available for Sun Solaris (using Sun compiler) and two different Linux distributions (using GNU g++). Unix versions of NW support multiple users, each with a separate `working` directory.

Linux Unix

If NW is not already installed on your computer, you will need to take these steps to install it under Linux. There are two versions of NW for Linux, one for "vanilla" Linux 2.2, the other for Red Hat Linux 6.0. They differ in the executable code libraries, which have different internal conventions.

Installing

If you do not have a distribution CD-ROM.

{

- download `nw*.linuxdist.tar` or `nw*.redhatdist.tar` to a temporary directory

- `cd` to that temporary directory

- type "`tar xvf nw*linuxdist.tar`" or "`tar xvf nw*redhat-dist.tar`" to extract `nw*` and its subdirectories

- at this point you are done with the tar file, if you wish to delete it type "`rm nw*.tar`"

- `cd` to the `nw*` directory (for example type "`cd nw40`")

}

else (you do have the CD-ROM)

- `cd` to the top-level directory on the CD-ROM

Now type "`./install-linux x`" or "`./install-redhat x`" where x is the path of the parent directory for NW, for example "`./install-linux /home/mpullen`"

Setup

1. The files in `nw*` can be shared by all users of your Unix system. Each user must have a separate working directory. These directions tell how to set up the working directory and NW files in Linux for one user. They must be repeated by each user.

2. The parent directory for NW will be represented by "`nwparent`" below. For example, nwparent at GMU is `/home/courses/csnets`.

3. To set up the Workbench files, `cd` to `nwparent/nw40/linux`, then type "`./setup6 x`" where x is the directory in which you want your working directory built, for example "`./setup6/home/mpullen`".

4. The above is for six-node network; for seven nodes substitute `setup7`, etc.

5. This will create a working directory and copy the NW program files you need to it. It will also copy data files and a compile shell program "`cwkb`". (See additional documentation in `nw*` for details.)

Running

1. `cwkb` is a shell program that will bring in your code and compile and link it with the provided workbench modules.

2. To run `cwkb`, type "`cwkb wan1`" (where `wan1` is the project) If the compile is successful, the resulting program will be in `NWxxxn`; just type, for example, `NWwan1` to invoke it. (NOTE: If your Linux `PATH` does not include your working directory, you may need to type "`setenv PATH .:$PATH`" for `cwkb` to work.)

   NW provides copies of all required routines in a library file. In the `nwmain.cpp` main program, any code you provide as input automatically takes the place of the Workbench modules. In other projects, the library is used to provide the module required for the project part if you do not provide it. If you comment out the "`#include topo.cpp`" in `wan1.cpp`, you will get a stack generated completely by the Workbench, so you can see how the Workbench authors solved that problem.

Sun Solaris Unix

If NW is not already installed on your computer, you will need to take these steps to install it in Sun Solaris. Remember the Unix version of NW supports multiple users.

Installing

1. If you do not have a distribution CD-ROM

   {

   - download `nw*sundist.tar` to a temporary directory

   - `cd` to that directory

   - type "`tar xvf nw*sundist.tar`" to extract `nw*` and its subdirectories

   - at this point you are done with the tar file, if you wish to delete it type "`rm nw*.tar`"

   - `cd` to the `nw*` directory (for example type "`cd nw40`")

   }

   else (you do have the CD-ROM)

   - `cd` to the top-level directory on the CD-ROM

2. now type "`./install-sun x`" where x is the path of the parent directory for NW, for example "`./install-sun /home/courses/csnets`".

Setup

Once NW has been installed, you need to set up the Workbench files.

1. These instructions assume NW is already installed on your computer.
2. The files in nw* can be shared by all users of your Unix system. Each user must have a separate working directory. These directions tell how to set up the working directory and NW files in Sun Unix for one user.
3. The parent directory for NW will be represented by "nwparent" below. For example, nwparent at GMU is /home/courses/csnets.

To set up the Workbench files, cd to nwparent/nw40/sun, then type "./setup6 x" where x is the directory in which you want your working directory built.

4. The above is for six-node network; for seven nodes substitute `setup7`, etc.

5. This will create a working directory and copy the NW program files you need to it. It will also copy data files and a compile shell program "cwkb." (See additional documentation in nw* for details.)

Running

1. `cwkb` is a shell program that will bring in your code, and compile and link it with the provided Workbench modules.

2. To run `cwkb`, you would type "cwkb wan1" (where the `wan1` is the project). If the compile is successful, the resulting program will be in `NWxxxn`; just type, for example, `NWwan1` to invoke it.

3. NW provides copies of all required routines in a library file. In the `nwmain.cpp` main program, any code you provide as input automatically takes the place of the Workbench modules. In other projects, the library is used to provide the module required for the project part if you do not provide it. If you comment out the "`#include topo.cpp`" in `wan1.cpp`, you will get a stack generated completely by the Workbench, so you can see how the Workbench authors solved that problem.

Network Workbench Header File nw.h

```
// last changed 8-28-99
#include "compiler.h"
//
//   Network Workbench (NW) Version 4.0
//   Copyright 1997-1999 J. Mark Pullen/George Mason University
//
//   STUDENTS MAY APPEND TO END OF THIS HEADER FILE BUT SHOULD
//   NOT CHANGE FILE CONTENTS (RESULTS OF MODIFYING COULD BE DISASTROUS)
//
//   This header file is organized as follows:
//
//   1. Narrative description of the Network Workbench (NW)
//   2. Compilation constant definitions
//   3. Global NW type definitions
//   4. NW Class definitions
//       a. class simulation_control
//       b. class utility
//       c. class GUI
//       d. class network
//       e. class stack
```

```
//
//  NW is highly modular.  Module assignments for each C++ function are
//  shown in the class definitions below, as ***** module xxx.cpp *****
//
//  Header file sections are separated by lines of ***** for example:
//*********************************************************************
//  SECTION 1 of header file: Narrative description of NW
//
//      Header file for Network Workbench, a tutorial programming
//      environment created by J.M. Pullen and various students
//      at George Mason University.  The intent of the Workbench is
//      to provide an abtracted form of the generic networking
//      problem that will simulate performance of a moderate-sized
//      packet network in such a way that its behavior under specified
//      node and link performance characteristics can be observed
//      and measured, while at the same time a student can create
//      a new software module that contains the essential functionality
//      of real networking software, written in C++.  A fundamental
//      aspect of the approach is use of Discrete Event Simulation (DES)
//      control software that causes the networking software to be
//      invoked at the order and timing that would be associated with
//      real networking software.
//
//      A major revision produced version 2 of Workbench in March 1998,
//      making the code more accessible and object-oriented. Internetting
//      with LANs added July 1998 as version 3. The most recent revision,
//      Version 4 in Summer 1999 by JMP altered the simulation
//      architecture such that functions in class "stack" see only the
//      state data present at an actual network node, whereas functions
//      in class "network" provide a representation of the network
//      environment and are able to access data for the state of all
//      network elements.
//
//      The NW project includes a serious attempt to provide code that
//      students can understand and expand on to create a simulation
//      of a working network.  Toward this end a number of  "include" C++
//      modules are specified; library code exists for all of these,
//      but in the general case students can replace the code with their
//      own simply by providing a different version with the same name,
```

```
//     in the directory under which compilation occurs.
//
//     The major modules that of the NE stack are:
//
//        topo.cpp      - topology matrix computations
//        al.cpp        - application layer code (email)
//                        specialized versions: ual (best-effort transport)
//                                               ral (reliable transport)
//                                               mal (multicast sending)
//        tl.cpp        - transport layer code (UDP-like or TCP-like)
//                        specialized version: utl for best-effort, like
//                        UDP, also used with multicast (generic tl.cpp can
//                        be parameterized in tlsend.cpp)
//        nl.cpp        - network layer code, IP-like (generic nl.cpp has
//                        packet forwarding in nlsend.cpp; multicast
//                        behavior is in mcsend.cpp)
//        dl.cpp        - data link control layer, ARQ or no ARQ (generic
//                        dl.cpp can be parameterized in dllogic.cpp; CRC
//                        FCS calculation in crc.cpp, stuff/unstuff in
//                        stuff.cpp)
//        mac.cpp       - MAC sublayer: mac.cpp is used with DLC for LAN
//                        simulation (CSMA/CD backoff in backoff.cpp and
//                        token handling in token.cpp)
//        pl.cpp        - physical layer (serial link with nominal errors)
//
//     While intending flexibility for student work, the workbench
//     establishes firm interface criteria that are included in this
//     header and are not intended to be changed by the student.
//
//     This header file is divided into major areas by rows of *******;
//     this is intended as an aid to studying its properties.
//
//   Data inputs to the Workbench are four primary network files:
//     nnets.txt     contains the number of subnets (and therefore of
//                   routers) and network diameter
//     wan.txt       contains node/link topology and link capacity
//     lan.txt       for eacn LAN, contains whether LAN is CSMA or token,
//                   and number of hosts
//     mc.txt        contains number of multicast hosts for each LAN
```

```
//     emailn.txt   application data files representing "email"
//                (n = 1,2,3).
//
//  Outputs come on the standard output screen, and are also copied into
//  file "diskout.txt" for later review and submission for grading.
//
//     Object-oriented modifications made 3-98 by JMP.  The hierarchy of
//     classes used is:
//
//       1. base classes
//          a. simulation control: control of Workbench
//          b. utility:            general-purpose manipulation and
//                                 output
//          c. GUI:                support for unimplemented GUI
//       2. network:               elements of network; nodes, links and
//                                 shared media, with DES "glue"; global
//                                 network data is private to this class
//       (class network is derived from simulation_control and utility)
//       3. stack:                 protocol stack layers,
//       (class stack is derived from class network)
//**********************************************************************
// SECTION 2 of NW header file: compilation constant definitions
//
//  The following are generic data types and constants created for the
//  simulation. The NW convention is that names of constants are
//  completely capitalized, where names of variables contain at least
//  one lower case letter.
//
#define HEADERFILE 1
#define SUCCESS 1
#define FAILURE 0
#define TRUE  1
#define FALSE 0
#define MAX_BYTE 255
#define WRAND_MAX 32767
#define MAX_MSG_PAYLOAD 100
#define MAX_SEG_PAYLOAD (MAX_MSG_PAYLOAD + 6)   // MESSAGE_HEADER_OFFSET
#define MAX_PKT_PAYLOAD (MAX_SEG_PAYLOAD + 11) // SEGMENT_HEADER_OFFSET
#define MAX_DLC_FRAME_PAYLOAD (MAX_PKT_PAYLOAD + 8)
```

```
                                            // PACKET_HEADER_OFFSET
#define MAX_DLC_FRAME_SIZE (MAX_DLC_FRAME_PAYLOAD + 11)
                            // FRAME_HEADER_OFFSET + FRAME_TRAILER_OFFSET
#define MAX_BIT_FRAME_SIZE (10*MAX_DLC_FRAME_SIZE)
                            // 10 is conservative stuffing factor
#define MAX_PHYS_FRAME_SIZE MAX_BIT_FRAME_SIZE
#define MAX_NETS 27                 // max number of nets in internet
#define MAX_HOSTS 7                 // max number of hosts in any net
#define MAX_NETHOSTS MAX_NETS*MAX_HOSTS
#define MAX_INTERFACES 6            // max number of interfaces in any node
                                    // including interface 0 which is LAN
#define DL_WINDOW_FRAMES 2          // for DLC (no more frames than this
                                    // pending ACK at any time)
#define DL_WINDOW_MAX 8             // max values of SN/RN (equivalent to
                                    // 3-bit field important for modulo
                                    // arithmetic)
#define FIREWALL_CAPACITY 10        // size of firewall list of trusted_LANs
#define DEFAULT_LINK_BIT_ERROR_RATE 0
#define DEFAULT_LINK_QUEUE_MAX 5 // size of link queue buffer
#define DEFAULT_LINK_LATENCY 1E-5// default delay for WAN links (.01 ms)
#define DEFAULT_CSMA_BIT_RATE 1E7// default parameters for CSMA/CD LANs
#define DEFAULT_CSMA_BIT_ERROR_RATE 0
#define DEFAULT_TOKEN_BIT_RATE 1E8
                                    // default parameters for token LANs
#define DEFAULT_TOKEN_BIT_ERROR_RATE 0
#define DEFAULT_TOKEN_LINK_LATENCY 2E-6
#define DEFAULT_PACKET_TTL 15       // default time to live in hops
#define DEFAULT_LINK_RTT 5000       // default link round trip in ticks
#define DEFAULT_NET_RTT_TIMEOUT 50000
                                    // default net rtt ticks for
                                    // nl timeout
#define DEFAULT_ROUTING_INTERVAL 200000
                                    // ticks between invocations of routing
#define TL_SEGMENT_DATA_SIZE 20     // segment payload size in bytes
#define TL_WINDOW_SIZE 60           // window size in bytes
#define TL_MAX_BUFFER_SEGS 3        // number segments in max window
#define EMAIL_DIRECTORY ""          // directory for email file names
#define NNETS_FILE """nnets.txt"""
                                    // directory/name of file  nnets
```

```
#define WAN_FILE """wan.txt"""      // directory/name of WAN links file
#define LAN_FILE """lan.txt"""      // directory/name of LAN hosts file
#define MC_FILE """mc.txt"""        // directory/name of mctopo file
#define DISK_OUTPUT """diskout.txt"""
#define AL_PROCESSING_TICKS 10      // ticks for al to process message
#define TL_PROCESSING_TICKS 50      // ticks for tl to process segment
#define NL_PROCESSING_TICKS 20      // ticks for nl to process packet
#define DL_PROCESSING_TICKS 10      // ticks for dl to process frame
#define MAC_PROCESSING_TICKS 10     // ticks for mac to process frame
#define CSMA_PROCESSING_TICKS 10    // ticks for CSMA/CD LAN interface
                                    // to process frame
#define TOKEN_PROCESSING_TICKS 10   // ticks for token LAN interface
                                    // to process frame
#define ROUTING_PROCESSING_TICKS 20
                                    // ticks for routing protocol layer
#define SLOT_TICKS 20               // LAN backoff parameter
#define COLLISION_THRESHOLD 5       // less ticks than this between two LAN
                                    // frames is considered a collision
#define JAMMING_TICKS 50            // time for jamming to take place
#define CSMA_BIT_RATE 10E6          // CSMA/CD LAN channel bits per second
#define TOKEN_BIT_RATE 10E7         // token LAN channel bits per second
#define BITS_IN_TOKEN_FRAME 56      // token LAN token frame length
#define TOKEN_INTERFACE_TICKS 1     // ticks for token interface to pass
                                    // token LAN frame
#define MC_NET_ADDR 254             // unique network code for multicast
#define MC_MAC_ADDR 254             // port code for MAC multicast groups
#define BC_NET_ADDR 255             // unique network code for broadcast
#define BC_MAC_ADDR 255             // port code for MAC broadcast
#define DEFAULT_MC_GROUP 1          // default multicast group (netnum)
#define DEFAULT_MCTREE_ROOT 1       // default root of multicast tree
#define STREAM_MESSAGE_CHAR '@'     // fill character for multicast
                                    // messages
#define STREAM_MESSAGE_LENGTH 30    // characters in multicast message
#define HUGEFLOAT 1E10              // very large floating point number
                                    // used in initialization
#define LIST_SERVER_CAPACITY 10     // possible number of forwarding
                                    // entries
#define LIST_SERVER_NET 2           // netnum of email list server
#define LIST_SERVER_HOST 2          // hostnum of email list server
```

```
#define DEFAULT_LS_TEST_TICKS 50000
                                    // default time to send list server
                                    // test email
#include <stdlib.h>
#include <fstream.h>
#include <iostream.h>
#include <stdio.h>
#include <math.h>
#include <stdlib.h>
#include <string.h>
//*********************************************************************
// SECTION 3 of NW header file: global NW type definitions
//
//   data types for the Network Workbench
//

typedef unsigned char bit;
typedef unsigned char byte;
typedef unsigned long int Sim_Timer;
typedef unsigned long int Event_Number;

typedef struct {bit file_read[MAX_HOSTS];
              } status;

enum interlayer_type{ file_send_interface,
                      umessage_send_interface,
                      rmessage_send_interface,
                      segment_send_interface,
                      routing_send_interface,
                      packet_queue_interface,
                      packet_send_interface,
                      dlc_init_interface,
                      frame_send_interface,
                      mac_send_interface,
                      physical_send_interface,
                      token_send_interface,
                      csma_send_interface,
                      csma_clear_interface,
                      token_receive_interface,
```

```
                    frame_receive_interface,
                    packet_receive_interface,
                    routing_receive_interface,
                    usegment_receive_interface,
                    rsegment_receive_interface,
                    message_receive_interface,
                    DES_schedule_event,
                    DES_next_event,
                    bit_error_generate,
                    bit_error_detect,
                    packet_drop,
                    csma_collision,
                    csma_backoff,
                    list_server_message,
                    firewall_action,
                    module_authors,
                    run_parameters,
                    routing_table,
                    multicast_tables,
                    message_stats,
                    segment_stats,
                    packet_stats,
                    frame_stats,
                    last_interface_type};

// application layer
 typedef struct {    // email file number input to application layer
   int file_number;
   } filein;

#define MESSAGE_HEADER_OFFSET 6 // message header has 6 bytes

enum al_message_types{email, stream};

typedef struct {        // email message output from application layer
   byte size;
   byte source_net;
   byte source_host;
   byte dest_net;
```

```
    byte dest_host;
    byte message_type;
    char text[MAX_MSG_PAYLOAD];
    } message;


typedef struct {          // inter-message interval statistics
    float ual_msg_delay; // best-effort transport mean inter-message
                         // seconds (not ticks)
    float ral_msg_delay; // reliable transport mean inter-message seconds
    float mal_msg_delay; // multicast mean inter-message seconds
                         // =0. for no messages, -1. for only one message
    unsigned ual_msg_randseed;
                         // seed values for random number generators
    unsigned ral_msg_randseed;
    unsigned mal_msg_randseed;
    Sim_Timer next_ual_msg_start;
                         // event times for al messages
    Sim_Timer next_ral_msg_start;
    Sim_Timer next_mal_msg_start;
    } al_msg_stats;


// transport layer
enum possible_tl_send_state {closed, syn_sent, tl_sending, close_wait};

#define SEGMENT_HEADER_OFFSET 11 // segment header has 11 bytes

typedef struct {          // transport layer segment, simplified TCP
    byte size;            // size includes header
    byte source_net;
    byte source_host;
    byte dest_net;
    byte dest_host;
    byte seqno;
    byte ackno;
    byte window;
    bit ack;
    bit syn;
    bit fin;
    message msg;
```

```
    } segment;

// network layer
enum packet_protocol { udata_pkt, rdata_pkt, null_pkt, control_pkt,
                       routing_pkt, send_supv_pkt };


enum payload_protocol {utransport, rtransport, SPF_routing};


#define PACKET_HEADER_OFFSET 8 // packet header has 8 bytes


typedef struct pkt     { // packet format
  byte size;              // size includes header
  byte source_net;
  byte source_host;
  byte dest_net;
  byte dest_host;        // or dest_group, for multicast
  byte ttl;
  byte pkt_protocol;
  byte reserved;
  segment seg;           // or SPF_message, for routing
  } packet;

typedef struct pkt_queue{// queue of packets at an outgoing interface
  struct pkt_queue* next_in_queue;
  packet* queue_packet;
  } packet_queue_item;


typedef struct {
  byte link_ifacenum;   // NOTE: netnum and hostnum are in routing header
  byte link_SN;         // sequence number
  byte queue_length;    // length of queue for interface, in packets
  } SPF_LSA_entry;

typedef struct { // shortest-path-first routing packet payload
  byte size;      // = 3*number of interfaces + 6
  byte source_net;
  byte source_host; // always = 1 (router)
  byte dest_net;
  byte dest_host;
```

```
   byte number_of_interfaces;
   SPF_LSA_entry link_states[MAX_INTERFACES];
   } SPF_segment;

typedef struct { // routing database for a router
   SPF_LSA_entry routing_database[MAX_NETS+1][MAX_INTERFACES];
   } SPF_database;

typedef struct { // selected next hop routers to reach all other routers
   byte router[MAX_NETS+1];
   } next_hops;

// datalink layer
typedef struct {           // generic char data
   byte chars[MAX_DLC_FRAME_SIZE];
   } char_data;

enum frame_type { data_frame, init_link, receiver_ready,
                  receiver_not_ready, disc_link, mac_frame };

#define FRAME_HEADER_OFFSET 8   // frame header has 8 bytes
#define FRAME_TRAILER_OFFSET 3 // frame trailer has 3 bytes

typedef struct {       // DLC layer frame (simplified HDLC)
                       // used to build bit_frame
   byte start_flag;    // size includes headers, FCS and flags
   byte frame_size;    // (in bytes) but no stuffed bits
   byte from_port_id; // globally unique port identifier of source
   byte to_port_id;    // globally unique port identifier of dest
   byte frame_type;
   byte SN;
   byte RN;
   byte reserved;
   packet pkt;
   byte FCS[2];        // FCS and finish_flags are only in this
   byte finish_flag;  // position if packet is max size, otherwise they
   } DLC_frame;        // come at end of actual packet bits

typedef struct {       // generic bit data
```

```
  bit frame_bits[MAX_BIT_FRAME_SIZE];
  }bit_frame;

typedef struct{ bit FCS_bits[16];} FCS;


// physical layer
typedef struct {        // generic bit data
  bit frame_bits[MAX_PHYS_FRAME_SIZE];
  } physical_frame;

typedef struct{char parm_chars[MAX_PHYS_FRAME_SIZE];}interlayer_args;


// union spanning all layers for DES
typedef union {// union means storage in these types of structure
               // overlaps, thus for data_units x; the descriptions
               // x.packet_args.size and x.segment_args.size
               // refer to the same storage by different names
               // (this is required to make the unified DES event
               // list work)
               filein file_args;
               message message_args;
               segment segment_args;
               SPF_segment SPF_segment_args;
               packet packet_args;
               char_data char_args;
               DLC_frame frame_args;
               bit_frame bit_args;
               physical_frame phys_args;
               } data_units;

class stack;   // this just tells the compiler that stack is a class
               // to be defined later

// state descriptors for network elements (subnet, hosts, interfaces)

typedef struct{                 // LAN state value for mac send
          Sim_Timer frame_start_time;
```

```
                    Sim_Timer frame_finish_time;
                    } csma_lan_state;


    typedef struct{                  // interface state values for mac send
            float bitrate;           // bits per second
            float errrate;           // errors per second
            float latency;           // delay in segment
            Sim_Timer simtime_next_error_due;
            Sim_Timer frame_complete_time;
            Event_Number frame_event_SN[MAX_HOSTS+1];
            csma_lan_state* timing; // frame start and finish times
            int csma_send_state;     // next state in csma_send
            unsigned randseed;       // seed for random errors
            unsigned random_backoff_seed;
            int max_backoff_slots;
            int backoff_count;
            int number_bits_in_frame;
            int collisions;
            byte netnum;             // netnum associated with this
                                     // MAC interface
            byte hostnum;            // hostnum "
            byte portnum;            // portnum "
            byte hosts_this_lan;     // number of hosts in this LAN
                                     // (including router)
            byte timeout_SN;
            byte to_portnum;
            bit in_token_lan;        // TRUE if token, FALSE if CSMA/CD
            bit in_multicast_group;  // TRUE if this host is in group
            bit_frame* current_frame;
            } mac_interface_state;


    typedef struct {
                    DLC_frame buffer[DL_WINDOW_MAX];
                    } iface_frame_buffer;


    typedef struct {
                    packet_queue_item* queue_head;
                                         // -> first packet in queue
                    mac_interface_state* mac;// -> mac_state_data for this
```

```
                                        // interface if it is MAC
                                        // (otherwise NULL)
                iface_frame_buffer* pending_frames;
                                        // buffered frames for DLC ARQ
                float bitrate;          // bits per second
                float errrate;          // errors per second
                float latency;          // end to end delay in sec
                Sim_Timer simtime_next_error_due;
                                        // saves errors between frames
                Sim_Timer supv_frame_intvl;
                                        // number of ticks to wait
                                        // for frame round-trip
                unsigned randseed;      // seed for random errors
                int queue_depth;        // number of packets in queue
                int dl_send_state;      // state in dlc_send (dl.cpp)
                byte netnum;            // netnum associated with
                                        // interface
                byte hostnum;           // hostnum "
                byte ifacenum;          // ifacenum "
                byte portnum;           // portnum "
                byte SN;                // SN contained in last frame
                                        // sent
                byte RN;                // RN contained in last frame
                                        // received
                byte SNmin;             // lower bound of sliding window
                byte SNmax;             // upper bound of sliding window
                bit supv_frame;         // supervisory frame in dlc_send
                bit link_active;        // status bit for interface
                byte routing_SN;        // SN for routing packets
                }link_interface_state;

typedef struct{
        Sim_Timer sent_time;
        segment sent_seg;
        } tl_storage;

typedef struct {
        tl_storage tl_buffer[TL_MAX_BUFFER_SEGS];
        }host_tl_buffer;
```

```
typedef struct {
        int last_char_sent;        // send side index of last char sent
        int send_window_start;     // send side index of first char
                                   // in current sending window
        int send_window_size;      // last window send has received from
                                   // other end
        int last_char_acked;       // receive side index of last char
                                   // ACKed
        int tl_receiving_from_net; // receive side - net/host to which
        int tl_receiving_from_host;// it is connected
        int tl_receive_state;      // state of trans_receive
        int tl_send_state;         // state of rtrans_send
        byte current_timeout_seq;  // seq no for timeouts
        byte number_of_fins_sent;  // counts FIN segments sent at close
        segment last_reply;        // receive side places here replies
                                   // (but not receive data) from other
                                   // end to send side here
        message outgoing_message;
        message incoming_message;
        }transport_state;


typedef struct { // state elements for a subnet and its router
    SPF_database* routingdb; // dynamic routing updates
    next_hops* routes;          // selected neighbor routers to send
                                // a packet toward its destination
    csma_lan_state csma_lan_busy;
                                // holds sim_timer current LAN frame done
    byte netnum;                // number of subnet described
    byte nports;                // number of ports (interfaces) on router
    byte hosts_in_mc_group;     // number of subnet hosts in multicast group
    byte lan_hosts;             // number of hosts on LAN in this subnet
    bit token_lan;              // FALSE for CSMA/CD LAN, TRUE for token LAN
    bit mc_iface[MAX_INTERFACES];// 1 if router interface
                                // participates in multicast tree
    } subnet_state;


typedef struct {                       // state elements for a host
    subnet_state* subnet;              // host's parent subnet
```

```
      link_interface_state* linkstate[MAX_INTERFACES];
                                    // link states for this host
    host_tl_buffer* host_tl_segs;   // reliable tl segments pending ACK
    transport_state* host_tl_state; // state variables for tl
    al_msg_stats* al_msg_intervals; // statistics for message generator
    SPF_database* routingdb;        // dynamic routing updates (-> same
                                    // element as subnet_state does)

    next_hops* routes;              // -> same routes as subnet_state
    byte netnum;                    // (sub)set number of host
    byte nports;                    // number of ports (interfaces)
    byte hostnum;                   // host number within subnet
    } host_state;


enum possible_dl_send_state {waiting, dl_sending, sending_supv};


typedef struct {  // statistics for output
        int frames_sent[MAX_INTERFACES];
        int frames_received[MAX_INTERFACES];
        int frames_with_errors_generated[MAX_INTERFACES];
        int frames_with_errors_detected[MAX_INTERFACES];
        int packets_dropped[MAX_INTERFACES];
        int uc_packets_sent;
        int uc_packets_received;
        int uc_packets_forwarded;
        int uc_packets_dropped;
        int routing_packets_sent;
        int routing_packets_received;
        int mc_packets_sent;
        int mc_packets_received;
        int mc_packets_forwarded;
        int mc_packets_dropped;
        int bc_packets_sent;
        int bc_packets_received;
        int bc_packets_forwarded;
        int bc_packets_dropped;
        int u_segments_sent;
        int u_segments_received;
        int r_segments_sent;
        int r_segments_received;
```

```
            int email_messages_sent;
            int email_messages_received;
            int stream_messages_sent;
            int stream_messages_received;
            } stats;


typedef struct{          // topology structure for interfaces
            byte net;        // values set in create_topology()
            byte host;
            byte ifacenum;
            byte other_end;
            } iface;


enum possible_csma_send_state {csma_ready, csma_waiting,
            csma_send_complete, csma_doing_backoff};


typedef struct {
            byte net;                    // net number
            byte host;                   // host number
            } email_address;

// discrete event simulation
typedef struct  // for DES
{
   Sim_Timer time_stamp;              // ticks when event happens
   Event_Number event_SN;            // unique sequence number
   mac_interface_state* state;       // pointer to state of mac interface;
                                     // also used for state of link
                                     // interface,state of host, and state
                                     // of net by typecasting
   byte action_index;                // used to indicate action by event
                                     // function; the specific action
                                     // depends on semantics of the event
   interlayer_type func_index;       // determines event function
   data_units args;                  // data unit argument of event
                                     // function
} Event_Info;


typedef struct tag // for DES
```

```
{
    Event_Info  event_info;
    struct tag *next_time_next_event;
    struct tag *this_time_next_event;
} Event_Item;

//
//    interface data types for GUI
//

typedef struct{ int packets_sent;        // host statistics
                int packets_received;
                int packets_forwarded;
                int packets_dropped;
              } host_stats;

typedef struct{ int frames_sent;         // link statistics
                int frames_received;
              } link_stats;

//*************************************************************************
// SECTION 4 of NW header file: NW class definitions
//
// SECTION 4a of NW header file: class simulation_control
//
//    top-level control of the simulation
//
class simulation_control          // shared control variables
{
 public:
    FILE *diskout;                // disk copy of screen output

// network
    bit lan;                      // TRUE if one or more LANs in network
    bit wan;                      // TRUE if one or more WANs in network
    bit reliable_dlc;             // TRUE if reliable DLC is being used
    bit multicast;                // TRUE if network uses multicast
    bit internet;                 // when TRUE internet notation is used
```

```
                                        // (INTERNET must be TRUE if both
                                        // LAN and WAN are TRUE)
    bit dynamic_routing;                // FALSE if routing is static
    bit cycle_email;                    // if TRUE, al loops on email input
    bit firewall;                       // if TRUE, nl uses allow_packet
                                        // filter
    bit default_lan_is_token;           // if TRUE and not WAN, LAN will be
                                        // token not CSMA/CD
    bit run_list_server;                // if TRUE node 2 acts as list server
    Sim_Timer ls_subscribe_ticks;       // time list server subscriptions sent
    Sim_Timer ls_test_ticks;            // time list server test email sent
    float time_step;                    // real-time increment
                                        // per Sim_Timer tick
    int number_of_hosts_sending_email;
                                        // number of email files to startup
    fstream infile[MAX_NETHOSTS];       // input files
    status inputopen;                   // whether input file is open
    status notopen();                   // sets input file status=not open
    int print_at[last_interface_type];
                                        // turns on print output at interface
    float link_bit_error_rate;          // network-wide average BER (can be
                                        // overridden for separate link BER)
    float csma_bit_error_rate;          // separate network-wide CSMA/CD LAN
                                        // BER (can be overridden for
                                        // individual LANs)
    float token_bit_error_rate;         // separate network-wide token LAN
                                        // BER (can be overridden for
                                        // individual LANs)
    float csma_bit_rate;                // bit rate for all CSMA/CD LANs
                                        // (can be overridden for individual
                                        // LANs)
    float token_bit_rate;               // bit rate for all token LANs (can
                                        // be overridden for individual LANs)
    float token_link_latency;           // segment delay for all token LANs
                                        // (can be overridden for individual
                                        // LANs)
// ***** interactive run mode *****
    bit interactive;                    // determines whether to pause
                                        // between outputs
```

```
   bit started_run_interactive;    // determines whether final statistics
                                    // are presented interactively
   bit keep_running;               // determines whether simulation will
                                    // continue past sim_time = 0;
// ***** discrete event simulation *****
   Sim_Timer sim_time;             // current value of DES timer
   Sim_Timer max_DES_ticks;        // limit on DES timer
   Event_Number next_event_SN;     // unique number for each event
// ***** module ualintd.cpp *****
   long ticks_to_next_ual_msg(host_state*);// message interval generator
                                       // for best effort transport
// ***** module ralintd.cpp *****
   long ticks_to_next_ral_msg(host_state*);// message interval generator
                                       // for reliable transport
// ***** module malintd.cpp *****
   long ticks_to_next_mal_msg(host_state*);// message interval generator
                                       // for multicast
// ***** module linkerrm.cpp *****
   long int ticks_to_next_bit_error(link_interface_state*);
                                       // bit error interval
// ***** module lanerrm.cpp *****
   long int ticks_to_next_lan_error(mac_interface_state*);
                                       // bit error interval
// ***** module printout.cpp *****
// generic output functions; use for standard output
// (a copy of all output goes to file diskout.txt)
   int interact(void);             // interacts with user, control output

   void output(char*);             // writes a character string to screen
                                   // and diskout.txt
   void output(char*,char*);       // overloaded for two inputs
   void output(char*,char*,char*);                 // " three inputs
   void output(char*,char*,char*,char*);           // " four inputs
   void output(char*,char*,char*,char*,char*);     // " five inputs
   void output(char*,char*,char*,char*,char*,char*);// " six inputs
   void outputn(int);              // outputs int as six digits
   void outputn(int,int);          // overloaded for two inputs
   void outputn(int,int,int);                      // " three inputs
   void outputn(int,int,int,int);                  // " four inputs
```

```
    void outputn(int,int,int,int,int);              // " five inputs
    void outputn(int,int,int,int,int,int);          // " six inputs
    void outputc(char);               // outputs single char
    void print_bits(bit_frame*);      // formats and prints a bit_frame
    void print_chars(char_data*);     // formats and prints a char_frame
    void print_email(message*);       // formats and prints an email message
    char outnum[10];                  // stores up to 9 digits for output
    char* onedig(int);                // formats one digit char string
    char* twodigs(int);               // formats two digit char string
    char* threedigs(int);             // formats three digit char string
    char* fourdigs(int);              // formats four digit char string
    char* fivedigs(int);              // formats five digit char string
    char* sixdigs(int);               // formats six digit char string,
                                      // blanks removed
    char* routerout(int);             // formats router number n to char
                                      // string n.1 if INTERNET, otherwise n
    char* hostout(int,int);           // formats host number n.m to char
                                      // string n.m if INTERNET, otherwise n
    char* pointout(char*);            // formatted pointer output for debug
    void showbits(bit*, int);         // sends bit array to output()
    void show_host(host_state*,char*);
                                      // describes host to output()
    void show_host_iface(link_interface_state*,char*,char*);
                                      // describes host and link to output()
    void show3(char*,byte,byte,byte);
                                      // outputs text and three numeric
                                      // bytes for debug
    void printall();                  // turns on all print interfaces
                                      // for debug
    void printnone();                 // turns on all print interfaces
                                      // for fast run
    void fopen_error(char*);          // file open error message
// ***** module wrand.cpp *****
// random number generators
    unsigned wrand(unsigned);         // generates random number given seed
    float fwrand(unsigned*);          // generates random number in (0,1]
                                      // given pointer to int seed
};
```

```
//***********************************************************************
// SECTION 4b of NW header file: class utility
//
//    utility bit and character manipulation functions
//
class utility
{
public:
// ***** module bitwork.cpp *****
// generic bit string and array manipulation functions
  int framesize(bit_frame*);          // counts bits in bit_frame
  int framesize(physical_frame*);     // counts bits in physical_frame
  void bytetobit(bit*,byte*,int);     // moves bytes into bit*
  void bytetobit(int,bit*,byte);      // moves 1 byte into bit* at offset
  byte* bittobyte(bit*,int);          // turns bits (each stored in a
                                      // byte) into bytes
  byte bittobyte(bit*);               // turns eight bits into one byte
  byte bittobyte(int,bit*);           // turns eight bits starting at
                                      // offset into one byte
  byte threebits(bit*);               // turns three bits into one byte
  void bitcpy(bit*, bit*, int);       // copies stated number of bits
  void bitcpy(bit*, bit*, int, int);  // copies bits between arrays
                                      // starting at offset
  void bitcpy(int, bit*, bit*, int);  // copies bits from array
                                      // starting at offset to array
  void bitcpy(bit_frame*,physical_frame*);
                                      // copies all bits from
                                      // physical_frame to bit_frame
  void bitcpy(physical_frame*,bit_frame*);
                                      // copies all bits from bit_frame
                                      // to physical_frame
  void bitcpy(bit_frame*,bit_frame*); // copies all bits from bit_frame
                                      // to bit_frame
  void bitcpy(physical_frame*,physical_frame*);
                                      // copies all physical_frame bits
                                      // to physical_frame
  bit scan_flags(bit_frame*);         // verifies a bit_frame contains
                                      // two flags (0x7e)
// generic character string and array manipulation functions
```

```
   char_data* message_to_char(message*);// retypes message to char_data
   char_data* DLC_to_char(DLC_frame*);  // retypes DLC_frame to char_data
   void cinsert(char,char*,int);        // inserts character in string
   void bytecopy(byte*,byte*,int);      // copies bytes between arrays
   void bytecopy(char*,byte*,int);      // copies bytes to char array
   void bytecopy(byte*,char*,int);      // copies chars to byte array
   void bytecopy(char*,char*,int);      // copies chars between arrays
   void message_copy(message*,message*,int);
                                        // copies message data units
   void segment_copy(segment*,segment*);// copies segment data units
   void packet_copy(packet*,packet*);   // copies packet data units
};


//*********************************************************************
   *
// SECTION 4c of NW header file: class GUI
//
//    hooks for graphical user interface (not implemented at present)
//
class GUI
{
public:
 void graph_hosts(host_stats*);        // draws the hosts with statistics
 void graph_links(link_stats*);        // draws the links with statistics
};



//*********************************************************************
// SECTION 4d of NW header file: class network
//
//    attributes of a network: nodes, links, statistics
//
//    NOTE: in general the range of netnum is 1:MAX_NETS and hostnum is
//    1:MAX_HOSTS; netnum=0 and hostnum=0 are not used in the Workbench
//    IP-like protocol

class network : public simulation_control, public utility, public GUI
{
public:
```

```
      network();                    // constructor to initialize network storage
// global variables- set once for duration of a simulation at outset
   int link_queue_max;          // max queue depth allowed at link interface
   byte packet_ttl;             // time-to-live assigned to every packet
   Sim_Timer max_link_rtt;      // max expected link round-trip time (ticks)
   Sim_Timer net_rtt_timeout;// max expected round-trip time thru net
    (ticks)
   byte mc_tree_root;           // root router of multicast tree
   int mc_grp_size;             // number of routers in MC group
   int lan_ports;               // number of ports in all LANs combined
   int total_ports;             // total number of ports in WAN + LAN
   int routing_update_interval;
                                // ticks between routing protocol activity
   byte mc_group[MAX_NETS+1];// netnums of routers in MC group


// topology and simulation results
   int nnets;                   // number of subnets in internet simulated
   int nhosts;                  // number of hosts in internet simulated
   int nlinks;                  // number of links in internet simulated
   int WAN_diameter;            // max number of links between any 2 routers
   int links[MAX_NETS+1][MAX_NETS+1];
                                // links[router1][router2] = link data rate
                                // in kbps if there is a link from router1
                                // to router2; if there is no link it is 0
   byte trusted_nets[FIREWALL_CAPACITY];
                                // list of subnets in trusted community
   int number_of_trusted_nets;
                                // number of elements used in trusted_nets


// ***** module setparms.cpp *****
   void set_runparms();         // sets run parameters from constants
   char* parms_author();        // author of set_runparms module
// ***** module defaults.cpp *****
   void set_defaults();         // sets network defaults from
                                // startup parameters
// ***** module readnet.cpp *****
   int read_net();              // reads in network links matrix
// ***** module topo.cpp *****
   char* topo_author();         // author of create_topology module
```

```
   void create_topology();    // creates network topology matrice
// ***** module mtopo.cpp *****
   char* mc_topo_author();    // author of mtopo.cpp
   void create_mc_topology();// creates multicast topology matrices
// ***** module cost.cpp *****
   float cost(byte,byte,byte);
                             // returns cost function for a link
                             // in context of a router's LSA DB
// ***** module printout.cpp *****
   void print_topology();     // prints network topology matrices
   void print_mc_topology();  // prints multicast topology matrices
   void statistics(void);     // prints network statistics for run
   void print_routes(byte,next_hops*);
                             // prints forwarding tables as matrix
   void lookup_error(byte,byte,byte);
                             // print error message for lookup
   void collect_bc_mc_stats(host_state*,byte);
                             // collects broadcast/multicast stats
   void count_lan_error(mac_interface_state*);
                             // counts total lan errors
   void count_link_error_frame(link_interface_state*);
                             // counts total link errors
   void collision_message(mac_interface_state*);
                             // prints CSMA collision
   void backoff_message(Sim_Timer,mac_interface_state*);
                             // prints CSMA backoff
   void flag_error(link_interface_state*);
                             // prints flag error message
   void FCS_error(link_interface_state*);
                             // prints FCS error message
   void ttl_expired_message(link_interface_state*,byte);
                             // message for ttl-expired packet drop
   void queue_full_message(link_interface_state*,byte);
                             // message for queue-full packet drop
   void firewall_drop_message(byte,byte);
                             // message for firewall packet drop
   void segment_ignore_message(host_state*,byte);
                             // message for reliable transport
                             // drop of segment when busy
```

```
    void lan_bit_error_message(mac_interface_state*,int);
                            // message when bit error is generated
    void link_bit_error_message(link_interface_state*,int);
                            // message when bit error is generated
// ***** module fwdopt.cpp *****
    byte forward_iface(subnet_state*,byte);
                            // determines output interface
                            // for packet forwarding
// ***** module bitwork.cpp *****
    void routecopy(next_hops*,next_hops);
                            // copies routes between arrays
// ***** module init.cpp *****
    void startup_simulation();// sets up initial values and events
    byte lookup(byte,byte,byte);
                            // looks up (netnum,hostnum,ifacenum)
                            // combination in topology table
    void zero_errors(void);    // zeros bit_error_rate for all links
    void start_email(host_state*);
                            // starts up "email" sending
    void startup_routing();    // starts routing function
                            // (including initial static routes)
// ***** module mac.cpp *****
    byte next_token_host(mac_interface_state*);
                            // returns portnum of next host
                            // in token LAN rotation
// ***** module makeframe.cpp ******
    byte otherend(byte);      // returns other end of a WAN link
    byte porttonet(byte);     // returns netnum for a portnum
    byte porttohost(byte);    // returns hostnum for a portnum
// ***** discrete event simulation *****
 Event_Item *head;          // event list head
// a separate DES interface function is required for each send and
// receive in the stack; this function schedules call with appropriate
// delay to the appropriate interface (e.g. appl_send to trans_send)
// after collecting statistics and optionally printing a trace and any
// user-specified output
//
// because of the DES supporting functions, each of the stack functions
// must have the same parameter sequence: data_units, x_state*, byte
```

```
//
// NOTES: 1. x_state means subnet_state,host_state,link_interface_state
//           or mac_interface_state
//        2. the byte may be missing; its use is determined by the
//           semantics of the stack module involved
//
// ***** module interlyr.cpp *****
 void al_to_utl(message*,host_state*);
 void al_to_rtl(message*,host_state*);
 void tl_to_al(message*,host_state*);
 void delay_to_al_send(Sim_Timer,host_state*,filein*);
 void invoke_routing_send(Sim_Timer,message*,host_state*);
 void utl_to_nl(segment*,host_state*,byte);
 void rtl_to_nl(segment*,host_state*,byte);
 void routing_to_nl(SPF_segment*,host_state*,byte);
 void nl_to_utl(segment*,host_state*);
 void nl_to_rtl(segment*,host_state*);
 void nl_to_routing(segment*,host_state*);
 void delay_to_tl_send(Sim_Timer,message*,host_state*);
 void nl_to_dl(packet*,host_state*,byte);
 void dl_to_nl(packet*,link_interface_state*);
 void delay_to_nl_receive(Sim_Timer,packet*,host_state*);
 void dl_to_pl(bit_frame*,link_interface_state*);
 void dl_to_mac(bit_frame*,link_interface_state*,byte);
 void nl_to_dl_init(packet*,link_interface_state*);
 void wakeup_dl_send(Sim_Timer,link_interface_state*,byte);
 void wakeup_dl_send(Sim_Timer,byte,byte);
 void delay_to_mac_send(Sim_Timer,bit_frame*,mac_interface_state*,byte);
 void clear_sender(byte);
 void send_across_link(Sim_Timer,physical_frame*,link_interface_state*);
 void send_across_token_lan(Sim_Timer,physical_frame*,
                            mac_interface_state*,byte);
 void send_across_csma(Sim_Timer,physical_frame*,
                       mac_interface_state*,byte);
 void broadcast_csma(Sim_Timer,physical_frame*,mac_interface_state*);
 void jam_csma(Sim_Timer,physical_frame*,mac_interface_state*);
 void multicast_csma(Sim_Timer,physical_frame*,mac_interface_state*);
 void delay_to_token_receive(Sim_Timer,bit_frame*,mac_interface_state*);
 void pl_to_dl(bit_frame*,link_interface_state*);
```

```
  void mac_to_dl(bit_frame*,mac_interface_state*);
// user output stubs are available to support user-generated output that
// will take place upon transfer of data across each layer interface
// ***** module userout.cpp *****
  void message_send_user_out(message*,host_state*);        // al to tl
  void message_receive_user_out(message*,host_state*);     // tl to al
  void segment_send_user_out(segment*,host_state*);        // tl to nl
  void segment_receive_user_out(segment*,host_state*);     // nl to tl
  void routing_send_user_out(SPF_segment*,host_state*);    // routing to nl
  void routing_receive_user_out(SPF_segment*,host_state*);
                                                           // nl to routing
  void packet_send_user_out(packet*,link_interface_state*);
                                                           // nl to dl
  void packet_receive_user_out(packet*,host_state*,byte);// dl to nl
  void dlc_send_user_out(bit_frame*,link_interface_state*);
                                                           // dl to pl
  void dlc_receive_user_out(bit_frame*,link_interface_state*);
                                                           // pl to dl
  void dlc_init_user_out(packet*,link_interface_state*); // dl_init
  void mac_send_user_out(bit_frame*,mac_interface_state*,byte);
                                                           // dl to mac
  void physical_send_user_out(physical_frame*,link_interface_state*);
                                                           // link pl
  void csma_send_user_out(physical_frame*,mac_interface_state*,byte);
                                                           // CSMA LAN pl
  void token_send_user_out(physical_frame*,mac_interface_state*,byte);
                                                           // token LAN pl
// ***** module des.cpp *****
  Event_Number schedule_event (Sim_Timer,interlayer_type,data_units&,
                          host_state*,byte);
  Event_Number schedule_event (Sim_Timer,interlayer_type,data_units&,
                          link_interface_state*,byte);
  Event_Number schedule_event (Sim_Timer,interlayer_type,data_units&,
                          mac_interface_state*,byte);
  bit next_event();                    // discrete event function execute
  bit delete_event(Event_Number);   // discrete event delete
// ***** private network class data ******
// this data is hidden from the stack class, to ensure that
// each stack module uses only data that would be available
```

```
// within a network node; thus class network can  see the whole
// simuilated networkt, but class stack can see only local data
private:
   int exit_interfaces[MAX_NETS+1][MAX_NETS+1];
                                  // = interface number, starting 0,
                                  // router1 to router2, -1 if no link
                                  // between router1 and router2
   iface interfaces[MAX_BYTE];      // WAN topology decription

   iface lan_interfaces[MAX_BYTE]; // saves LAN interfaces until after
                                  // create_topology() is finished
   stats netstats[MAX_NETS+1][MAX_HOSTS+1]; \
                                  // statistics collected for
                                  // printout at simulation end
   subnet_state* net_state_data[MAX_NETS+1];
                                  // net state - pointers to state
                                  // for each subnet
   host_state* host_state_data[MAX_NETS+1][MAX_HOSTS+1];
                                  // host state (including embedded
                                  // pointers to link state)
   mac_interface_state* mac_state_data[MAX_BYTE];
                                  // interface state - holds state
                                  // of ongoing MAC activity
};


//*********************************************************************
// SECTION 4e of NW header file: class stack
//
// The following class defines an Internet-like 5-layer protocol stack
//
//
class stack : public network
{
public:
   stack();                     // constructor to initialize stack
   int simulation();
   void print_startup();        // prints version, copyright, date/time
   void print_authors();        // invokes all *_author modules
```

```cpp
// application layer
   ***********************************************************************
   **
// ***** module al.cpp *****
   bit send_email(message*,host_state*,bit);
                                       // sends an email message
   bit send_subscribe(host_state*);    // send a list_server subscription
   bit appl_send(filein*,host_state*); // al send
   bit uappl_send(filein*,host_state*);// ual send
   bit rappl_send(filein*,host_state*);// ral send
   bit mappl_send(filein*,host_state*);// mal send
   bit appl_receive(message*,host_state*);
                                       // al receive
// ***** module lstserv.cpp *****
   char* ls_author();                  // author of al.cpp module
   void list_server(message*,host_state*);
                                       // adds a subscriber to the list
                                       // or generates outgoing mail to
                                       // the list
   email_address list_server_addresses[LIST_SERVER_CAPACITY];
   int server_list_count;              // number of entries in preceding
// transport layer **************************************************
// ***** module tl.cpp *****
// transport layer
   bit utrans_send(message*,host_state*);// utl send
   bit rtrans_send(message*,host_state*);// rtl send
   bit utrans_receive(segment*,host_state*);
                                       // utl receive
   bit rtrans_receive(segment*,host_state*);
                                       // rtl receive
   message timeout_message(host_state*); // creates unique SNs for tl
   int send_seg(segment&,host_state*,int);
                                       // sends and buffers segments
// ***** module makseg.cpp *****
   segment make_segment(message*,int);   // makes segment from piece
                                       // of a message
// ***** module tlsend.cpp *****
   char* tl_author();                  // author of tlsend.cpp module
   segment send_rtl_segments(host_tl_buffer*,segment*,host_state*,byte,
```

```
                              byte,byte);
// network layer ******************************************************
// ***** module nl.cpp *****
  bit in_community(byte);                     // test whether subnet is in
                                              // community of trust
  bit net_send(segment*,host_state*,byte);
                                              // nl send
  bit net_receive(packet*,host_state*,byte);
                                              // nl receive
// ***** module makpak.cpp *****
  packet make_packet(segment*,byte);     // makes packet from a segment
  segment unpack_segment(packet*);       // removes segment from packet
  SPF_segment make_routing_segment(SPF_database*,host_state*);
                                              // makes routing segment from
                                              // local routing database
// ***** module firewal.cpp *****
  char* firewall_author();                    // author of firwall.cpp module
  bit allow_packet(packet*);                  // firewall packet filter
// ***** module mcsend.cpp *****
  bit mcsend(packet*,host_state*,byte); // sends multicast packets
// ***** module fwdopt.cpp *****
  char* fwdopt_author();                      // author of fwdopt.cpp module
  next_hops optimize_routes(byte);            // computes optimal next_hops
                                              // for routing
// ***** module routing.cpp *****
  bit routing_send(message*,host_state*);
  bit routing_receive(SPF_segment*,host_state*);
  bit routing_flood(packet*,host_state*);
                                              // test for continued flooding
// ***** module rteupdt.cpp *****
  char* routing_author();                     // author of rteupdt.cpp module
  SPF_LSA_entry update_LSA(link_interface_state*,byte);
                                              // routing LSA generation
// datalink layer ****************************************************
// ***** module dl.cpp *****
  bit dlc_send(packet*,link_interface_state*);
                                              // dl send
  bit dlc_receive(bit_frame*,link_interface_state*);
                                              // dl receive
```

```cpp
// ***** module dlinit.cpp *****
  bit dlc_init(packet*,link_interface_state*);
                                        // dl link initiatialization
// ***** module queue.cpp *****
  bit enqueue(packet*,link_interface_state*);
                                        // adds a packet to the
                                        // outgoing interface queue
  packet dequeue(link_interface_state*);// removes a packet from the
                                        // outgoing interface queue
// ***** module makframe.cpp *****
  void make_frame(link_interface_state*,DLC_frame*,packet*,byte);
                                        // makes a frame from a packet
  void finish_frame(bit_frame*,DLC_frame*,byte);
                                        // completes a frame for DLC
  packet unframe_packet(DLC_frame*,int,link_interface_state*);
                                        // removes packet from frame
                                        // wrapper
  packet dummy_packet(byte,byte,byte,byte);
                                        // creates placeholder packet
// ***** module stuff.cpp *****
  char* stuff_author();                 // author of stuff.cpp module
  void zero_bits(bit_frame*);           // fills a bit frame with zeros
  void stuff(bit_frame*,bit_frame*);    // stuffs a frame
  void unstuff(bit_frame*,bit_frame*);  // unstuffs a frame
// ***** module crc.cpp *****
  char* crc_author();                   // author of crc.cpp module
  FCS generate_FCS(bit_frame*);         // generates the frame check
                                        // sequence (FCS) of CRC
// ***** module dllogic.cpp *****
  char* dl_author();                    // author of dllogic.cpp module
  bit LTwindow(byte,byte);              // DLC flow control logic
  bit INwindow(byte,byte);              //             "
  bit window_full(link_interface_state*);          //    "
  bit frames_remain_unacked(link_interface_state*);//    "
  void increment_SNmax(link_interface_state*);     //    "
  void update_SNmin(link_interface_state*,byte);   //    "
  void update_RN(link_interface_state*,byte);      //    "
  bit accept_frame(byte,byte);                     //    "
// MAC sublayer **************************************************
```

```
// ***** module mac.cpp *****
   bit mac_send(bit_frame*,mac_interface_state*,byte);
                                        // sends MAC frame
   bit csma_send(bit_frame*,mac_interface_state*,byte);
                                        // sends CSMA/CD frame
   bit csma_receive(physical_frame*,mac_interface_state*,byte);
                                        // receives a frame
   void clear_csma_send(mac_interface_state*);
                                        // clears state of csma_send
   void insert_lan_errors(physical_frame*,mac_interface_state*);
                                        // applies errors to frame
   bit forward_token(mac_interface_state*);
                                        // injects token in token LAN
   bit start_token_timeout(mac_interface_state*);
                                        // initiates timeout event
                                        // for token LAN
   bit token_present(bit_frame*);       // test for token frame
   bit mac_buffer_contains_frame(mac_interface_state*);
                                        // test for MAC frame available
   bit timeout_code_present(bit_frame*); // test for timeout event code
   byte extract_timeout_SN(bit_frame*,byte);
                                        // frame timeout SN in token LAN
   byte fromport(bit_frame);            // extracts from_port
   byte toport(bit_frame);              // extracts to_port
   void clear_mac_buffer(mac_interface_state*);
                                        // clears data from mac_buffer
   bit token_interface(physical_frame*,mac_interface_state*);
                                        // physical interface
                                        // for token LAN data frame
   bit token_send(bit_frame*,mac_interface_state*);
                                        // sends token LAN data frame
// ***** module backoff.cpp *****
   char* backoff_author();              // author of backoff.cpp
   int backoff(mac_interface_state*);   // updates the backoff interval
                                        // for CSMA/CD LAN
```

```
// ***** module token.cpp *****
  char* token_author();                    // author of token.cpp
  bit token_receive(bit_frame*,mac_interface_state*);
                                           // receives token LAN frame
// ***** module randex.cpp *****
  void RN_example();                       // demo random number generate
// ***** module crcex.cpp *****
  void CRC_example();                      // CRC generation example
  FCS generate_FCSex(bit_frame*);          // FCS generation example
// physical layer *****************************************************
// ***** module pl.cpp *****
  char* pl_author();                       // author of pl.cpp module
  bit phys_send(bit_frame*,link_interface_state*);
                                           // pl send
  bit phys_receive(physical_frame*,link_interface_state*);
                                           // pl receive
};
extern stack sim;                          // stack class reference
```

Using This Book with Networking Textbooks

Y ou can use this book by itself to gain a basic understanding of the Internet protocols, or you can use it the way my students do: with a textbook intended to provide in-depth coverage of data communications and networking principles and protocols. For those interested in the second approach, this appendix provides suggested pairings of the chapters and projects in this book with several major textbooks.

Douglas Comer, Computer Networks and Internets,
Second Edition, Prentice Hall, 1999

COMPUTER NETWORKS & INTERNETS	UNDERSTANDING INTERNET PROTOCOLS
Chapters/Sections	Chapter and Project
1	1
3–5	3, DLC1
6	4, DLC2
7–10	6, LAN1; 7, LAN2
12, 13, 14.1–14.9	2, WAN1
14.10–14.12	5, DLC3
15–21	8, WAN2; 9, WAN3
22	10, TRN1
23, 25–31, 33	12, INT1; 14, INT3
34	13, INT2

William Shay, Understanding Data Communications and
Networks, Second Edition, PWS Publishing Company, 1995

UNDERSTANDING DATA COMMUNICATIONS AND NETWORKS	UNDERSTANDING INTERNET PROTOCOLS
Chapters/Sections	Chapter and Project
1 except 1.2	1
1.2	2, WAN1
2–3	3, DLC1
4	4, DLC2; 13, INT2
5	5, DLC3
6. –6.2	6, LAN1
6.3–6.5	7, LAN2
7.1–7.4	8, WAN2; 9, WAN3
7.5	10, TRN1
8.1–8.3	12, INT1; 14, INT3

William Stallings, Data and Computer Communications, Sixth Edition, Prentice Hall, 2000

DATA AND COMPUTER COMMUNICATIONS	UNDERSTANDING INTERNET PROTOCOLS
Chapters/Sections	Chapter and Project
1	1
2–6	3, DLC1
7.2	4, DLC2
7 except 7.2	5, DLC3
9.1	2, WAN1
13.1–13.3, 14.1	6, LAN1
13.4–13.7, 14.2	7, LAN2
15.1–15.4	8, WAN2
15.5	11, WAN4
16	9, WAN3
17	10, TRN1
18	13, INT2
19	12, INT1; 14, INT3

Andrew S. Tanenbaum, Computer Networks,
Third Edition, Prentice Hall, 1996

COMPUTER NETWORKS	UNDERSTANDING INTERNET PROTOCOLS
Chapters/ Sections	Chapter and Project
1	1,2,WAN1
2	3, DLC1
3.1–3.2	4, DLC2
3.3–3.7	5, DLC3
4.1–4.3.1	6, LAN1
4.3.2–4.7	7, LAN2
5 except 5.5.5–5.5.6	8, WAN2
5.5.5–5.5.6	9, WAN3
5.3 and 7.7	11, WAN4
6	10, TRN1
7 except 7.1 and 7.7	12, INT1
7.1	13, INT2
8	14, INT3

APPENDIX E

Resources

T here are many good books, Web sites, and technical documents associated with Internet protocols. This appendix is intended only to give you a basic set of one or two useful information resources on each important topic for further study. Each of these will lead you to many more resources.

Books

Bertsekas, D., and R. Gallager, *Data Networks, Second Edition*, Prentice Hall, 1992

Rigorous mathematical theory of network performance.

Cheswick, W., and S. Bellovin, *Firewalls and Internet Security: Repelling the Wiley Hacker*, Addison-Wesley, 1994

Practical, down-to-earth description of how firewalls work and how to assemble one.

Comer, D., *Computer Networks and Internets, Second Edition*, Prentice Hall, 1999

A thorough and basic presentation of networking principles and technology at an undergraduate level.

Comer, D., *Internetworking with TCP/IP, Volume. I: Principles, Protocols, and Architectures, Third Edition*, Prentice Hall, 1995

A classic that provides working-level detail on the Internet protocols.

Comer, D., *Internetworking with TCP/IP, Volume. III: Client-Server Programming and Applications, Second Edition*, Prentice Hall, 1996

Details needed to create working programs that use the Internet for communication.

Goldman, J.E., *Local Area Networks Networks: A Client/Server Approach*, John Wiley & Sons, 1997

A wealth of detail on the ins and outs of LANs.

Oppliger, R., *Internet and Intranet Security*, Artech House, 1998

Comprehensive overview of network security technologies and methods.

Shay, W., *Understanding Data Communications and Networks*, PWS Publishing Company, 1995

An excellent undergraduate-level introduction to networking technology.

Stallings, W., *Data and Computer Communications, Fifth Edition*, Prentice Hall, 1997

A very broad and deep resource for networking technology at the graduate level.

Stallings, W., *High Speed Networks: TCP/IP and ATM Design Principles*, Prentice Hall, 1998

Details of advanced networking technologies.

Stevens, W., *TCP/IP Illustrated, Volume I: The Protocols*, Addison-Wesley, 1994

Detailed, working-level explanations of the Internet protocols.

Stevens, W., *Unix Network Programming, Volume I, Second Edition*, Prentice Hall, 1998

A classic with many details on writing programs that communicate over networks.

Tanenbaum, A., *Computer Networks, Third Edition*, Prentice Hall, 1996

Another very broad and deep resource for networking technology at the graduate level.

Web Sites

`http://standards.ieee.org`

Homepage for the IEEE standards; particularly important in LAN technology.

`http://www.ietf.org`

Homepage for the Internet Engineering Task Force; starting here you can find all Internet standards.

RFCs

Historically known as "Request for Comments," these are the archival documents of the IETF. The ones listed here relate to the protocols described in this book. For access to the entire RFC repository, see the IETF Web page listed above.

`RFC768 User Datagram Protocol (UDP)`

Standard best-effort transport protocol for the Internet.

`RFC791 Internet Protocol (IP)`

Standard way to exchange information over the Internet as packets.

`RFC792 Internet Control Message Protocol (ICMP)`

Used by routers to pass information other than data packets and routing information; for example, an echo request (ping).

`RFC793 Transmission Control Protocol (TCP)`

Standard reliable transport protocol for the Internet.

`RFC821 and RFC822 Simple Mail Transfer Protocol (SMTP)`

Standard mechanisms for exchange and formatting of Internet electronic mail.

`RFC826 Address Resolution Protocol (ARP)`

Enables a host to find the Ethernet or other MAC address associated with an IP address.

`RFC854 and RFC855 TELNET`

Standard remote terminal emulation protocol for the Internet.

`RFC903 Reverse Address Resolution Protocol (RARP)`

Enables a diskless system to find its IP address from a server on its LAN.

`RFC959 File Transfer Protocol (FTP)`

Standard way to transfer files between computers on the Internet.

RFC977 Network News Transfer Protocol

Standard way to transfer Network News between servers.

RFC1035, RFC1035 Domain Name System (DNS)

Defines the operation of the distributed system that maps DNS names to Internet addresses.

RFC1058 Routing Information Protocol (RIP)

Distance vector routing protocol for Internet unicast.

RFC1075 IP Distance Vector Multicast Routing Protocol (DVMRP)

Distance vector routing protocol for Internet multicast.

RFC1112 Internet Group Management Protocol (IGMP)

Used between routers and subnet hosts to establish multicast group membership.

RFC1157 Simple Network Management Protocol (SNMP)

Defines a way for all Internet systems to communicate information to remote management stations.

RFC1421 to RFC1424 Privacy Enhanced Mail (PEM)

Encrypted Internet electronic mail.

RFC1517, RFC1518, and RFC1519 Classless InterDomain Routing (CIDR)

Defines a way other than the historic standard classes A, B, and C for Internet addresses to be grouped for routing.

RFC1584 Multicasting Extensions to OSPF (MOSPF)

Link state routing protocol for Internet multicast.

RFC1661 Point-to-Point Protocol (PPP)

A standardized data link layer for use with Internet connections, widely used for dial-up links.

RFC1825 to RFC1928 Security Architecture for IP

This was developed for IPv6 but can be used with IPv4 to provide for confidentiality, integrity checking, authentication, and non-repudiation of IP packets.

RFC1866 Hypertext Markup Language (HTML)

Standard language used to create World Wide Web documents.

RFC1883 IPv6 Specification

Next version of the Internet Protocol (the current version is IPv4).

RFC1889 Transport Protocol for Real-Time Applications (RTP)

Used as transport layer for multimedia streams.

RFC2045 Multimedia Internet Mail Extensions (MIME)

Defines how Internet electronic mail can carry multimedia data.

RFC2068 Hypertext Transfer Protocol (HTTP)

Standard way to transfer World Wide Web information over the Internet.

RFC2131 Dynamic Host Configuration Protocol (DHCP)

Mechanisms used by a host to obtain an IP address from a server.

RFC2205 Resource reSerVation Protocol (RSVP)

Quality-of-service signaling protocol for the Internet.

RFC2328 Open Shortest Path First Version 2

Link state routing protocol for Internet unicast.

RFC2362 Protocol Independent Multicast (PIM)

Hybrid routing protocol for Internet multicast.

RFC2400 Internet Official Protocol Standards

Master index of Internet Protocols in the IETF standards process.

Terms in these definitions that also appear in this Glossary are shown in **boldface**.

Abstracted. Simplified in such as way as to retain only those attributes appropriate to a particular purpose.

Access control. Network function that limits **ingress** at some point to only those data units meeting some criterion.

ACK (*acknowledgement*). Aspect of a message that confirms receipt of some other message.

Active open. In **TCP**, the process of attempting to establish a connection; the other host must be prepared to accept the connection (normally by a **passive open**).

Addressing. In a network, a function that provides for unique identification of a node, allowing delivery of packets.

Address space. The range of addresses that is possible within a particular addressing structure, such as the Internet Protocol's 32-bit address.

Agent. A software element that performs some function autonomously (*e.g.*, fulfilling **SNMP** queries).

Algorithm. A procedure for solving a problem, used to program the function to solve that problem.

Anonymous FTP. A mode of operation for the File Transfer Protocol (FTP) that permits a remote user to obtain transfer of a particular collection of files without authentication.

Applet. A **Java** program that is downloaded from a Web server and runs in a Web browser.

Application layer. The highest layer in the protocol stack, occupied by software that performs the end function desired by the user.

Application-level protocol. A set of rules for transfer of information between distributed instances of an application.

ARP (*address resolution protocol*). Internet protocol by which a host identifies its **MAC** address when an ARP broadcast identifies the corresponding IP address.

ARQ (*automatic repeat request*). A data communication or network function where, when data is detected to be missing from a received sequence, a request for retransmission is generated by the receiving protocol layer; transparent to higher layers except for delay in receipt.

Array. A programming language abstraction representing a sequence of data elements where the individual element is identified by a **subscript**, an integer representing its offset from the beginning of the sequence.

ASCII (*American Standard Code for Information Interchange*). Provides a seven-bit pattern for each of 128 common characters; often used in an eight-bit form by appending a zero bit or parity bit.

Asynchronous transmission. Sends data as individual characters; timing is established separately for each character.

Authentication. A security function where the data received is confirmed to have been sent by a particular party.

Autonomous system. Network, among those that form the Internet, that is managed independently from its neighbors; for example, a network operated by an Internet Service Provider.

Backbone. Portion of a network intended to be shared by many users; normally it is provided with high capacity for this purpose.

Bandwidth. Range of frequencies present in an analog signal; also the range of frequencies that an analog channel will transmit; often used as a synonym for digital channel capacity, to which it is related by **Shannon's law**.

Base class. In C++, a **class** from which another class derives its properties through **inheritance**.

Best-effort service. Network service that is implemented without mechanisms intended to meet quality of service specifications.

Best-effort transport. Protocol such as UDP that facilitates end-to-end transmission, but does not attempt to provide reliable transmission.

Binary digits (bits). Values 0 and 1.

Binary exponential backoff. Technique used by Ethernet to deal with collisions, where each of 10 successive collisions results in doubling of a range of time values; from this range, the backoff interval is chosen at random.

Bit error rate. Average frequency with which single-bit errors occur in a digital channel, normally expressed as a ratio; for example, one error in every million bits is $1/10^6 = 10^{-6}$.

Bit stuffing. Process of inserting bits in a data stream to prevent patterns that have a special meaning; generally, inserting zero after every string of five consecutive ones to avoid having the pattern 111111 in the stream.

Bits per second. Unit for send/receive rate of digital information.

Block parity. Error detection scheme that adds a pattern at the end of a block, where each bit of the pattern represents a parity calculation taken across the position of that bit in all bytes of the block.

Border gateway. Network router that interconnects an autonomous system with one or more other autonomous systems, also called **exterior gateway**.

Bridge. Device that interconnects two or more **LAN** segments; frames are passed among the segments based on layer-2 (**MAC**) addresses.

Broadcast. Process whereby a message sent by one network station is received at all other stations.

Broadcast network. Uses broadcast to route data among nodes; this is simple, but does not make effective use of transmission media, so it is normally done only in **local area networks,** where the media are relatively inexpensive.

Buffer. Memory allocated to storing data pending its use by some other process; in the context of this book, the memory would hold information sent to or received from a data communication link or network.

Burst error. An error in a digital channel, that changes the value of two or more successive transmitted bits.

Bus. Hardware for data transmission allowing multiple devices to be connected at different points on the same transmission line.

Bus topology. Network configuration where the stations all are connected to the same transmission line, and each message is broadcast to the whole network.

Byte. Eight bits of data used as the code for one character; generally, the code is **ASCII**.

Byte-oriented transmission. Approach to synchronous transmission where all frames consist of an integer number of characters; any character in the data stream that otherwise would have a special significance for communication must be preceded by a data link escape (DLE) character.

Carrier. 1. Signal in a data channel, upon which information to be transmitted is impressed. 2. Organization (normally, commercial) that provides communication services among geographically dispersed locations.

Category five. Wiring standard using **UTP**, capable of supporting 10BASET and 100BASET Ethernet.

Category three. Wiring standard using **UTP**, capable of supporting 10BASET Ethernet.

CGI (*Common Gateway Interface*). Specification for an approach whereby a Web server can accept input through remote clients and invoke external processes to generate new Web pages dynamically in response.

CDDI (*copper distributed data interface*). A variation on **FDDI** where the channel consists of copper wire rather than optical fiber.

Channel. Path for data communication, also called **link** or **circuit**.

Channel capacity. Digital transmission rate in bits per second of which a channel is capable, also called **data rate**.

CIDR (*Classless InterDomain Routing*). Approach to determining paths for Internet packets, where addresses are grouped as subnets without regard to historic classes A, B, and C; this allows smaller routing tables and reduced address allocation.

Circuit. In electronics, a closed path through which a signal current can pass; in telecommunication, a path from one point to another through which a signal can pass.

Circuit-level gateway. Describes a **firewall** implemented by a TCP connection between the Internet and a protected subnet, where the only transmissions passed are those using the designated TCP port numbers.

Class. 1. historically, in the Internet protocol, a category of network address that designated the number of address bits used to specify the subnet. 2. In the C/C++ programming languages, a data type whose members are **object**s, that is, data structures and the functions defined to manipulate them.

Client-server model. An approach to distributed information processing where a station (the **server**) provides specific application services over the network to multiple other stations (the **client**s).

Closed list. List server that supports input from and output to only a specified list of users, for which it is configured.

Cloud. Generic term for a network of unspecified size, intended to represent a "black box" that transmits data among stations that are connected to it.

Collision. Event that occurs in a broadcast MAC system when multiple stations attempt to send at the same time.

Complex data type. A data type built up from multiple simpler data types.

Compress. To reduce the number of bits in a message or other collection of data, using a different coding to take advantage of the fact that the information content can be represented more concisely; trades processing to compress and decompress for channel capacity to transmit.

Compromised. Security status of a system or element that has been penetrated by an untrusted party and must be assumed untrustworthy.

Confidentiality. Exists when information is disclosed only to those intended to receive it.

Congestion. In a network, excessive traffic which causes delays and possibly loss of data.

Congestion control. Methods and procedures that reduce congestion in order to maintain satisfactory network performance.

Contention. Method for sharing a medium, defined by the **MAC** sublayer; stations contend for use of the medium, and a protocol is provided for dealing with inevitable **collisions**.

Controlled Load QoS. Category of Internet Integrated Services quality of service where the data transmitted is limited to fall within specific transmit rate characteristics, defined by a burst rate and a time average; the network contracts to assure QoS on a statistical basis.

CRC (*cyclic redundancy check*). Technique for error detection based on appending a **Frame Check Sequence (FCS)** computed as the remainder when a number representing the coefficients of a polynomial divides the data, treated as another polynomial, using ones complement addition.

CSMA (*carrier sense multiple access*). **MAC** method whereby stations sharing a medium sense the presence of a carrier and do not send if the carrier is present. However, if a **collision** occurs when sending, the stations cannot detect it so they continue sending even though the transmission cannot be received effectively.

CSMA/CD (*carrier sense multiple access with collision detection*). **MAC** method whereby stations sharing a medium sense the presence of a carrier and do not send if the carrier is present; if a **collision** occurs when sending a frame, they are able to sense it and stop sending.

Data communication. Passing information from a transmitting computer to a receiving computer.

Data rate. Digital transmission rate (in bits per second) of which a channel is capable, also called **channel capacity**.

Data unit. The aggregate of data communicated by a message for a particular protocol, also called a **protocol data unit**; examples are **packet** at the network layer and **frame** at the DLC layer.

Datagram. A data message together with source and destination addresses, plus any other information needed to deliver it; **IP** packets are datagrams.

Decryption. Process of decoding an encrypted message, resulting in the original message that was encrypted.

Default route. In a router, the route to be used for any packet for which no other route is already contained in the routing table.

Destination. In a protocol header, the address of the intended receiver.

DHCP (*dynamic host configuration protocol*). Provides for automatic distribution of **IP address** within a subnet, based on broadcast requests from hosts.

Dial-up link. Data communication link derived by signaling a circuit-switched network, using the circuit-switched address (usually, a telephone number) of the other end of the link.

DiffServ (*Differentiated Services*). Internet standards approach that determines at the network **ingress** point the **quality of service** to be provided to each packet, in order to provide a contracted level of service to some packets.

Directory service. In a network, an automated support service such as **DNS** that supports locating network users and resources.

Distance vector. Approach to distributing reachability data among routers based on the distance (usually in **hops** to the destination router) using a **routing protocol**.

Distributed system. Organized collection of cooperating processes using computers interconnected by networks.

DLC layer (*data link control layer*). In the five-layer augmented Internet protocol stack, the layer between the bottom (physical) and middle (network/internet) layers. The DLC layer is responsible for controlling operation of a single data communication link so as to move information efficiently from end to end, even though the link may be experiencing transmission errors.

DNS (*Domain Name System*). Distributed Internet service that provides for lookup of the **IP address** associated with a particular name (such as netlab.gmu.edu) or vice-versa.

DVMRP (*Distance Vector Multicast Routing Protocol*). Internet routing protocol using a distance vector method to support IP multicast.

Dynamic routing. Process that updates routes used within a network during operation, based on state of the network.

Edge. Entry or exit (**ingress** or **egress**) point, where a packet is transferred between a network and an attached subnet.

Egress. Departure **edge** point, where a packet enters an attached subnet from a network.

Email. Electronic mail, carried over a network.

Encryption. Process of recoding messages into a form that is intended to make it very difficult for parties that are not trusted by the sender to understand them.

Encryption algorithm. Definition of a procedure to encrypt and decrypt messages.

End-to-end. Refers to a process that takes place at two hosts in arbitrary locations on a network, and is supported transparently by the intervening network.

Enrollment. Process by which an email user joins a list server group.

Errors. Changes in data values arising from noise or faulty performance in a digital communication system.

Error control. Process responsible for detecting and dealing with errors in data communication link or a network.

Error rate. Average frequency with which data communication errors occur, due to combined effects of **bit errors** and **burst errors**.

Even parity. Technique for detecting data communication errors, based on adding a redundant bit with value selected such that the number of bits with value 1 is even.

Exterior gateway. Network router that interconnects an autonomous system with one or more other autonomous systems; also called **border gateway**.

FCS (*frame check sequence*). The remainder code generated by the CRC process, used for error detection.

FDDI (*fiber distributed data interface*). Standard defining a token ring **local area network** operating at 100 Mbps over optical fiber.

Firewall. Network element used to protect hosts (typically, on a subnet) from packets sent by potentially hostile sources in a larger network (typically, the Internet).

First-come, first-served (FCFS) queue. See **first-in, first-out (FIFO) queue**.

First-in, first-out (FIFO) queue. Process in which workload is maintained in order of arrival and the least recently arrived workload is served first.

Flooding. Process by which information is distributed throughout an area of a router-based network; each router passes a copy of each flooding packet to all of its neighbors.

Flow control. In data communication link or a network, process responsible for ensuring that the sender does not transmit data units at a rate that the receiver is not prepared to receive.

Forward error correction. In data communication, a method whereby redundant data is transmitted and used to determine a correction value for data corrupted by errors.

Forwarding. Process in a router that sends arriving packets toward their destination.

Fragment offset. Field in the IPv4 packet header, used to show how to reassemble a packet that has been fragmented because its size is greater than the **MTU** of a network through which it must pass.

Fragmentation. The process of breaking a message, or other aggregation of data, into fragments to be passed through a network.

Frame. The basic data unit at the **DLC layer** (including its **MAC** sublayer).

Framing. At the **DLC layer** and its **MAC** sublayer, placing data in the frame format required for transmission.

FTP (*file transfer protocol*). Internet application protocol for transfer of files between hosts.

Full duplex. Property of a communication link or network, whereby a node can both send and receive data simultaneously.

Gateway. Router that acts as the entry point to a subnet; used particularly to describe a router providing access to a network that is an autonomous system.

Geosynchronous satellite. Communication satellite that holds an orbit at about 22,300 miles above the equator, with the result that the satellite stays stationary with respect to the earth because its period of revolution matches that of the earth's rotation.

GIF (*Graphic Image Format*). Standardized format for a computer image composed of individual pixels.

Guaranteed QoS. Category of Internet **Integrated Services quality of service** where the rate of data transmission must be less than an absolute limit; the network contracts to pass this traffic without loss unless some part of the network breaks.

Half duplex. Property of a communication link or network whereby a node can either send or receive data, but not do both simultaneously.

Hamming code. Method of coding data that permits correction of single bit errors without retransmission.

HDLC (*High Level Data Link Control*). Important **DLC** standard from the **ISO**.

Header. The part of a protocol data unit that provides parameters used to control how the payload (data) is delivered, or treated upon delivery.

Hop. In a packet network, incremental progress across the link to the next router along the route from source to destination.

Host. Computer connected to a network, capable of communicating data between its applications and those of other computers on the network.

Host to network layer. In the Internet protocol stack, collective term for the layers below the **network** (internet) **layer**; details for these layers generally are not specified by the Internet protocols.

HTML (*Hypertext Markup Language*). Formal language, derived from Standard Generalized Markup Language (SGML), that supports hypertext plus various MIME types such as **GIF**, **JPEG**, **MPEG**, etc.

HTTP (*Hypertext Transfer Protocol*). Application-layer protocol used to transfer HTML for the Web.

Hypertext. Elaborated text, which can be specified as to font, color, size, etc., and may contain symbolic links that can be followed automatically to other text, either within the hypertext document or to external documents and multimedia objects.

IANA (*Internet Addressing and Naming Authority*). Organization that issues unique names and addresses required for functioning of the Internet Protocol Suite.

ICMP (*Internet Control Message Protocol*). Defines a set of functions for exchange of information between routers and hosts, necessary for operations other than passing data; examples are **ICMP Echo** and **ICMP Unreachable**.

ICMP Echo. Function of **ICMP** that provides for automatic, network-layer reply to an ICMP packet by a remote host or router; used for **ping**.

ICMP unreachable. Function of ICMP that provides for a router to inform a host or another router that it has no route available reach a particular IP address.

IEEE (*Institute of Electrical and Electronics Engineers, Inc*). International technical/professional society; produces a series of technical standards that include specifications for **local area networks**.

IETF (*Internet Engineering Task Force*). Organization that provides technical standards and implementation guidance for the Internet Protocol Suite.

IGMP (*Internet Group Management Protocol*). Defines procedures for communication of multicast group memberships between an IPmc router and multicasting hosts in its supported subnet.

Ingress. Entry **edge** point, where a packet enters a network from an attached subnet.

Inheritance. In C++, deriving properties from a **base class**.

Instability. Generally, inability to maintain a consistent state (see Bertsekas and Gallager *Data Networks* for a rigorous treatment of stability in networks).

Integrity. Property of a system or data unit indicating it is intact or "whole"; in other words, not **compromised** from a security standpoint.

Interactive mode. Way of operating a computer system such that it responds with output for each human input.

Inter-domain routing. Selecting paths to relay communication traffic among Internet autonomous systems.

Interface. Point where two system elements come together; an example is the boundary between any two layers in a protocol stack.

internet. Network of networks.

Internet. The global set of interconnected networks that use the **Internet Protocol Suite**.

Interoperate. To work together providing network functions; generally, this applies to systems that embody separate implementations of network standards and are able to work together to fulfill the specified functions.

Intranet. A corporate internet, which may or may not be connected with the Internet.

IntServ (*Integrated Services*). Internet standards approach that provides a capability to define a quality of service for delivery of packets between any source and destination host.

Inverse DNS. Function of the Domain Name System that returns a DNS name, given an **IP address**.

IP (*Internet Protocol*). Primary network-layer protocol of the **Internet Protocol Suite**; defines format and procedures for transmission of packets between Internet hosts and routers; the Internet currently uses **IPv4**.

IP address. Network address used by the **Internet Protocol**; for **IPv4**, it is 32 bits, for IPv6, it is 128 bits.

IPmc (*Internet Protocol— multicast*). Feature set of IP that supports multicasting; not a separate protocol, but not supported in all implementations of IP.

IPS (*Internet Protocol Suite*). Collection of network protocols standardized for use in the Internet by the **IETF** and defined by the **RFC** standards.

IPv4 (*Internet Protocol version 4*).

IPv6. (*Internet Protocol version 6*).

IPX (*Internetwork Packet Exchange*). Proprietary protocol of Novell, Inc. that allows their proprietary LAN protocols to function as an **internet** (not used in the **Internet**).

ISO (*International Standards Organization*). Responsible for a range of commercial standards; the one mentioned in this book is HDLC.

ISP (*Internet Service Provider*). Organization that operates a network providing access to the Internet for users.

ITU-T (*International Telecommunication Union—Telecommunication Standardization Sector*). Standards body responsible for various network standards including **HDLC** and ISDN.

Java. A programming language used to create programs that run on Web client computers and interact with the users of Web browser.

Jitter. Property of electronic communication that defines variation in latency.

JPEG (*Joint Photographic Experts Group*). Standard for compression of still images, name taken from the group that defined it; used in **MIME** and therefore with **HTML**.

Key. Data used with an encryption algorithm such that the algorithm can be known, yet encrypted data is very hard to decrypt without knowing the key.

Key distribution. Function of a cryptographic system providing for distribution of keys in such a way that, with a high confidence, they are available only to trusted parties.

LAN (*local area network*). Data communication system that interconnects multiple stations in a geographically small area (generally a building or campus); usually offers a relatively high data rate (2 Mbps or more) and is owned by the organization that uses it.

LAN segment. Portion of a **LAN** that supports physical transmission.

Latency. Delay from the time a particular bit of a message leaves the sender until the same bit reaches the receiver; in data communication, it is due to propagation delay; in packet networks, it is due to queuing delay plus propagation delay.

Leased links. Data communication links leased from a carrier; also called leased lines and leased **circuits**.

Link. Path for data communication, also called **channel** or **circuit**.

Link initialization. Process whereby the DLC at each end of a link completes initial communication with the other end to bring the link into a usable state.

Link management. Function of DLC dealing with **link initialization** between connected stations, and operation of **polling** arrangements in **master-slave links**.

Link state. In a router, the status of an interconnection link, including the operational status (ON or OFF) and utilization (particularly the size and performance of the packet queue awaiting transmission over that link).

Link state routing. Method of dynamic routing where a **routing protocol** is used to exchange **link state** in order to allow **optimization** of routes under network loading.

List server. Application that receives email and forwards it to members of a list.

Load balancing. Function of network routing that attempts to even out traffic load over network resources.

MAC (*media access control*). Sublayer of **DLC layer**; enables sharing of media on a peer basis by providing a mechanism for sharing, typically a **contention** or **token-passing** protocol.

Mail alias. List of email addresses intended to be substituted by an email server for some incoming message and transmitted; provides a simple form of **list server**.

Mail reflector. Another name for a **list server**.

Mailfile. A computer file containing one or more email messages.

Master-slave link control. Function used by data communication systems in **multidrop mode;** allows multiple stations to share one link by having one that is in charge, the **master**, which communicates with the others by **polling**.

Media. Plural of **medium**.

Medium. The communication path or channel "in the middle," where the signal propagates for telecommunication.

Mesh topology. Network configuration where nodes are interconnected by multiple paths, with more than two links terminating on the average node.

Message. The information passed between sender and receiver via a communication system.

Message digest. A technique for summarizing a message such that it is difficult to create another message with a matching digest; used to ensure message **integrity**.

MIB (*management information base*). A collection of data maintained by an **SNMP agent** and provided over the network in response to **SNMP** queries.

MIME (*multipurpose Internet mail extensions*). Formats of multimedia information usable in **email** and **HTML**.

Moderated list. Server operation where a human reviews email messages and decides which ones are to be forwarded to the list.

Modular. Consisting of small, easily assembled pieces.

Modular number system. Counting system where the allowable numbers range from zero to some maximum; the result of operations outside this range can be determined as the remainder when the true result is divided by the **modulus**.

Modulo two sum. Result of adding two binary numbers, expressed as a remainder when divided by two; the function is identical with the exclusive or logic function.

Modulus. In a **modular number system,** the number one greater than the largest number that can be represented in the system.

MOSPF (*Multicast Open Shortest Path First*). An extension to the **OSPF** Internet routing protocol that supports routing for **IPmc.**

Most significant bit (MSB). The leftmost bit in a binary number, which has the greatest weight in binary arithmetic.

MPEG (*Motion Picture Experts Group*). Family of standards for compressing of moving images, name taken from the group that defined it; used in **MIME** and therefore with **HTML.**

MTU (*maximum transfer unit*). The largest data unit allowed by a particular network or protocol.

Multicasting. Sending information over a network to a group of hosts having multiple individual network addresses; replication of packets to the individual hosts is performed by the network, based on the group address.

Multidrop mode. Arrangement where a single communication link is connected to more than two stations.

Multimedia. Communication involving more that one medium; for purposes of this book, the medium in question is the one used to convey information to human senses.

NACK (*negative acknowledgement*). Aspect of a message that confirms nonreceipt of some other message; sometimes abbreviated NAK.

NAT (*network address translation*). Method for extending Internet address space; one address is used to represent many logical addresses behind a gateway, by mapping various TCP flows onto different addresses and thereby sending them to different hosts.

Network. Collection of processing elements (**nodes**) that have the ability to communicate with each other through **links**; each has the ability to communicate with all others, either by direct connection or by passing the information through intermediary nodes.

Network news. Application providing for selective distribution of "news" articles in a format similar to email, using **NNTP.**

Network prefix. The high-order bits (leftmost) of an IP address, ending where the host identifier field for the **subnet** starts.

NNTP (*Network News Transfer Protocol*). Used to transfer **network news.**

Node. Network element interconnected by links; processing and storage takes place here.

Noise. Unwanted signal in a communication system; results in corruption of transmitted information.

Nonrepudiation. Property of a system whereby it is probably very unlikely that a particular party did not send a message that is attributed to them.

Nyquist rate. Frequency of sampling that will capture all information in an analog signal; it is equal to twice the bandwidth of the signal (for audio, the sampling rate typically used is twice the highest frequency in the signal).

Object. In C++, a variable that is defined by a collection of data structures and program functions; a type whose variables are objects is called a **class**.

Octet. Eight bits of data.

Odd parity. Technique for detecting data communication errors based on adding a redundant bit with value selected such that the number of bits with value 1 is odd.

Open standards. Have the properties that standards development is fully visible to all participants, and anybody can propose new standards features.

Optimization. Process of finding the best possible value of a function.

OSI (*Open Systems Interconnect*) **Reference Model.** Seven-layer protocol stack used to characterize open data network standards and often cited as a paradigm for networking software; more detailed and generally more complex than the stack used in the **Internet Protocol Suite**.

OSPF (*Open Shortest Path First*). Internet **routing protocol** that provides for **link state routing**.

Packet. The **data unit** of the **network layer**; in IP packet consists of the data to be delivered plus a header consisting of source address, destination IP address, and other information needed to deliver the packet.

Packet loss. Rate of packets being dropped due to network problems (generally, errors and/or congestion); specified as a ratio, for example 1 packet in 20 or .05; may be of concern either on an end-to-end basis, or within any defined portion of a network.

Padding. Extra unused data, provided to make some part of a data unit come out right; for example, the IP packet header length must be a multiple of four bytes in length, so the header is padded at the end to achieve this.

Passive open. In TCP, the process of preparing to accept a connection; for the connection to be completed, an **active open** must be completed by TCP at the other end of the connection.

Peer connection. Virtual connection between protocols at the same level in the stack (it is virtual because, except at the physical layer, the data actually pass through other layers to complete communication).

Peering. Providing a direct gateway interconnection between two autonomous systems in the Internet.

PEM (*privacy enhanced mail*). Version of email that provides standardized **encryption** to improve the privacy of Internet communication.

Physical layer. The layer at the bottom of the protocol stack, at which actual (but unreliable) communication of bits takes place.

Physical security. Protecting things by denying physical access to untrusted people.

Piggyback. Method where information is imbedded in a data stream being sent for other purposes; an example is ACKs from a receiver to a sender, which where possible are imbedded in data units being transmitted the other direction (receiver to sender).

PIM (*Protocol Independent Multicast*). Protocol for exchange of routing information in support of IP multicast routers; similar to DVMRP, but has a separate sparse mode intended to replace the role of hand configured **tunnels**.

Ping. An application of **ICMP echo** that shows whether a particular **IP address** is reachable and how long the round-trip for echo request and reply takes.

Pixel. Abbreviation for "picture element," an individual grayscale or colored dot in an image.

Plaintext. Encryption jargon for unencrypted data.

Pointer. In C/C++, a variable that is used to refer to another variable; it is indicated by a * after the variable name, for example `packet* this_packet`; it is used like this in coding programs: `this_packet->size=0;`

Polling. In **master-slave link control**, a process whereby the link master station requests data from a slave, which is not permitted to send a frame until the poll is received.

Port. Abstraction used in Internet transport protocols TCP and UDP to subdivide an IP address, providing multiplexing between IP hosts and the associated ability to identify applications with particular ports.

Port number. Identifier associated with a TCP or UDP port; length is 16 bits.

PPP (*Point to Point Protocol*). Internet DLC protocol, similar to HDLC, used to interconnect various devices that might otherwise not be interoperable; widely used as a means of establishing **dial-up links** that can work with Internet routers.

Preamble. The beginning part of an Ethernet frame, used to synchronize receivers with the sender.

Prefix notation. A way of showing a block of Internet addresses that indicates the unique **network prefix** used for Internet routing followed by and slash and then the number of bits in the prefix, for example 129.174.65/24.

Primary nameserver. In **DNS**, the nameserver that is responsible for providing name-to-address mappings for a particular domain, such as gmu.edu.

Propagation. Process whereby an electromagnetic wave moves between two points.

Propagation delay. Time required for an electromagnetic wave to move between two points; proportional to the distance and the velocity of electromagnetic propagation in the **medium** (often called the **speed of light**).

Protocol. A set of rules for transfer of information under a specified set of conditions.

Protocol data unit. Aggregate of data communicated by a message for a particular protocol; examples are **packet** at the network layer and **frame** at the DLC layer; also called **data unit**.

Protocol stack. An arrangement of software modules, each interfaced with the one below it, which provides the required functionality for network communication.

Proxy server. Webserver that obtains and caches a copy of pages from remote Webservers; this reduces time for repeated access and also provides a Web application gateway for use with **firewall** security.

Public key encryption. Cryptographic system where the encryption and decryption are complementary but not symmetric; receiving key is very difficult to determine from sending key, thus the sending key can be made public with confidence that other parties cannot decrypt the encrypted data.

Pull. In NNTP, a mode where the client must ask for each network news article.

Push. 1. In NNTP and Web-based information services, a mode where the server automatically offers information based on a profile provided by the user. 2. In TCP, an option for the application program to have TCP send data immediately rather than waiting to fill a segment before sending it.

QoS (*quality of service*). Specification for network performance providing acceptable level **packet loss, latency**, and/or **jitter** associated with a given traffic level; the traffic level may be described in bits per second or packets per second.

Queue. Sequence of objects ordered by a queueing discipline (such as **FIFO**).

Queueing delay. Time between arrival in a queue and processing; at a router interface, this is directly related to the length of queue, which grows with loading, increasing dramatically if there is congestion arising from traffic levels near the capacity of the link associated with the interface.

RARP (*Reverse Address Resolution Protocol*). Used by a host that needs to be told what its IP address is; usually, this will be a device with no persistent storage to record the IP address.

Real-time. Characteristic of a process requiring that it receive a response to a message in a time (normally, short) that is required to influence an ongoing process; frequently, the process is interacting with a person and needs a response in a sufficiently short time to be acceptable to that person.

Receiver. The destination in a communication process.

Redundant. Duplicative; in data communication systems, controlled amounts of data redundancy are included to enable error detection and correction.

Reliable service. In network communication, a service that is specified to detect and automatically replace data that is missing or corrupted;

this process is transparent to the user of the service, except for delays that are necessary for repairs to be accomplished.

Reliable transport protocol. Provides **end-to-end** communication as a **reliable service**.

RFC (*Request for Comments*). Internet standards document; letters stand for "Request for Comments."

Ring topology. Network configuration where each node is connected to exactly two neighbors, such that the whole system forms a single closed loop.

RIP (*Routing Information Protocol*). **Distance vector routing protocol** widely used in the Internet.

RN (*request number*). Header field in a reliable DLC or transport protocol; used to identify message being **ACK**ed or **NACK**ed.

Root domain. Any of the possible rightmost identifiers in a DNS name, such as "edu" in netlab.gmu.edu; two or more root name-servers are associated with each root domain.

Router. Computer that performs packet switching; that is, **forwarding** arriving packets toward their destination.

Routing. Process of selecting paths to relay communication traffic; in a packet network it results in creating or updating a **routing table**.

Routing policy. Predetermined decision rule to use certain routing, if available, based on management considerations.

Routing protocol. Used to exchange **routing** information among **routers**.

Routing table. Data structure designating an outgoing interface, and thereby a next-hop router, for the destination address of arriving packets.

RSVP (*Resource reSerVation Protocol*). Provides **signaling** for setup of **Integrated Services** in the Internet.

RTP (*Real-time Transfer Protocol*). Provides a generic transport framework for real-time data **streams** within the **Internet Protocol Suite**.

RTCP (*RTP Control Protocol*). Provides control information to supplement data transmitted using **RTP**.

RTT (*round trip time*). Elapsed time from transmission of a reliable transport layer segment until the associated **ACK** returns.

Scalar. Program variable that stands alone; it is not part of a larger data structure.

Secondary nameserver. In DNS, a nameserver that automatically maintains a complete copy of DNS information stored by the **primary nameserver** of a domain, and is known by other DNS servers as an alternate source of this information.

Segment. Data unit of the Internet **reliable transport protocol, TCP.**

Sender. The source in a communication process.

Server. Software (and/or the associated computer) that provides application services over the network to software at other stations (the **clients**).

Service. Functionality offered by a protocol to the protocol in the layer above it.

Shannon's law. Relates digital channel capacity to analog bandwidth.

Shared symbol set. Common representation of information; both parties in a communication process must have the same understanding of the meaning of each symbol in the set.

Signaling. Process of communicating setup information for a connection.

Simulation. Models a process or system in such a way that its important aspects are **abstracted** for study.

Single-bit error. Change to the correct value of a bit (making it incorrect) that does not affect neighboring bits.

Sliding window. Protocol mechanism that implements error and/or flow control by allowing multiple data units to be outstanding between sender and receiver; the window moves forward when the earliest sent data unit is **acknowledged**.

Slow start. Feature of **TCP** that presents data to the network slowly after initial connection, increasing the rate until/unless congestion is sensed by increase in the **RTT**; the intention is to avoid causing congestion.

SMTP (*Simple Mail Transfer Protocol*). Internet standard for email.

SN (*sequence number*). Header field in a reliable DLC or transport protocol; used to identify message being sent.

SNA (*Systems Network Architecture*). Proprietary network protocol suite of IBM Corporation.

SNMP (*Simple Network Management Protocol*). Internet standard for network management.

SNMP agent. Autonomous software that monitors a network resource, maintains a **MIB**, and responds to **SNMP** queries.

Socket. Abstraction for the concatenation of an **IP address** and **port number**; uniquely identifies one end of a TCP connection.

Source. Sender in a communication process.

Spam. Unwanted Internet email, usually generated in bulk.

Speed of light. Velocity of light and other electromagnetic waves, in a vacuum unless stated otherwise; in air or vacuum it is about 186,000 miles per second or 300,000,000 meters per second; in other materials it is slower.

Stack. See **protocol stack**.

Star topology. Network configuration where multiple nodes all connect to one central node.

State-transition diagram. Shows the possible conditions of a process along with the inputs that cause the process to change condition, and possibly the outputs that occur along with the changes.

State variable. Uniquely determines the state (condition) in which the function operates.

Static routing. Establishes a routing table and does not change it.

Station. Generic name for a **DLC** node.

Stream abstraction. Pertaining to an extended, continuous flow of data.

Streaming audio and video. Web delivery mechanism for continuous multimedia data; provides highly compressed **streams** delivered as sound and moving images; an initial delay in delivery allows the client to **buffer** sufficient data to avoid jerkiness from jitter.

Strong encryption. Hard to break; uses advanced encryption algorithms and long keys.

Subnet (*subnetwork*). Generically, any part of the Internet that can be reached using a single network address (the **network prefix** part of the **IP address**); generally used for the address space associated with a **LAN**.

Subscript. In C/C++, notation indicating a position in an **array**; for example, A[i] indicates the ith position of A, where the smallest acceptable value of i is zero.

Subscription. Process by which an email user subscribes to a listserver group.

Switch. Network element that determines which of two or more possible paths will be used to send data.

Switched LAN. Interconnected by a switch rather than the more common bus or ring, with the result that multiple transmissions among nodes may take place simultaneously as long as no two involve the same station.

Switched network. Uses switching as its basic means of forwarding data; this method is almost always used for a **WAN**, whereas it is typical for a **LAN** to operate as a **broadcast network**.

Symmetric. Property of a matrix wherein elements are reflected across the diagonal; $a[i][j] = a[j][i]$.

Symmetric encryption. Uses the same key to encrypt and decrypt.

Synchronous transmission. Sends each frame as a continuous stream of bits with no breaks; timing is established for the whole frame.

TCP (*Transmission Control Protocol*). Primary transport protocol of the **Internet Protocol Suite**; provides for **reliable transport** using a **stream** model of data and multiplexing of streams using **ports**.

Telecommunication. Passing information from a sender to a distant receiver by electromagnetic means.

Teleconferencing. Meeting conducted by people at different locations, using **telecommunication**.

Telephony. Telecommunication using sound; normally the encoding is a natural language produced by spoken voice.

Telnet. Application protocol for remote terminal emulation via the Internet.

Thin client. A **client-server** approach where programmed functionality in the **client** is designed to be small, placing a correspondingly larger burden on the **server**.

Throughput. Rate at which usable information passes through a system.

THT (*Token holding time*). Parameter of some **token-passing LAN** protocols that establishes the maximum period of time one station may hold the token before passing it on.

Token. Pattern used to indicate the holder has some special status within a system; for example, in a **token-passing LAN** normally only the station having the token is allowed to transmit a frame.

Token bus. A token-passing LAN that uses a single shared transmission path.

Token ring. A token-passing LAN where each station is connected to two neighbors, such that the whole forms a closed ring.

Token-passing LAN. Passes a **token** from station to station as a means of controlling media access.

Topology. 1. Mathematical study of internal connection properties of "graphs," which are abstract structures consisting of connection points called **nodes** interconnected by lines called **links**. 2. A graph that is topologically equivalent to a network, because the nodes and links are connected the same on a one-to-one basis.

Traceroute. Application that allows a user to observe the sequence of routers that will be used by the Internet to reach a given **IP address**.

Transparent bridge. Self-configuring **LAN bridge**; works by observing frame addresses to infer which **LAN segment** holds a given address, and bridging frames between segments accordingly.

Transport layer. Responsible for packaging data for host-to-host delivery; for long streams of data this requires dividing the information into **segments**; also provides a means to identify how messages are to be used in the receiving host in that a set of messages is associated with a particular application.

Truncation. Computational process where some part of a number is dropped; for example, the fractional part of the number held in a floating point variable is dropped when its value is assigned to an integer variable.

TTL (*time to live*)**.** Misleading name designating the field in the **IP** header indicating how many **hops** the **packet** is allowed to progress through the network before it is dropped.

Tunnel. Network function that moves data between two points without modifying it, by encapsulating it in some other format; for example, **IP multicast** packets can be moved through parts of the Internet that do not support multicasting, by carrying them as the payload of **unicast** IP packets.

Type. In C/C++, a collection of attributes that can be associated with a **variable**; a simple example is `int` meaning "integer."

Typecasting. In C/C++, notation that indicates a **pointer** is to be treated as a different **type** than another pointer, the value of which is transferred to it.

Unicast. Ordinary network transmission, from one **source** to one **receiver**.

UDP (*User Datagram Protocol*). Transport protocol of the **Internet Protocol Suite,** an alternate to **TCP**; provides for **best-effort transport** of individual **datagrams** provided by applications.

USENET. Collective name for hosts supporting **network news** distribution.

UTP (*unshielded twisted pair*). Wire used for 10BASET and 100BASET Ethernet.

Value-added network provider. Organization that provides packet-switched network services over links leased from a carrier, and charges for use of the services.

VC (*Virtual circuit*). Path from a sender to a receiver through a packet-switched network; consists of a sequence of switches (or **routers**) and links that will carry every packet of the call that is using the VC.

Virtual. Effectively true.

Virtual reality. Three-dimensional graphic environment, intended absorb the user's spatial attention.

Well-known port. TCP or UDP **port number** that is recognized as being an appropriate place to connect with a given application.

Weak encryption. Relatively easy to break, but also easy to perform.

WAN (*wide area network*). A network that spans a sizable geographic area, such that its links normally are leased from carriers, with capacity only sufficient to serve requirements.

Web. See **WWW**.

Window. Number of frames in DLC, or total bytes in TCP, which can be transmitted before the sender must wait for an **acknowledgement**.

WWW (*World Wide Web*). Virtual network of sites that use the Internet to exchange multimedia files in HTML using HTTP; often abbreviated to Web; client is a Web browser that provides visual and audio output from the contents of the files, or starts another program to do so.

XOR (*exclusive or*). Digital logic function defined by a table showing that its output is TRUE (one) when its inputs are different, and FALSE when they are the same.